Democracy in Social Movements

Also by Donatella della Porta

GLOBAL DEMOCRACY AND THE WORLD SOCIAL FORUM (*co-authored*)

THE GLOBAL JUSTICE MOVEMENT: Cross National and Transnational Perspectives (*edited*)

THE POLICING OF TRANSNATIONAL PROTEST (*co-edited*)

GLOBALIZATION FROM BELOW (*co-authored*)

SOCIAL MOVEMENTS: An Introduction (*co-authored*)

TRANSNATIONAL PROTEST AND GLOBAL ACTIVISM (*co-edited*)

SOCIAL MOVEMENTS IN A GLOBALIZING WORLD (*co-edited*)

SOCIAL MOVEMENTS, POLITICAL VIOLENCE AND THE STATE

Democracy in Social Movements

Edited by

Donatella della Porta
European University Institute, Italy

palgrave
macmillan

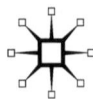

First published 2009 by
PALGRAVE MACMILLAN

Palgrave Macmillan in the UK is an imprint of Macmillan Publishers Limited,
registered in England, company number 785998, of Houndmills, Basingstoke,
Hampshire RG21 6XS.

Palgrave Macmillan in the US is a division of St Martin's Press LLC,
175 Fifth Avenue, New York, NY 10010.

Palgrave Macmillan is the global academic imprint of the above companies
and has companies and representatives throughout the world.

Palgrave® and Macmillan® are registered trademarks in the United States,
the United Kingdom, Europe and other countries.

ISBN-13: 978–0–230–21883–3 hardback

This book is printed on paper suitable for recycling and made from fully
managed and sustained forest sources. Logging, pulping and manufacturing
processes are expected to conform to the environmental regulations of the
country of origin.

A catalogue record for this book is available from the British Library.

A catalog record for this book is available from the Library of Congress.

Printed and bound in Great Britain by
CPI Antony Rowe, Chippenham and Eastbourne

Contents

List of Tables

List of Figures

Acknowledgements

This book reports the results of part of the comparative research project Democracy in Europe and the Mobilization of the Society – DEMOS (http://demos.iue.it). The DEMOS project is financed by the European Commission, 6th FP Priority 7, Citizens and Governance in a Knowledge Based Society, and (for the Swiss case) the Federal Office for Education and Science, Switzerland. It is co-ordinated by Donatella della Porta (European University Institute); partners are University of Kent at Canterbury, UK, Christopher C. Rootes; Wissenschaftszentrum Berlin fuer Sozialforschung, Germany, Dieter Rucht; Università di Urbino, Italy, Mario Pianta; Centre de recherches politiques de la Sorbonne (CRPS), Universitè Panthéon-Sorbonne, France, Isabelle Sommier; Instituto de Estudios Sociales de Andalucía, Centro Superior de Investigaciones Científicas (IESA-CSIC), Spain, Manuel Jiménez; and Laboratoire de recherches sociales et politiques appliquées (resop), Université de Genève, Switzerland, Marco Giugni. Collaborators to the research included, at different times, Massimiliano Andretta, Marko Bandler, Angel Calle, Hélène Combes, Nicolas Haeringer, Nina Eggert, Raffaele Marchetti, Lorenzo Mosca, Alessandro Nai, Herbert Reiter, Clare Saunders, Simon Teune, Mundo Yang and Duccio Zola.

Hundreds of representatives of social movement organizations trusted us, participating in our interviews and other research activities. We are very grateful to all of them.

As has very often been the case in the past, Sarah Tarrow helped us enormously with a most careful and gently handled editing of our text.

Notes on Contributors

Hélène Combes is a CNRS Research fellow with the Centre de recherches politiques de la Sorbonne (Paris 1 University). Her PhD in political science scrutinized the relationship between political parties and social movements in Mexico. She currently works on protest in Mexico City and partisan activism in a number of Latin American countries.

Donatella della Porta is Professor of Sociology in the Department of Political and Social Sciences at the European University Institute. Among her recent publications on social movements are: *The Global Justice Movement*; (with Massimiliano Andretta, Lorenzo Mosca, and Herbert Reiter) *Globalization from Below*; (with Abby Peterson and Herbert Reiter) *The Policing of Transnational Protest*; (with Manuela Caiani) *Quale Europa? Europeizzazione, identità e conflitti*; (with Mario Diani) *Social Movements: An Introduction*, 2nd edn; (with Sidney Tarrow) *Transnational Protest and Global Activism*.

Marco Giugni is a researcher at the Laboratoire de recherches sociales et politiques appliquées (resop) and teaches in the Department of Political Science at the University of Geneva. He has authored or co-authored several books and articles on social movements and contentious politics. His research interests include social movements and collective action, immigration and ethnic relations, unemployment and social exclusion.

Nicolas Haeringer is a doctoral researcher at the CERSO (Centre d'étude et de recherche en sociologie des organisations), Université Paris-Dauphine. His PhD thesis aims at defining the World Social Forum as an emerging form of socialization and also addresses the European Social Forum. It focuses on its main features and dynamics, through participant observation and action research conducted on the memory and the electronic tools of both the WSF and the ESF.

Raffaele Marchetti is Lecturer on International Relations at LUISS University and John Cabot University. He co-ordinates the FP6 Strep project SHUR – Human Rights in Conflicts: The Role of Civil Society. Recent works include *Global Democracy: For and Against. Ethical Theory, Institutional Design, and Social Struggles.*

Lorenzo Mosca holds a PhD degree from the University of Florence (2004). He received a postdoctoral fellowship at the European University Institute and is currently Assistant Professor at the University of Roma Tre. Mosca has been involved in several European projects such as YOUNEX, DEMOS, and EUROPUB. He has published extensively in international peer-reviewed journals and articles in books translated into English, Spanish, French, German and Italian.

Alessandro Nai works as a teaching and research assistant at the University of Geneva (Political Science), where he is completing his PhD dissertation. His works deal with cognitive strategies used by citizens in decision making, focusing especially on their determinants (individual and contextual) and effects on the quality of the decision. He is a visiting scholar at Rutgers University (NJ, USA) during the academic year 2008–09.

Mario Pianta is Professor of Economic Policy at the University of Urbino and has been a visiting fellow at the European University Institute, the London School of Economics, and the Université Paris 1 Panthéon Sorbonne. He works on international economic policy and social movements.

Herbert Reiter is a historian and researcher at the European University Institute in Florence. Among his recent publications, with Donatella della Porta, Massimiliano Andretta and Lorenzo Mosca, *Globalization from Below*; with Donatella della Porta and Abby Petersen (eds), *The Policing of Transnational Protest.*

Dieter Rucht is Professor of Sociology and co-director of the research group 'Civil Society, Citizenship and Political Mobilization in Europe' at the Social Science Research Center, Berlin. His research interests include political participation, social movements, and political protest.

Clare Saunders is a lecturer (RCUK Fellow) in Politics and International Relations at the University of Southampton. Prior to this, she was a Research Associate at the University of Kent, working with Christopher Rootes on the DEMOS project.

Isabelle Sommier is a professor at the Sorbonne, Paris. Among her books are *Le renouveau des mouvements contestataires à l'heure de la mondialisation*; (with Olivier Fillieule and Eric Agrikoliansky, eds) *Généalogie des mouvements altermondialistes en Europe. Une perspective comparée*; and (with Eric Agrikoliansky, eds) *Radiographie du mouvement altermondialiste*.

Simon Teune works at the Social Science Research Center, Berlin. His research interests are social movements, protest and culture. He is preparing a PhD dissertation dealing with the communication strategies of global justice groups during the 2007 anti-G8 protests in Germany.

Duccio Zola is currently a PhD student in philosophy at the University of Rome 'La Sapienza'. He is the author of research and articles on deliberative democracy, transnational social movements, the participation of civil society actors in contexts of local governance, the crisis of institutional politics, and the party system in modern democracies.

Organizational Structures and Visions of Democracy in the Global Justice Movement: An Introduction

Donatella della Porta

Organizational structures and visions of democracy

Social movements do not limit themselves to presenting demands to decision makers; they also more or less explicitly express a fundamental critique of conventional politics, thus shifting their endeavours from politics itself to meta-politics (Offe 1985). Their ideas resonate with 'an ancient element of democratic theory that calls for an organisation of collective decision making referred to in varying ways as classical, populist, communitarian, strong, grass-roots, or direct democracy against a democratic practice in contemporary democracies labelled as realist, liberal, elite, republican, or representative democracy' (Kitschelt 1993, p. 15). Their critique has traditionally addressed the representative element of democracy, with calls for citizen participation.

While participatory aspects have long been present in theorizing about democracy and social movements, some emerging developments can be usefully discussed in light of the growing literature on deliberative democracy, with its focus on communication (della Porta 2005b) and locating democratic deliberation in voluntary groups (Cohen 1989), social movements (Dryzek 2000), protest arenas (Young 2003, p. 119) or, more in general, enclaves free from institutional power (Mansbridge 1996). Deliberative participatory democracy refers to decisional processes in which, under conditions of equality, inclusiveness, and transparency, a communicative process based on reason (the strength of a good argument) may transform individual preferences, leading to decisions oriented to the public good. Some elements of this definition echo those already included in the participatory models we have just described as typical of (new) social movements, although with an emerging emphasis on the quality of discourse. In

1

particular, deliberative democracy 'requires some forms of apparent equality among citizens' (Cohen 1989, p. 18); in fact, deliberation takes place among free and equal citizens (as 'free deliberation among equals', ibid., p. 20). At a minimum, 'all citizens must be able to develop those capacities that give them effective access to the public sphere', and 'once in public, they must be given sufficient respect and recognition so as to be able to influence decisions that affect them in a favourable direction' (Bohman 1997, pp. 523–4). Deliberation must exclude power deriving from coercion but also an unequal weighting of the participants as representatives of organizations of different sizes or as more influential individuals.

Also common to traditional conceptions of participatory democracy is the emphasis on inclusiveness. All citizens with a stake in the decisions to be taken must be included in the process and able to express their views. This means that the deliberative process takes place under conditions of plurality of values, including people with different perspectives but facing common problems. This is also a central premise of deliberative conceptions, as deliberation (or even communication) is based upon the belief that, while not necessarily giving up my perspective, I might learn if I listen to the other (Young 1996). Moreover, transparency resonates with direct, participatory democracy: assemblies are typically open, public spheres. In Joshua Cohen's definition, a deliberative democracy is 'an association whose affairs are governed by the *public* deliberation of its members' (1989, p. 17, emphasis added).

However, what seems especially new in the conception of deliberative democracy, and in some contemporary movements' practices, is the emphasis on preference (trans)formation with an orientation to the definition of the public good. In fact, 'deliberative democracy requires the transformation of preferences in interaction' (Dryzek 2000, p. 79); it is 'a process through which initial preferences are transformed in order to take into account the points of view of the others' (Miller 1993, p. 75). In this sense, deliberative democracy differs from conceptions of democracy as the aggregation of (exogenously generated) preferences. A deliberative setting facilitates the search for a common end or good (Elster 1998b). In this model of democracy, 'the political debate is organized around alternative conceptions of the public good', and, above all, it 'draws identities and citizens' interests in ways that contribute to public building of public good' (Cohen 1989, pp. 18–19).

In particular, deliberative democracy stresses reason, argumentation, and dialogue: people are convinced by the force of the better argument. Deliberation is based on horizontal flows of communication, multiple producers of content, wide opportunities for interactivity, confrontation based on rational argumentation, and attitude to reciprocal listening (Habermas 1981; 1996a). Decisions rely upon arguments that participants recognize as reasonable (Cohen and Sabel 1997). These conceptions also often refer to practices of consensus, with decisions approvable by all participants – in contrast with majority rule, where decisions are legitimated by vote.

The central focus of our research is the vision of democracy in social movement organizations. We do not wish, however, to measure degrees of democracy, but to conceptualize the various models of democracy that are present, in more or less 'pure' form. A main assumption of our research is that the general principles of democracy such as power (*kratos*) by/from/for the people (*demos*) can be combined in different forms and with different balances: representative versus participatory, and majority versus deliberative (see below). We assume that the plurality of repertoires that we have identified in contemporary movements (see della Porta 2007b) is also reflected in the variety of conceptions of democracy they express.

We look at the conception of democracy in social movement organizations (SMOs). Attention to social movement organizations has been at the core of the resource mobilization approach, whose proponents stress 'both the rational-economic assumptions and formal organizational thrusts' (Zald and McCarthy 1987, p. 45). Social movement organizations must mobilize resources from the surrounding environment, whether directly in the form of money or through voluntary work by their adherents; they must neutralize opponents and increase support from both the general public and the elites (for examples, McCarthy and Zald 1987b, p. 19). Stressing its instrumental role, a social movement organization can be defined as a 'complex, or formal, organization which identifies its goals with the preferences of a social movement or countermovement and attempts to implement those goals' (ibid., p. 20). However, SMOs are also sources of identity for the movements' constituencies as well as their opponents and the public (della Porta and Diani 2006). In fact, SMOs play an identification function, being defined as 'associations of persons making idealistic and moralistic claims about how human personal or group life ought to be organized that, *at the time of their claims making*, are marginal to or excluded from mainstream society' (Lofland 1996, pp. 2–3).

In this volume, we look at organizations both as mobilization agents and as spaces of deliberation and value construction. In social movement literature, the first approach has been dominant. As Clemens and Minkoff (2004, p. 156) have recently noted, with the development of the resource mobilization perspective, 'Attention to organization appeared antithetical to analysis of culture and interaction. As organizations were understood instrumentally, the cultural content of organizing and the meanings signalled by organizational forms were marginalized as topic for inquiry.' In recent approaches, however, SMOs are increasingly considered as 'contexts for political conversation', characterized by specific etiquettes (Eliasoph 1998, p. 21).

This evolution reflects changes in the sociology of organizations from the closed to the open system approach, and then to neo-institutionalism. These approaches can be distinguished mainly by the relative role assigned to environmental influence and the role of organizational agency (see Table I.1). With the development of organizational sociology, the so-called 'closed system approach' presented internal organizational factors as 'the prime causal agents in accounting for the structure and behaviour of organizations' (Scott 1983, p. 156). In the 1960s, an open system approach stressed instead the technical interdependence of organizations and their environments, while later the metaphor of a 'garbage can' was used to describe decision making in conditions of high ambiguities of preferences and low information on environmental constraints and opportunities (see March 1988). More recently, with the neo-institutional approach in organizational theory, the focus has shifted from the technical to the sociocultural environment (Scott 1983, p. 161). According to two proponents of this approach: 'The new institutionalism in organizational theory and sociology comprises a rejection of the rational-actor models, an interest in institutions as independent variables, a turn towards cognitive and cultural explanations, and an interest in properties of sovra-individual units of analysis that cannot be reduced to aggregations

Table I.1   Approaches to organizational sociology

		Environmental influence	
		−	+
Organizational	−	[Garbage can]	Open system
Agency	+	Closed system	Neo-institutionalism

or direct consequences of individuals' attributes or motives' (DiMaggio and Powell 1991a, pp. 8–9).

In our research, we share some of the concerns expressed by the neo-institutional approach in an attempt to combine the analysis of environmental impacts (with a particular focus upon the cultural dimension) with that of organizational choices (as determined by their norms). First, we consider organizations as socializing agents and norms producers, which 'do not just constrain options: they establish the very criteria by which people discover their preferences' (ibid., p. 11). Organizations are therefore not just means for mobilization, but also (or even mainly) arenas for experimentation.

Second, we look at formal as well as informal practices. Within the neo-institutional approach, 'The relevance of relationships was no longer defined by the formal organization chart; forms of coordination grounded in personal networks as well as non authoritative projects of mobilization were made visible, as were influences that transgressed the official boundaries of an organization' (Clemens 2005, p. 356). Thus, our analysis will go beyond the formal organizational charts and look at the practices and ideas embodied in each organization.

Third, we share with the neo-institutional approach a focus on cognitive mechanisms: organizations do not automatically adapt to their environments; environmental pressures are filtered by organizational actors' perceptions. Neo-institutionalists marked a shift from Parsons' conception of internalization (with utilitarianism derived from Freud) to an emphasis on cognitive processes, derived from ethnomethodology and phenomenology and their focus on everyday action and practical knowledge (DiMaggio and Powell 1991a, pp. 15ff.) based upon the assumption that 'organization members discover their motives by acting' (ibid., p. 19). Important for this analysis is Bourdieu's notion of *habitus* as 'a system of "regulated improvisation" or generative rules that represents the (cognitive, affective and evaluative) internalization by actors of past experiences on the basis of shared typifications of social categories, experienced phenomenally as "people like us"'' (ibid., p. 26). In our research, we aim at combining an analysis of formal organizational roles with that of informal practices, general values, and participation in protest campaigns. While considering environmental constraints as potentially important in shaping organizational behaviour, we believe that organizations play an important and active role in shaping their environments. For social movements, as for other social actors, the organization is therefore not just a means, but also an end in itself.

We shall focus on the visions of democracy present in one particular movement, which became especially visible with the protest at the
Summit of the World Trade Organization in Seattle: the Global Justice
Movement (GJM), defined as the loose network of individuals and organizations (with varying degrees of formality), engaged in collective
action of various kinds, on the basis of the shared goal of advancing the
cause of justice (economic, social, political, and environmental) among
and between peoples around the globe (della Porta 2007b). Conceptions of democracy emerge as particularly relevant for this movement,
committed to addressing external as well as internal transformation.
Regarding the external, the movement must adapt to challenges to representative democracy: the shift of power from the state to the market;
the increasing power of transnational institutions, with their lack of
electoral accountability; the decline of mass parties (della Porta and
Tarrow 2005). As for internal transformation, the open and inclusive
structure already typical of other movements (particularly the women's
and peace movements) appears in the Global Justice Movement in a version with heightened reticularity: international counter-summits and
campaigns, but also local-level protests, are normally organized by structures co-ordinating hundreds if not thousands of groups (della Porta
2005c).

Leaving for the next chapter a more in depth conceptualization of the
relevant dimensions of democracy, I shall, in what follows, address some
methodological choices of our research.

Multi-method research: advantages and caveats

The research presented in this volume is part of the Democracy in
Europe and the Mobilization of the Society (DEMOS) project, which
focuses on the attitudes towards democracy of social movement organizations active in the GJM. The research admittedly covers only a limited
part of the GJM – looking at social movement organizations from six
European countries (Italy, Germany, France, Spain, Great Britain, and
Switzerland) as well as transnational ones. Many of them participated in
the European Social Forums, where, since the first edition in Florence in
2001, thousands of groups and tens of thousands of activists have met
and networked towards the building of 'another Europe' (della Porta
2009). However, it addresses not only the largest European countries,
but also the two main constellations that converged in the GJM: one,
especially in Central and Northern Europe, where NGOs (often coming from the New Social Movements of the past) are more visible; and

one where unions and social issues appear as more central (della Porta 2007b).

The research we present here consists of an analysis of documents and Web sites of GJM organizations; semi-structured interviews with movement organizations; surveys of movement activists; and participant observation of movement groups and their experiences with participatory and/or deliberative decision making. In contrast to most social movement research done in the past, we aimed at collecting information on a relatively large number of organizations/groupings per country and on very different organizational models. In the various parts of our research, we combined qualitative in-depth analysis of a few organizations with quantitative analysis of a large number of cases. One of the rationales for enlarging the number of selected cases was the heterogeneity of the GJM, particularly in terms of organizational designs. In order to reflect this heterogeneity, we needed to select a large number of different groups. This book presents the results of an analysis of the Web sites of 266 SMOs; the fundamental documents of 244 SMOs; and interviews with representatives of 210 SMOs.

The first part of our research focuses on e-democracy as conceived of and implemented in the Web sites of 266 social movement organizations involved in protest campaigns on global justice. Social movement organizations use the Internet as an instrument for spreading information, constructing identities, involving new members, and mobilizing on- and off-line. Given not only its low cost but also the potential for horizontal participation, in recent years the number of movement organizations with an online presence has grown dramatically. Building upon previous research (on Eastern European NGOs: Vedres et al. 2005; on European parliaments online: Trechsel et al. 2003), the analysis of the GJM organizations' Web sites was carried out using a structured codebook in order to collect information on the characteristics that might affect the extent to which online organizations fulfil the democratic potential of the Internet.[1] The codebook was structured around the following dimensions:

a) *general information provision*, including variables aimed at estimating the dissemination of information and analysing how information is organized on the Web site (information usability);
b) *identity building*, focusing on the use of a Web site for internal, multilateral communication;
c) *transparency*, with a set of variables on the online publication of information on statutes, organizational structure, work agenda,

physical existence and reachability, activities, economic situation, number of Web site users, as well as information useful to accessing members of the organization – often referred to as *bilateral interactivity*, that is, an organization's willingness to offer channels of direct communication with citizens, creating more participative organizational structures (Rommele 2003, p. 10);

d) *mobilization*, through variables aimed at measuring the use of Web sites for protest, both offline (demonstrations, events, and so on) and online (petitions and electronic disturbance actions such as netstrikes, mailbombing, and so on);

e) *intervention on the digital divide*, based on the presence of opportunities for training and providing a series of resources to socialize their users to the Internet.

The Internet is not only an interesting object of study, but also a rich source for analysing the written production of social movement organizations. Although not relying only upon the Web, a second part of our research analysing the fundamental documents of 244 social movement organizations focuses on the general tensions between deliberative participatory and representative patterns, both in the internal dynamics of social movements and in their relationships with institutions. This part of the research is not meant to capture the actual functioning of the organizations/groupings (to be addressed in other parts of the DEMOS project based on interviews, Web analysis and participant observation), but rather their organizational ideology. The assumption is that when a group has strong normative statements about internal democracy, these tend to be written in a 'visible' document such as a constitution, mission statement, 'about us' section on the organization's Web site, and so on. We are aware that in some cases constitutions or mission statements are strategically instrumental – that is, they can be adapted to the requirements of external sponsors/state institutions and so on, in order to obtain funds and influence. Formalized decision-making procedures tend, however, to constrain organizations' institutional structures and frames.

The analysis focused on the following organizational documents:

a) the constitution of the organization;
b) a document of fundamental values and/or intent;
c) a formally adopted program;
d) the 'mission statement';
e) the 'about us' section of the Web site;

f) the 'frequently asked questions' section of the Web site; and
g) equivalent or similar material on the Web site expressing the 'official' position of the organization as a whole (for example, internal documents referred to in documents a)–f) such as annual reports, membership application forms, and so on).

Many, but not all of these materials were available on the sites. After an analysis of the Web sites, we contacted the organizations to request missing documents in an effort to complete, as much as possible, our collection.

For the quantitative part of the research, we developed a codebook aimed at a structured analysis of visions of democracy. This part is quite new from a methodological point of view. Documents describing the structure of social movement organizations have been analysed in various research projects but mostly within qualitative in-depth analyses of a few groups, which had the advantage of 'thick' description but were difficult to summarize in larger comparison (for a review of the literature, see Rootes 2000; Clemens and Minkoff 2004; della Porta and Diani 2006).

We built our codebook around the following sets of variables:

a) general information on the organizational characteristics (including country and date of foundation, territorial level of activity, numbers of individual and collective members);
b) membership rules (including requirements for admission and procedures for admission as well as expulsion);
c) organizational structures and decision-making methods (including, if mentioned, the role of assemblies, executive committees, and presidents or general secretaries; their composition and functioning; methods for choosing delegates; limits on delegation; incompatibility rules);
d) relationships with public institutions (distinguishing among collaboration, democratic control and refusal of relationships with local institutions, national institutions, and international governmental institutions, as well as with economic actors);
e) identity and conceptions of democracy (including references to internal organizational values such as limitation of delegation, inclusiveness, deliberation, general democratic values such as participation, equality, and dialogue; themes covered, such as democracy, social justice, human rights, and ecology; specific functions of the organization, such as protest or lobbying).

To our knowledge, this is the first attempt to develop a systematic content analysis of SMOs' organizational documents on democratic values. We therefore invested considerable energies in the preparation of the codebook, taking into account both our main research questions and the characteristics of the available materials. For the development of this instrument, we were able to rely upon some previous experiences in other fields of research. In particular, the constitutions of political parties have been studied in research on party organizational models, and party electoral manifestos analysed as important sources of information on party ideology (see Klingeman et al. 1994).

The challenge in our research, however, is the presence of very different types of organizations: from political parties to unions, from large associations to small informal groupings, from transnational networks to local groups. Of course, we could have focused our attention only on organizations of the same type – for instance, organizations with a constitution. However, this approach would have excluded some relevant alternative organizational forms from our analysis. We must therefore accept that the quantity and character of written material varies a great deal by group: in fact, substantial written production makes it more likely that we will find statements about democracy, while the absence of a formal constitution makes it less likely that we will find detailed information about the formal rules of decision making. In the interpretation of our results, we take into account these differences and their consequences. A related problem is that, while formal organizations often provide easy access to the selected documents (generally on their Web sites; see della Porta and Mosca 2006), this is not always true for less formalized organizations. In addition, informal organizations also proved more reluctant to provide documents offline. This meant that, especially in some countries, the corpus of documents on some groups was reduced.

These limits are to be addressed, among other methods, through the triangulation of the results with those from a survey of (whenever possible) the same organizations analysed in the previous parts. Like the document analysis, the semi-structured interviews focused on conceptions of democracy, but shifted the attention to the way in which they are addressed by representatives of a sample of social movement organizations belonging to the GJM. The semi-structured questionnaire, administered by phone to key informants covering 210 SMOs, concerned organizational characteristics (name, year of foundation, internal decision making, types of activity, types of campaigns, type of organization, types of members, type of budget and sources of revenue) and relationships with the organizational field (connections with other groups/networks/campaigns of the GJM, interactions with institutions at different territorial levels). The interview campaign ran between January and August 2006.[2]

Before moving to the results of our empirical analysis, some brief remarks on the sampling strategies are in order. For the quantitative part, we have selected in each country organizations that had been involved in the main initiatives of the GJM (among them the European Social Forums), insuring variance especially on the main issues addressed. Since the GJM has been called 'a movement of movements', we have selected about 35 organizations per country and at the transnational level, including those we considered most representative of the various streams that converged in the GJM. Lists of organizations signing calls for action of social forums (at the national, European and global levels) and other important movement events were collected and used to identify the groups belonging to the 'core' of the GJM's networks. A common sampling strategy was agreed upon in order to collect comparable data, covering SMOs focusing upon different issues (environment, peace, women's rights, labour issues, solidarity, homosexual rights, migrant and human rights, and so on). Moreover, various kinds of media Web sites close to the GJM were also selected (periodical magazines, radio programs, newspapers, and networks of independent communication). Where present, local social forums were also included in the sample. Finally, groups critical of the social forum process were covered when symbolically influent upon the activists' debate on democracy.

Ours is not a random sample and therefore cannot be considered as representative of the composition of the GJM in each country. However, random sampling is only one of the possible ways of selecting cases; it has some obvious advantages, but difficult preconditions of applicability. As stated by King et al., among others, 'In qualitative research, and indeed in much quantitative research, random selection might not be feasible because the universe of cases is not clearly specified' (1994, p. 125). In our case, in fact, random selection was impossible given that the universe was unknown (there is no 'official' list of GJMOs). Additionally, 'even when random selection is feasible, it is not necessarily a wise technique to use' (ibid.), since there is the risk of 'missing important cases'. This reflection also applies to our research design, where (given the time-consuming tasks of acquiring and coding documents) we could select only about 30 to 40 groups per team. King et al. warn us that 'if we have to abandon randomness, *as it is usually the case in political science research*, we must do with caution' (ibid., p. 124, emphasis added).

In fact, we did not use randomness as a criterion in our sampling strategy, but tried instead to select in each country and at the supranational level organizations at the core of the Global Justice Movement. Additionally, we tried to reflect the heterogeneity of the movement by issues covered and ideological leanings. In this sense, we were careful not to sample on our dependent variables (conceptions of democracy), following the criterion that 'the best intentional design selects observations to ensure variation in the explanatory variable (and any control variables) without regard to the values of the dependent variables' (ibid., p. 140).

Because of this sampling strategy, we cannot say that our national samples are representative of the (unknown) universe of GJM organizations in each country. However, since our case selection also respected the principle that 'we must not search for those observations that fit (or do not fit) our a priori theory' (ibid., p. 141; see also p. 142), we do feel confident that the selection choices did not bias the statistical correlations among the coded variables. The sampling strategy for the interviews adapts the lists used for the analysis of documents, which were (when possible) substituted for with similar organizations, when unavailable. This happened in 19.5 per cent of the cases; these were concentrated in the Spanish and transnational samples (with about 50 per cent substitutions each), while ranging from 0.0 per cent substitution in the Swiss case to 2.7 per cent in the Italian, 7.7 in the German, 10.7 per cent in the French, and 13.8 per cent in the British.

This volume

In this volume we discuss the impact of different sets of variables on conceptions and practices of democracy. The mentioned databases, integrated with qualitative information, are used with different statistical techniques in an attempt to build up generalizable statements that speak to the large social science literature on social movement organizations.

In Chapter 1, on 'The Organizational Population', Donatella della Porta justifies the choice of the Global Justice Movement as the focus of our analysis. She addresses the issue of the plurality of the movement, looking at the ways in which the sample organizations define the GJM, as well as the issue of its 'global' nature.

In Chapter 2, Herbert Reiter addresses the meaning of participation as a value, and participatory democracy as a principle for the internal life of the group, for organizations belonging to various areas of the Global Justice Movement. While delegation emerges as correlated with some organizational characteristics, the mentioning of democracy as a value spreads across groups with different structural characteristics, testifying for the presence within the GJM of various participatory traditions. Old Left, New Left, new social movements, and groups in the New Global Movement areas all refer to participation, but with different nuances and consequences on internal democracy as well as interactions with institutions. The same is true when looking at groups involved in different organizational fields such as grass-roots social movement groupings, modern networks, formal NGOs, unions, parties, and co-operatives.

The aim of Chapter 3 on consensus in movements, by Donatella della Porta, is to conceptualize the contribution of the Global Justice Movement to reflections on deliberative democracy. Looking at normative theory on deliberative democracy and empirical research on deliberation in movements, it identifies some different meanings that similar concepts take in organizations with different historical traditions as well as involvement in different arenas (for example, NGOs, unions, squatted centres). Additionally, explanations of the emphasis on consensual decision making are discussed by looking at the structural and cultural characteristics of the organizations that mention consensus.

Chapter 4, again by Donatella della Porta, addresses the movement's attitudes towards the institution of multilevel governance. The chapter looks, in particular, at how social movement organizations respond to contemporary challenges to the representative model of democracy. Based on organizational documents and interviews, it conceptualizes attitudes towards institutions (working upon the distinction among collaboration, critical control, and refusal) and investigates explanations for the diverse attitudes. In particular, the effects of structural as well as cultural organizational characteristics are addressed.

In Chapter 5, Marco Giugni and Alessandro Nai explore possible explanations for differences in internal decision making observed among organizations of the Global Justice Movement. In particular, they investigate some structural and cultural determinants for the adoption of a deliberative participative model by organizations active in the movement. They do so by triangulating various methods. First, a logistic regression is run in order to control which of the organizational structural and cultural characteristics have an impact and to assess their relative weight. Second, qualitative comparative analysis (QCA) is used to explore multiple and conjunctural effects.

In Chapter 6, on the impact of organizational resources on democratic conceptions, Clare Saunders discusses the main sociological theories on organizational structures of social movements (iron law of oligarchy/institutionalization, tyranny of structurelessness, and so on).

In light of the interview data, size (in terms of operating budget, number of staff, number of volunteers/members, number of local groups) indeed emerges as leading to a more oligarchic organizational structure. A qualitative analysis of a few selected large organizations, however, allows us to go beyond the statement that 'big is ugly', identifying some organizational choices that can keep the oligarchical tendency in check.

In Chapter 7, Dieter Rucht and Simon Teune focus on the forms of action of the sampled organizations. After mapping some general trends in GJMOs' repertoires, the authors distinguish two clusters of organization, one consisting of groups that only use moderate forms, others that also employ confrontational ones. Based on various sources, including the groups' Web sites, key documents, and interviews conducted with group representatives, the different action choices are then explained looking at both internal and external factors.

In Chapter 8, 'Mediating the Movement', Lorenzo Mosca and Donatella della Porta focus on the use of the Internet by Global Justice Movement Organizations. This chapter describes how activists and organizations employ Computer Mediated Communication in the internal lives of their organizations, as well as for external mobilization. Through a systematic analysis of the organizational Web sites, the chapter conceptualizes their different qualities and looks for explanation in the environmental opportunities as well as the internal characteristics of the groups.

In Chapter 9, by Hélène Combes, Nicolas Haeringer and Isabelle Sommier, practices and conceptions of democracy as they emerged in interviews are analysed in relation to the 'generation' to which the different organizations belong. Indeed, the GJM is considered by its actors as a *new* form of engagement, an *innovative* form of struggle – that is to say, an unprecedented form of collective engagement. However, being a 'movement of movements', it gathers organizations that were created at different times. Different generations do indeed emerge as reflecting some characteristics of the periods in which they were created, with the most recent groups characterized by more direct and consensual visions and practices of democracy.

In Chapter 10, Mario Pianta, Raffaele Marchetti and Duccio Zola investigate the transnational dimension of activism in the Global Justice Movement, considering cross-border activism as the cause for the major novelties in social movement organizations. The move to transnational action is conceptualized as a broadening of the understanding of global issues and an evolution of political objectives and relationships to economic and political power, leading to forms of action and organization that largely differ from domestic activism. Based on the empirical evidence drawn from the interviews, an index of transnational activism is proposed, combining information on participation in transnational events and linkages with transnational networks and campaigns. The results of this analysis show that key determinants affecting the degree of transnational activism of the Global Justice Movement include global justice identity, field of activity, size, a network/campaign form of organization, the use of demonstrations as a form of action, and national specificities.

In the concluding chapter, Donatella della Porta reflects on the visions of democracy emerged from the empirical analysis as well as on the structural and cultural explanations for them.

Notes

1. In order to have a reliable instrument for Web sites coding, the codebook was tested several times by all coders. Two reliability tests were carried out on two different Web sites each. After the second test, we intervened in particular upon variables that had not worked well (scores of intercoder reliability below 50 per cent). Variables that had not worked since they were interpreted differently by different coders were eliminated and only when possible replaced with new ones. To make the coding process more reliable, we instructed the coders to follow some general rules, such as: a) to limit some searches to specific parts (i.e. the homepage) or sections of the Web site; b) to use the internal search engine (when present) or an equivalent searching function of Google that allows the search for specific information, limiting the search to a single Web site. In order to complement the quantitative coding with additional information, we asked the coders to record some Web pages (statistics, Web site map, statute, links page, etc.) and to add a final note about peculiarities of the Web site with a particular emphasis on symbols, discourses, actions and co-ordination to whom the organizations belong (and how they make this affiliation public). The codebook can be downloaded at: http://demos.iue.it/PDFfiles/Instruments/wp2codebook_final.pdf.
2. Considering the range of issues covered by the questionnaire, we decided that the person to be interviewed had to be somebody knowledgeable about the history of the organization, and that in some cases it would be necessary to interview two persons (e.g. for questions concerning the budget). Especially for trade unions, political parties, or large NGOs we interviewed the person responsible for protest campaigns, for international relations or for relations with social movements. For more informal groups, lacking clear organizational roles, we interviewed activists with long-standing experience in the group.

1
Global Justice Movement Organizations: The Organizational Population

Donatella della Porta

A new global movement? An introduction

Our research focuses on the Global Justice Movement. In general, social movements cannot be characterized as unified actors: by their very nature, they are made up of loose networks, their repertoire of action is varied, and their collective identity is not structured within specific organizational boundaries (della Porta and Diani 2006, chap. 1). This is all the more true for the actor we investigate, which has been described as organizationally fluid, strategically broad, and tolerant of diversity (della Porta 2007c).

As a result, the very presence of *a* global justice movement has been subject to debate. The use of the singular 'movement' or the plural 'movements' to refer to the groups and networks mobilizing on global justice is discussed among activists and scholars alike, with opinions reflecting in part the degree of harmony or divergence in mobilization at the national level (see, for example, della Porta 2005c; Rucht 2005). The heterogeneity of the movement, acknowledged as an asset by activists who talk of a 'movement of movements', has been considered by some scholars as a sign that the mobilizations on global issues do not share enough common meaning to allow us to speak of a social movement (Rucht 2005); by others as resonating with internalized values of tolerance and inclusiveness (della Porta 2005c). The question of the presence of 'a movement' has been addressed by looking at the intensity of activists' identification with the movement, the homogeneity of diagnostic and prognostic frames, the density of mobilizing networks, the continuity of action.

Among activists, the use of the singular or the plural varies. The Italian activists who organized the protest against the 2001 G8 summit in Genoa defined themselves as belonging to 'A movement of movements'. At the end of the 4th edition of the European Social Forum (a most prominent encounter of the European groups involved in the GJM), the Assembly of the Movements declared, 'We, women and men from social movements across Europe, came to Athens after years of common experiences, fighting against war, neoliberalism, all forms of imperialism, colonialism, racism, discrimination and exploitation, against all the risks of an ecological catastrophe' (ESF 2006).

Beyond the existence of 'a movement', the *global* nature of the phenomenon is also discussed. Some scholars stress that social movements still develop around national concerns and organize mainly at that level, while transnational groups are mainly ad hoc coalitions, weak in autonomous resources and individual commitment. Protest action, it is often noted, only very rarely happens beyond national borders, as it is mainly influenced by national political opportunities and aims to target national governments in particular. Together with the rareness of transnational protest events, the lack of duration of transnational networks and campaigns has been cited as a sign of weakness on other constitutional elements of social movements, such as action and networking (Tarrow 2005).

Finally, it is also contested to what extent we can single out *innovations* in the organizational models, issue framing and action repertoires in the recent mobilizations on global justice. To a certain extent, cycles of protest have always been laboratories for experimentation with new ideas (Tarrow 1998; Tilly 1978) and emerging movements bearers of new norms and codes (Melucci 1999; Rochon 1998). However, the definition of new social movements was already contested in the 1980s, and the tendency to see newness in each further wave of protest looked at with suspicion. This was all the more true for the mobilizations on global justice, which have been welcomed or criticized as a return of the (Old) Left, not only for their concern with 'materialist' themes but also because of the organizational resources provided by left-wing parties and unions alike (della Porta 2007c; Andretta and Reiter 2009).

The data we have collected allow for some specification on these (admittedly complex) issues. In what follows, I shall discuss the existence of a movement, the strength of its transnational dimension as well as its innovative versus traditional elements, while presenting some descriptive evidence on the organizational population studied in this volume in terms of cultural frames, forms of action and organizational models. Finally, I shall present the organizational conceptions of democracy that will be referred to broadly in the remainder of this volume.

Framing global issues

The establishment of a global movement requires, first of all, the development of a discourse that singles out a common identity as well as the target of the protest at the transnational level. Movement organizations should frame their action in terms of global identities and concerns, identifying themselves as part of a 'global movement' and targeting 'global enemies' within a global *enjeu* (or field of action).

The first finding from our research (confirmed by the survey of activists at the 4th ESF in Athens; see della Porta 2009) is the presence of high degrees of identification with a global movement. In our interviews with representatives of social movement organizations, we asked our respondents how close their group felt to the Global Justice Movement (see Table 1.1). As many as about 80 per cent answered that they identified fully, while only very few groups (less than 10 per cent) did not perceive themselves as being part of the movement or did not have a shared view on the question. The expression of a sense of belonging to the movement is all the more relevant since, among the organizations who declared feeling part of the movement, there are very different types of groups: from NGOs to political parties, from unions to more typical 'new social movement' organizations. Those who declared a lack

Table 1.1 Sense of belonging to the movement per country according to the interviews (%)

The group feels part of the movement	Country (% of Yes)							Total
	F	G	I	SP	SW	UK	TN	
No	17.9	23.1	13.5	0.0	0.0	0.0	0.0	7.6
The group doesn't have a shared view	14.3	0.0	2.7	2.9	3.6	0.0	0.0	3.3
Yes, but with reservations	14.3	15.4	5.4	11.4	0.0	10.3	11.1	9.5
Yes	53.6	61.5	78.4	85.7	96.4	89.7	88.9	79.5
Total	13.3	12.4	17.6	16.7	13.3	13.8	12.9	100.0
(N)	(28)	(26)	(37)	(35)	(28)	(29)	(27)	(210)

Notes: F = France; G = Germany; I = Italy; SP = Spain; SW = Switzerland; UK = United Kingdom; TR = Transnational. Cramer's V is 0.270***.

of identification were often media, which we sampled as sympathetic to the social forum process, as well as more radical (for example, anarchist) groupings. Additionally, the data indicate a high level of identification with the GJM by organizations that predate its emergence (we did not find a significant correlation between year of foundation and sense of belonging to the movement).

Actors' self-definition in terms of the existence of the movement and feelings of belonging might not be sufficient for assessing how much diverse actors and campaigns do conform to an analytic definition of social movements that stresses the need to subscribe to a 'shared belief'. As mentioned, the debate remains open, in politics as well as in the social sciences, to what extent a 'movement of movements' has enough core consensus to really qualify as such. The responses to an open question in our questionnaires to SMOs about the main aims of the GJM provide interesting material to address these issues.

The interviewed representatives perceived the Global Justice Movement in varied and multiple ways. As Table 1.2 shows, re-aggregating the answers to an open question, the main aims of the movement are defined as social by two-thirds of the groups, international by more than one-third. More than half of our groups point at new social movement issues, and around one quarter underline the issue of democracy. In a cross-national comparison, international aims are (unsurprisingly) mentioned especially by transnational groups, while national groups (with the exception of the Swiss ones) point at social issues; Swiss and Spanish groups address more new social movement issues, while a significant number of British, French, and Italian organizations see

Table 1.2 Perception of the movement per country (%)

Main aims of the movement	Country (% of Yes)							*Total*
	F	*G*	*I*	*SP*	*SW*	*UK*	*TN*	
Social issues	77.3	71.4	88.2	58.6	22.2	68.0	83.3	67.0
International issues	27.3	33.3	32.4	37.9	29.6	36.0	70.8	37.9
New social movement issues	50.0	47.6	52.9	65.5	88.9	24.0	54.2	55.5
Democracy / free access to information	45.5	9.5	38.2	27.6	3.7	40.0	29.2	28.0
Total	12.1	11.5	18.7	15.9	14.8	13.7	13.2	100.0
(N)	(22)	(21)	(34)	(29)	(27)	(25)	(24)	(182)

democracy (together with free access to information) as being at the core of the movement. Our respondents tend to underline positive aspects of the movement, with 85 per cent (especially British and transnational groups) supporting proactive claims while almost 40 per cent (especially French and Spanish groups) mentioned negative ones. As for the type of statement, most groups (around 80 per cent – especially Swiss and transnational groups) advance general statements (for example, equality for all, societal transformation), while one-third (especially Spanish and transnational groups) raise specific issues and/or policy proposals (for example, climate change, peace, Kyoto agreement, corporate accountability law, and so on).

Looking at the full answers, we can indeed observe that organizations tend to perceive the movement as a space in which their own specific concerns can find a larger audience. Our respondents do focus on some main issues that have converged in mobilizations on global justice. An important stream in our mobilizations is made up of organizations active on the South of the world. For them, the GJM represents an occasion for developing alternative mechanisms to regulate markets, trade and development (the Italian network Sdebitarsi), promoting 'a vision of the world based upon the dignity of the persons and the respect for human rights' (Amnistia Internacional Spain), asking for 'worldwide legislation for protection of labour rights according to ILO norm' (the German Kampagne für saubere Kleidung), aiming at eliminating the global inequalities that force people to migrate and fighting against the concept of a fortified Europe (Swiss Solidarité sans Frontières), promoting 'fair trade, in order to promote sustainable development and put at the centre the small producers' (International Fair Trade Association) and 'a change in the rules of international trade' (Altromercato). In fact, the Jubilee Debt Campaign puts alleviation of poverty and economic justice at the core of its concerns. For Medico International, the movement's main aims are 'to give human beings, who are permanently marginalized, access to resources like education, health service; to fight the logic of rating human beings according to their economic profitability'. The Italian Consortium of Solidarity criticizes the 'developmental models inspired by the neoliberal dogma'.

Issues of peace and war are also central. Peace and human security are considered as main values for the GJM (Stop the War Coalition). The eradication of poverty and hunger is considered as necessary in order to achieve peace through justice (Caritas Internationalis), as a main aim of the GJM is 'to prevent wars, accomplish disarmament, implement international standards' (Friedens- und Zukunftswerkstatt). In connection, ecological groups stress environmental issues, presenting the movement as seeking 'alternatives to the capitalist system that widens the gap between the rich and the poor and depletes natural resources' (Swiss Les Verts).

Traditional concerns for social justice are represented as central by the unions and left-wing parties. Thus, for the International Metalworkers' Federation, the GJM aims at ensuring 'basic human rights, democracy and social justice, through fighting for an alternative model of globalisation which put decent work at the centre of development and trade' and, for the Parti socialiste suisse – section genevoise, at 'providing global solutions that are not only based on profit'. Equality, and conversely the struggle against inequality, are stressed as central concerns by the associations of the 'have nots'. The GJM is seen as promoting the struggle against inequality, giving 'visibility to the excluded' (Agir contre le Chomage!), and fighting for a non-pauperizing guaranteed income (Arbeitslosengruppen Erwerbslos). In parallel, for the French association for the rights of migrants (Pajol), the aim of the movement is 'to make the struggles of undocumented migrants known' and for the Coordination des intermittents d'Ile de France, it 'struggles against precarious work'; while for the Italian Comitato Immigrati, it stresses the 'fight against the western model conceiving other peoples as colonies' and for the Muslim Association of Britain (Youth Section), equal rights.

These are not 'single issue' concerns, but clearly that which each organization considers as a core topic for the agenda of a complex movement. Additionally, the language used is often resonant with the various traditions. Religious organizations stress the 'the dignity of the person', unions and traditional left organizations 'equality'. For Hermandad Obrera de Acción Católica, the movement aims at 'spreading social justice and economic development in the whole planet'; it is a 'movement of universal brotherhood'. For the Sexual Freedom Coalition, the movement promotes analytical libertarian thinking. And, for the rank-and-file union Confederazione Unitaria di Base (CUB), it focuses on workers' rights, equal wages, freedom of organization, and unionism.

Notwithstanding these specific focuses and languages, however, there is common ground. Beyond the different accents are bridging themes that are shared by the respondents and underline core concerns. Over and over, the respondents locate four main concerns at the basis of the GJM: calls for rights, social justice, democracy from below, and the global nature of the action.

First of all, a *language of rights* is used by virtually all groups, with different emphasis on some specific ones. This is typical of unions ('individual and collective rights', CGIL), as well as organizations closer to New Social Movement concerns ('civil rights' for Arcigay). The organizations involved in campaigning on the South of the world spread a language of 'human rights', which in the GJM soon became 'global rights'. In the words of the representative of the European Global March Against Child Labour, the GJM is oriented to the 'promotion of human rights and of social sustainable development through strategies against poverty, illiteracy and exploitation'. However, the base of reference of the movement is rarely circumscribed to specific groups of the population, but rather defined by broad categories such as 'citizens of the humanity'. The language of human rights is not only used for the citizens of non-democratic countries. Citizenship is mentioned, but extended to all residents and beyond. The purpose of the GJM is 'to struggle against neo-liberal globalization and propose an alternative globalization based upon the respect of human rights for all' (Agir Ici, the French branch of Oxfam), as it is a 'movement that starts from the citizens' (Centre d'études et d'initiatives de solidarité internationale – CEDETIM), a 'world citizens' movement' (Centre de Recherche et d'Information pour le Développement – CRID). Civil rights are stressed, also, by gay associations. The representative of the largest Italian gay rights association declares that 'Arcigay follows the GJM as we think that together with economic globalization also civic and social rights should be globalized.'

Second, *social issues* are mentioned, in one way or another, by most respondents. Social justice is the most quoted aim (35 mentions of 'justice', plus 18 of 'fair' are present in open answers to the question about what the movement is about). As stressed by the Italian Emergency, the GJM aims at 'Engagement on concrete issues: stating equality among human beings, emphasizing human rights and reduction of differences. These aims can be summarized with the term social justice.' Social justice is framed in different terms according to different traditions. Social issues might be addressed in terms of 'poverty' in the NGOs' or religious language. Christian Aid works as part of the GJM in order 'to expose the scandal of poverty, to help in practical ways to root it out from the world, and to challenge and change the systems which favour the rich and powerful over the poor and marginalised'; for the Catholic Pax Christi, the movement aims at modifying the rules of the economy. Social issues are framed in terms of exploitation in the traditional left-wing jargon – thus for the Trotskyite Socialist Workers' Party, the GJM 'challenges capitalism and all of the negative effects that it has on people'. The mobilization is defined as mainly against neoliberal policies (mentioned 20 times by our respondents), but also (with 16 mentions) in the name of 'a clear anticapitalist identity that opposes a society based on goods, profit and war' (Confederazione dei COBAS, Italian rank-and-file union).

Social justice is, however, perceived as the 'broker frame' that connects all others – in the words of the representative of Espacio Alternativo, 'there is a great diversity, but also the trend to unify them in a general, pluridimensional idea of social justice: social, ecological, between genders, between peoples and cultures, democratic-participative and for the defence of the common good'. The GJM is in fact said to promote 'social justice in all the world, give priority to human beings over profit, reduce or redistribute economic, financial, cultural and military power' (Groupe pour une Suisse sans Armée, GSsA) and to 'seek economic, political, social alternatives to the prevailing model, in a decentralised and non-hierarchic way' (Marche Mondiale des Femmes, Switzerland). For Friends of the Earth International, the movement bridges 'environmental and social issues; it challenges the current model of economic and corporate globalisation, promotes the creation of solutions for environmentally sustainable and socially just societies'. For Greenpeace, its aim is 'to found a mondialization upon social and environmental rights and the rights of the human person, the respect for the environment, cultural diversity and pacifism'. Especially, but not only, by more 'political' groups, social justice is often mentioned at the top of long lists of goals that include:

- 'disarmament, new economic models, globalization of human rights, media democratization, environment and biodiversity protection' (Peacelink);
- 'redistribution of wealth, peace, freedom of movement for men and women all over the world, critics to all forms of intellectual propriety' (Giovani comunisti);
- 'reform of international institutions, European social constitution, struggle against precarity, more investments on developmental cooperation, strategic role of politics for sustainable development, right to education, culture and housing' (Sinistra giovanile);
- 'no war, social rights, ecology, end poverty, women's rights, migrants ... ' (Co.bas, sindicato de Comisiones de Base);
- 'participative democracy, sustainable development, alimentary sovereignty, gender equality, etc.' (Cordoba Solidaria);
- 'trade justice, debt cancellation, more and better aid (quality and quantity), human and workers' rights, social, cultural, economic and

political rights (e.g. being able to hold governments accountable), eradication of poverty' (Catholic Agency for Overseas Development);
- 'economic, social and environmental justice with a special focus on the economic, but not excluding other issues' (Make Poverty History);
- 'political, social, economic and cultural alternatives to globalisation and to international, regional or national policies' (ATTAC Swiss).

The quest for *another democracy*, built 'from below', is a third bridging theme, always linked with social justice. The movement is mainly about democracy, socioeconomic and environmental justice, and equity (Seattle to Brussels Network), 'another economy and a new democracy', which goes beyond the national and delegated institutions (the Italian journal Carta). It aims 'to reconstruct a public space and democracy' (ATTAC Italia).

Especially by the transnational organizations, attention to democracy is framed in terms of the reform of international governmental organizations. The movement aims at strengthening international law and institutions (Reclaim our UN); democratizing the international system (Food First Informations- und Aktions-Netzwerk); achieving 'democratization and accountability of international institutions' (EuroIFI, network for the reform of International Financiary Institutions); challenging and changing the dominant economic policies and the international decision-making architecture (the European Network on Debt and Development – EURODAD). The more traditionally 'political' organizations stress here the reform of existing institutions, the creation of 'democratic institutions without mercantilist aims' (Rifondazione Comunista), a more participatory governance of globalization, against economic power and transnational corporations and for a reform of the UN (Verdi, Italian Green party).

Additionally, however, democracy is perceived as the construction of participative and deliberative spaces. Democracy concerns '1) democratic participation at all levels; 2) transparency in production activities…, 3) to raise awareness of all actors' (Associazione Botteghe del Mondo), as well as requiring an 'innovation of the culture of traditional parties' (CTM Altromercato) and 'promoting a good politics coming from a vibrant and reactive civil society' (Campagn Banche Armate). The aim of the movement is 'to spread direct participation and citizenship to defend common goods from private economic aggression and to re-establish priority of politics on economics' (Venezia Social Forum[1]). Citizens' participation is presented as a requirement for social equality – the movement holds out for 'a transformation of society so that it is more just, egalitarian, solidarist, and in which all citizens have to decide on what concerns them, not only vote every four years' (Grupo Antimilitarista de Carabanchel). For London Rising Tide, the movement wants 'to change the current system of power to enable people to reclaim power over their own lives' and for the Welt-friedensdienst, democracy and participation belong to the basic form of living.

The demand for a return of politics against 'the market' is common. In most cases, the movement is seen as oriented 'to recuperate and expand the spaces that were lost for the community to the advantage of the financiary power; to oppose all the renunciations of compe-tences by the state that tend to privilege the rights of investors and traders' (ATTAC-Madrid). Similarly, the British journal *Red Pepper* per-ceives the movement as aiming at 'the creation of effective means of democratic control at all levels – local to global', and Euromovement points at the 'organization of politics under principles of participation and self-governing' in order to achieve 'global common goods'. The proposed solutions vary from the regulation of international financial markets (World Economy, Ecology and Development – WEED), to more co-management rights for the civil society (Aktion Finanzplatz), to what Rete Noglobal, a network linking squatted social centres and similar col-lectives, defines as 'a radical change in the forms of political decision and conditions of economic democracy'.

A fourth common element is the reference, explicit or implicit, to a *global* dimension, as expressed in the frequent use of words like global (77 mentions in the string variable database), international (40 mentions), or – simply – world (33 mentions, often as 'another world is possible'). In the words of an interviewee, the GJM 'pursues a change in the existing global structures that are based upon a neoliberal economic model that privileges that maximization of profits over distri-bution, equality, justice of human rights' (Organización de Cooperación y Solidaridad Internacional).

The international sphere, global perspective, and attention to the world are also framed with different focuses. Taking Swiss organizations as illustrations, in the definition of the GJM's aims we have references to: 'Balancing the power struggle between the North and the South, i.e. democratic consultation for international market regulations' (Jeunesse Socialiste Suisse); 'Seeking a fairer international economic order and give a human face to international relations' (Syndicat de l'Industrie et du Bâtiment, UNIA); changing the world in order to allow for more equality and freedom (Syndicat des Services Publics, SSP-VPOD, Section genevoise); 'Offering social, political and economic alternatives, implement international solidarity actions, be an instrument of reflection and criticism of neo-liberal policies' (Syndicat Interprofessionnel des travailleurs et travailleuses – SIT); 'improving the North-South relations and trying to abolish inequalities. Seeking a fairer world' (Solidarität mit Chiapas). In short, it is a movement for redistribution of global wealth (British Transport and General Workers' Union), which aims 'to stop the welfare cuts on the national, European and international level, to the realisation of social justice through reallocation of wealth from top to bottom' (Hamburger Sozialforum).

In fact, our data from the document analysis (see Table 1.3) on the basic themes and values mentioned in organizational documents confirms the 'bridging' function of such frames as 'alternative globalization' and 'democracy' (about half of the groups mention them) as well as 'social justice' (almost two-thirds of our groups), 'global justice', and 'workers' rights' (about half mention both). Ecological values also emerge as quite relevant (about half of the groups cite ecology, and the same proportion mentions sustainability, with much less frequent attention to animal rights). The Global South is mentioned by about half of the groups calling for solidarity with third world countries; but half of them also stress the importance of human rights, and one-third refer to fair trade. References to women's rights and peace are also commonplace (in half of the groups sampled), and the same is true for migrant rights. The big ideologies of the past, however, are less often mentioned by our groups (socialism: 7.8%; communism: 3.3%; anarchism: 3.7%; religious principles: 7%).

Table 1.3   Basic themes mentioned in fundamental documents (% yes)

Widespread themes		Little-spread themes	
Social justice	69	Socialism	8
Another democracy	52	Communism	3
Another globalization	50	Anarchism	4
Peace	50	Religious principles	7
Ecology	47		
Human rights	47		
Global justice	45		
Migrant rights	46		
Solidarity with the South	46		
Women's rights	43		

On the basis of bivariate correlations among all the themes, we recoded these variables, aggregating under 'new globalism' references to another globalization, democracy, and social justice. Almost all groups cite these fundamental themes (87.3 per cent). New social movement values (mentioned by 70.9 per cent of our organizations) refer to issues such as ecology, animal rights, women's rights, and anti-racism. Roughly the same number (69.3 per cent) focuses on issues of peace and non-violence. Values of solidarity, mentioned by 58.6 per cent of our sample, contain references to sustainability, solidarity with the third world, critical consumerism, and ethical finance. Anti-capitalism (26.6 per cent) also includes mentions of anarchism and autonomy and traditional left groups' references to socialism and communism (8.6 per cent). It is especially relevant that our organizations mention many of the listed themes as their main concerns (with an average of 7.6 themes per group), indicating a strong tendency to bridge issues beyond the original concern.

Concluding, it is difficult, for lack of comparative data, to say if this 'movement of movements' is more heterogeneous than previous ones, and, for lack of shared standards if it passes the threshold of 'shared belief' mentioned by social science definitions. The ways in which our respondents defined the main aim of the movement certainly indicate many specificities, but also common bridging themes, such as concerns with rights, social justice, democracy from below. Also common to our organizations, and supporting the definition of a *global* justice movement, is the identification of problems and solutions, identities, and targets as supranational – as seen in the frequent use of terms such as world, planet, and globe, as well as the reference to the Global South. Most of the mentioned themes are deeply rooted in the cultural traditions of the organizations and individuals joining the mobilizations. The bridging of the various themes resonates with a collective identification in the GJM. What seems new is the intensity of the frame bridging of issues and languages once considered as quite different, if not opposed to each other. Additionally, in the part of the research based on interviews we had to adjust the sampling in order to make up for the organizations, included in the document analysis, that for various reasons we could not interview.

Multilevel and multiform protest?

In order to be defined as global, a movement should engage in transnational forms of action. Just as protest actions concentrated at the national level with the creation of the nation-state, economic globalization and multilevel governance can be expected to move *protest* to the transnational level, against international actors. Although research on protest events has stressed that the nation-state remains the target of most claims-making, some of the new forms of protest that have emerged since Seattle are indeed transnational in nature. Counter-summits use the windows of opportunity and media attention offered by summits of international organizations to draw attention to criticisms against international policies on issues such as the depletion of natural resources or the violation of human rights, the promotion of communication rights or the struggle against copyrights on seeds. World or macro-regional social forums promote discussion beyond borders, and global days of action focus attention on common issues around the world.

Although they might be rare in absolute terms, transnational protest events – such as protest campaigns focusing on poverty in the South, taxation of capital, debt relief, fair trade, global rights, and reform of international intergovernmental organizations – are particularly relevant for their capacity to produce networking as well as their symbolic value (della Porta 2008a; della Porta and Caiani 2009; Reitan 2007). Contacts among different groups often developed at the transnational level, even before the national level. Campaigns such as the European Marches on unemployment and exclusion, the Euromayday against precarious jobs, or the global day of action against the war in Iraq have provided occasions for encounters 'in action', among activists of different national and social backgrounds, not only at the protest events but also during their preparation (see also Smith et al. 2007). Often, representatives of local groups or activists from different countries came together at the transnational level, with more openmindedness and curiosity about each other's histories than at the national level, where cleavages within and between social movements have consolidated along traditional fractures and personal enmities (Doerr 2006).

When asked about participation in events organized by the GJM (Table 1.4), our respondents indicated the transnational level as more relevant than the national and local ones, while the frequency of this participation testifies to a continuity that goes beyond ad hoc mobilization. In fact, almost 80 per cent of the groups had participated in a transnational event like a World Social Forum and/or European Social Forum; a similarly high share took part in Global Days of Action (that is, against war) and almost 75 per cent in counter-summits organized at meetings of International Governmental Organizations. Less than 60 per cent of the groups had participated in national or local social

Table 1.4 Participation in movement events per country according to the interviews (%)

Participation in movement events	Country (% Yes)							Total
	F	G	I	SP	SW	UK	TN	
World/European social forums	96.4	73.1	94.6	54.3	67.9	79.3	92.6	79.5
National/local social forums	82.1	73.1	54.1	48.6	71.4	17.2	59.3	57.1
Counter-summits	85.7	46.2	91.9	74.3	60.7	65.5	88.9	74.3
Global days of action	89.3	73.1	89.2	82.9	75.0	58.6	70.4	77.6
Total	13.3	12.4	17.6	16.7	13.3	13.8	12.9	100.0
(N)	(28)	(26)	(37)	(35)	(28)	(29)	(27)	(210)

Note: Cramer's V is: 0.354^{***} (WSF/ESF); 0.394^{***} (NSF/LSF); 0.317^{***} (counter-summits); 0.255^{**} (GDA).

forums. Regarding national specificities, the groups in the French and Italian samples appear to be the most engaged in the GJM events we listed. This reflects the organization of important movement events in those countries during the last decade (especially G8 counter-summits and European Social Forums). National and local social forums were also significant events for German (national social forum of Erfurt), Swiss, and transnational groups, while the 3rd European Social Forum (2004) in London was particularly important for the British groups. Global days of action figured prominently for French, Italian, and Spanish groups. With the significant exception of the German and Swiss samples, engagement in the GJM protests increases in all other countries when moving from local to national and transnational activities.

The relevance of the transnational dimension for our groups is also confirmed by the answers to the question about the five organizations, campaigns, and networks dealing with global justice issues with which the groups most intensively interacts. Table 1.5 presents the issue and the territorial level of these campaigns/networks. More than two-fifths of them address international issues (even more for the Swiss and transnational groups), around half social issues (even more for France and the UK); between 10 and 20 per cent national issues, democracy or new social movement issues. National issues are raised especially by German and Italian campaigns/networks, the issue of democracy mainly by Spanish groups, new social movement issues especially by British and transnational campaigns/networks. The data on the territorial level of the campaign confirms that most groups network transnationally

Table 1.5   Issues of networks/campaigns of the movement per country according to the interviews (%)

Issues of networks/campaigns	Country (% Yes)							Total
	F	G	I	SP	SW	UK	TN	
Social issues	66.7	45.5	56.7	38.5	36.8	81.5	33.3	53.3
International issues	70.4	81.8	76.7	88.5	94.7	85.2	100.0	84.0
National issues/political parties/think tanks	14.8	22.7	20.0	3.8	0.0	3.7	5.6	10.7
Democracy	7.4	4.5	10.0	34.6	5.3	7.4	5.6	11.2
New social movement issues	18.5	13.6	3.3	19.2	10.5	22.2	33.3	16.6
Total	16.0	13.0	17.8	15.4	11.2	16.0	10.7	100.0
(N)	(27)	(22)	(30)	(26)	(19)	(27)	(18)	(169)
Territorial levels of networks/campaigns								
Local	3.7	0.0	0.0	7.7	10.5	7.4	0.0	4.1
National	88.9	100.0	56.7	53.8	68.4	96.3	0.0	69.0
Transnational	96.3	70.8	86.7	88.5	89.5	66.7	100.0	84.4
Total	15.8	14.0	17.5	15.2	11.1	15.8	10.5	100.0
(N)	(27)	(24)	(30)	(26)	(19)	(27)	(18)	(171)

(almost 85 per cent; especially French and transnational organizations), with less emphasis on the national level campaigns (almost 70 per cent; especially German, French and British groups) and very low participation in (exclusively) local campaigns (4 per cent – with somewhat higher percentages for Spanish, Swiss and British groups).

While most of our groups take part in transnational action, their strategies do vary, as the multiplicity of concerns and values is reflected in a multiplicity of forms of action. Leaving to further chapters a more in-depth analysis of the groups' repertoires (see, in particular, Chapter 6), it is worth noting that the parts of the research based upon both documents and interviews contributed to confirming the presence of a broad and various repertoire, ranging from lobbying to direct action, from educational campaign to public protest. A plural repertoire confirms the pluralistic nature of the movement, with a (somewhat pragmatic) orientation towards the use of multiple tactics.

In the documents of the sampled organizations, while protest is mentioned by a large majority of our groups (69.3%), a similarly large share mentions influencing the media, spreading alternative information, and raising awareness as a main function of their groups (68.0%), and almost half of the organizations mention the political education of citizens (42.6%). Although smaller, the significant number of groups mentioning political representation (11.5%), defence of specific interests (18.4%), advocacy (27.5%), provision of services (21.7%) and self-help (13.9%) signals that most organizations engage in various types of activities. Even larger percentages also mention lobbying (35.7%). Most of our groups do not limit themselves to a single strategy but mix multiple strategies.

Similar results come from the interviews. As Table 1.6 shows, almost 90 per cent of the groups value cognitive activities such as disseminating information, organizing conferences, seminars and workshops, publishing research reports, and so on. Around three quarters of the groups report performing protest activities and the same proportion engaging in the construction of concrete alternatives. About half of the groups employ a strategy of lobbying with direct pressure on public decision makers. Contrary to the assumption that lobbying and protest are opposite strategies used by different actors, we found evidence of the use of both by a significant percentage of our groups. This result is consistent with most observations concerning the Seattle protests

Table 1.6 Main strategies of the groups by country according to the interviews (%)

Main strategies of the group	Country (% Yes)							Total
	F	G	I	SP	SW	UK	TN	
Protest	78.6	73.1	81.1	97.1	75.0	75.9	59.3	78.1
Building concrete alternatives	85.7	61.5	64.9	62.9	89.3	79.3	88.9	75.2
Lobbying	42.9	57.7	51.4	37.1	57.1	69.0	70.4	54.3
Political education/ raising awareness	78.6	100.0	89.2	82.9	96.4	89.7	92.6	89.5
Number of overlapping strategies								
0–1	10.7	7.7	8.1	5.7	3.6	10.3	7.4	7.6
2	21.4	34.6	21.6	31.4	10.7	6.9	22.2	21.4
3	39.3	15.4	43.2	40.0	50.0	41.4	22.2	36.7
4	28.6	42.3	27.0	22.9	35.7	41.4	48.1	34.3
Total	13.3	12.4	17.6	16.7	13.3	13.8	12.9	100.0
(N)	(28)	(26)	(37)	(35)	(28)	(29)	(27)	(210)

Notes: Cramer's V is: 0.257** (protest); 0.269** (alternatives); 0.232* (lobbying); n.s. (political education). Overall % of column can sum above 100% because of the possibility of multiple responses.

and similar events, where multiple strategies were planned and implemented. However, at least in our samples, organizations from different countries favour different strategies. While lobbying is more widespread among organizations belonging to the Northern European countries (Britain in particular) and to the transnational level, protest is more frequently used among those belonging to southern European countries (Spain in particular). Finally, almost all German and Swiss groups invest in the political education of citizens, while most of the French, Swiss, and transnational groups reported employing a strategy aimed at building concrete alternatives. Considering the use of multiple strategies, we can note that few groups (less than 10 per cent) focus on a single strategy. More than two-thirds employ at least three strategies at the same time, while one-fifth employ only two different strategies.

Groups very engaged with different forms of action (both conventional and unconventional) are more likely to be from southern European countries (Table 1.7). Petitioning and demonstrations are used by most of our surveyed organizations (over 75 per cent). Less widespread are more radical and/or innovative forms of action such as boycotts (especially common in Italy, Spain, and the UK), blockades (particularly mentioned for France, Germany, and Spain), occupations

Table 1.7 Repertoire of action of the groups per country according to the interviews (%)

Forms of action	Country (% Yes)							Total
	F	G	I	SP	SW	UK	TN	
Petition	82.1	76.9	67.6	88.6	53.6	72.4	88.9	75.7
Demonstration	92.9	61.5	91.9	85.7	75.0	75.9	66.7	79.5
Strike	21.4	11.5	37.8	45.7	21.4	13.8	7.4	24.3
Boycott of certain products	32.1	11.5	48.6	37.1	17.9	41.4	22.2	31.4
Blockade	35.7	34.6	32.4	40.0	25.0	10.3	11.1	27.6
Occupation of buildings	50.0	11.5	16.2	45.7	10.7	17.2	18.5	24.8
Civil disobedience	71.4	30.8	35.1	57.1	35.7	24.1	29.6	41.0
Artistic/cultural performance	64.3	57.7	67.6	71.4	46.4	65.5	40.7	60.0
Total	13.3	12.4	17.6	16.7	13.3	13.8	12.9	100.0
(N)	(28)	(26)	(37)	(35)	(28)	(29)	(27)	(210)

Note: Cramer's V is: 0.270** (petition); 0.275** (demonstration); 0.315*** (strike); 0.269** (boycott); 0.247** (blockade); 0.353** (occupation); 0.319*** (civil disobedience); n.s. (artistic/cultural performance).

and civil disobedience (especially widespread in France and Spain). The creative and symbolic side of collective action is highly valued by most groups: almost two-thirds of our organizations engage in artistic and cultural performances (especially in southern European countries and the UK). In some countries the strike is still limited to groups organizing workers, while in others (for example, Italy and Spain) it has spread from the trade union sector to the social movement sector.

The varied nature of the repertoire of action of our sampled organizations is confirmed by the answers to the open question about the movement's main aims, where respondents also addressed the ways in which the movement can help in reaching them. Different visions also affect the perception of the main means through which the movement acts. Respondents in fact stress political pressure (according to Swiss Radio LoRa, the movement 'Promotes better understanding of global links, brings together critical proposals, increase parliamentary and extraparliamentary pressure in order to achieve a fair distribution of material wealth and political power'); education of the people (among others, L'Autre Davos); 'conscientization' (Comité Catholique contre la Faim et pour le Développement); democratic control by citizens of economic and political development (Bewegung für den Sozialismus); social and cultural mobilization (Euromayday); alternative discourses and peaceful culture (Communication Rights in the Information Society). The main strategies of the movement can be presented in such different terms as 'public mobilization and teaching about the issues, raising trade profile as we see it as a key to lift people out of poverty' (Oxfam International) or 'to struggle against the barbarian consequences of the mondialized capitalism and discuss an alternative project' (LCR – Ligue Communiste Révolutionnaire).

However, the belief in the importance of 'building alternatives' is widespread across our organizations. In the database containing the string variables with answers to the open question about defining the movement, the word 'alternative' is counted 42 times; not only is the word 'revolution' completely absent, but even 'protest' is quoted only three times, with specification such as 'protest as the basis for the construction at the political level, not sterile protest' (Mouvement des Jeunes Communistes). Alternatives are conceived as concrete, implemented: for Rete Lilliput, the 'construction of other possible world' requires one 'to create evident contradictions through alternative practices'. The movement has, here, to 'publicize alternatives already practiced in the Global South' (Unimondo). But 'alternative' is also conceived as radically different, as the movement aims at 'unveiling/making visible/denouncing the different forms that the capitalist systems uses in order to legitimize itself and activate proposals or alternatives to this system' (Baladre). It implies 'radical change of society and lifestyles' (Italian Tavola della Pace) and 'offers an alternative to the capitalist model' (Swiss Les Communistes).

Concluding, document data and interviews testify to the relevance of transnational protest events in terms of networking as well as symbolic value for the groups participating in the GJM. At least for our organizations, participation in such events does not seem sporadic or occasional: to the contrary, a high percentage tends to take part in several and various types of transnational events. Once again, despite missing data on the role played by transnational events for other movements (for example, meetings of the Socialist International), it seems that in the perceptions of our activists the Global Justice Movement is mainly about action, not only at the local or national level, but also (and even more so) at the transnational level. Repertoires of actions seem to be not only multilevel but also multiform. Not only are groups preferring diverse strategies represented in our sample but, what is more, most groups tend to combine various forms (for example, protest and lobbying) once considered as quite far apart if not incompatible. Worth stressing as an innovation of recent mobilizations is the role given to the practice of alternatives as 'possible utopias'.

Networking: A movement of movements?

If social movements are *networks* of individuals and groups, a global movement should involve, on a stable basis, organizational nets active in various countries. The possibility of building up global networks, although enhanced by new technology such as the Internet, is of course constrained by material as well as symbolic limitations. World-wide events (such as the World Social Forum) are rare and involve mainly a cosmopolitan elite – so much so that networks such as No Vox have emerged to denounce the marginality of the 'have nots', not only in society, but also within the movement; these groups promote the presence of marginalized groups, especially at transnational events where the effects of the possession of cultural and material resources are more relevant.

Additionally, even when counter-summits are organized by transnational coalitions, their participants remain largely nationals. Transnational networks and campaigns, as well as transnational social movement organizations, are (with few exceptions) very poor in autonomous resources. Finally, in the global justice mobilization there is the convergence of different groups, not only with different values and forms of action, but also with different organizational models: a diversity that, according to some approaches, would make the development of common (even flexible) structures all the more difficult (della Porta 2005c; Juris 2005).

Our data from the interviews on the organizational characteristics of the sampled groups confirm the pluralistic and heterogeneous nature of the GJM, with very different organizational structures present in the same movement. First of all, resources vary. Our organizations cover a wide range in terms of *size* of individual and collective membership. While 21.6 per cent have fewer than 100 individual members, about half have between 100 and 10 000, and the remaining one-third have more than 10 000 members. Of the almost 65 per cent of our groups who have also collective members, one-fifth have up to ten, but one-third more than 100. As for their *budget*, while 16.7 per cent declare a variable or limited budget, and a quarter of them declare less than 50 000 euros, the remaining part is equally divided among those who declare between 50 000 and 500 000 and those who have more than 500 000. Similar variation exists on the presence of paid staff, with only one-third of our groups declaring none, 44.4 per cent up to 16, 14.1 per cent between 16 and 100, and 11.2 more than 100. Regarding number of *volunteers*, the groups are equally divided among those who declare less than 16, those who declare between 16 and 100, and those who declare more than 100.

On the basis of the organizational documents, we have been able to observe very different organizational features. A large majority of our groups (59.4%) has a positive score on an index of *structural participation* that we constructed by assigning a positive value to those organizations in which the assembly meets more than once a year, and/or the members of the executive/president/spokesperson are elected by the general assembly. A lower 39.3 per cent has a positive score on the index of *structural inclusiveness*, measured by the lack of requirements for membership (other than endorsing the principles of the organization) and of provisions to expel members. On an additive index of *formalization*, which includes the presence of a constitution, a document of fundamental values, a formally adopted program, formal membership, and membership cards (normalized to vary from 0 to 1), the average for our sample is 0.42. We could also classify our groups as belonging to different *organizational fields*: 9 per cent as unions; 9 per cent as parties; 2.9 per cent as co-operatives; 38.9 per cent as NGOs or formal SMOs;

4.9 per cent as grass-roots organizations; and 34 per cent as modern networks (1.2 per cent as others).

Our groups are also part of different *generations* of social movements: 18.6 per cent were founded before the mobilizations of 1968 and 19.8 per cent between 1968 and the fall of Berlin's wall (1989), while almost one-third (31.4%) were founded during the 1990s and almost another third (30.2%) after the protest of Seattle (1999). Linked to this, and resonating with the self-definitions of the GJM as a 'movement of movements', our sample in fact contains groups coming from different *movement areas*: 13.1 per cent of organizations we recoded as belonging to the Old Left; 11.5 per cent as New Left/anarchism/autonomy; 11.5 per cent as mobilizing on new social movement themes; 28.7 per cent on solidarity/peace and human rights; and 32.8 per cent that we defined as 'new global', having formed around issues of global justice (2.5 per cent were not classifiable).

If these are relevant differences, however, confirming the picture of a 'coloured', heterogeneous mobilization, our data point at some common features. First, the organizations belonging to our sample cover different territorial levels. As mentioned, our groups express high levels of participation in campaigns, forums, and global days of action, as well as in transnational umbrella organizations. If we look at the territorial levels covered, we notice that a local presence is considered to be important by three-quarters of the organizations in our sample (74.2%); this is all the more relevant for a sample that by definition (see above) under-covers local groups. However, the national level (with 83.6 per cent) is also very important, as is the international level: about one-third of our groups declare that they are organized at that level. Among the organizations with a supranational level, we can find hierarchical 'single' organizations (such as Greenpeace, 6.6 per cent of our sampled groups), traditional federations (such as ETUC, 11.5 per cent), modern/loose networks (such as ATTAC-International, 11.5%), and campaigns (such as Euromayday, 8.2%).

Especially significant for the GJM is the high presence of network organizations: in our sample, this is reflected in the fact that about half of our cases represent networks/federations or ad hoc umbrella organizations. An additional indicator of the high reticularity of the GJM organizations is that almost half of the groups in our sample allow for collective membership. Additionally, as many as about 80 per cent of our organizations mention in their documents collaboration/networking with national SMOs and about the same percentage with transnational SMOs. Of the organizations mentioning collaboration/networking, about one-third (slightly more at the transnational level) point at the relevance of collaboration with groups working on other issues than they do.

Recurrent in our interviews, bridging the different strategic visions, is an emphasis upon the role of the movement itself as a space for networking. First of all, the movement is perceived as an area for encounters, exchanges, networking, and also for collective mobilization. The GJM is about 'the critique of capitalist globalization and the proposals for economic, social and cultural alternatives, as well as the creation of nets between different movements, in the North as well as in the South' (the Spanish Red Ciudadana por la Abolición de la Deuda Externa), 'connecting and empowering people, especially those in the Global South' (the British People and Planet). Its main aim is 'to promote the coordination of movements that resist neoliberal globalization, define and implement alternatives' (Xarxa de Mobilitzaciò Global). Its main contribution is 'building/strengthening international civic networks' (Forum del III Settore), including 'the promotion of new relations between social movements and political parties' (Centre Internacional Escarré per a les Minories Ètniques i les Nacions). Among others, the representative of Indymedia Italia points at the plural nature of the movement as a sign of its richness: 'We feel close to the movement because we think it represents an umbrella of different movements.' Similarly stressed are the 'creation of ample social coalitions for an emancipatory movement, that presents an alternative to neo-liberal capitalism' (Initiative für ein Berliner Sozialforum); 'the development of better working relationships amongst NGOs' (Oxfam International); 'the strengthening of the coordination among national campaigns' (Our World Is Not For Sale).

In the net, the spread of information is often considered important. Many interviewees point at the cognitive richness of the GJM, which aims at 'spreading, reflecting and debating the different struggles at the local level' (Indymedia Euskal Herria) and promotes 'the crosscutting debate between the different social movements, international networking' (Forum Social Suisse). Information then allows for mutual understanding: a main aim of the movement is defined as 'to allow all forces that oppose the neoliberal mondialization to know each other and converge' (Forum social local d'Ivry), to be a space for 'an exchange of struggles and *savoir faire*' (DAL – NO VOX). Reciprocal knowledge then facilitates the 'common struggle', as 'this movement aims at an internationalization of resistances, to unite the local resistances and coordinate' (Jóvenes Izquierda Unida); 'federates social struggles' (L'autre Davos); allows for the convergence of the struggles against neoliberalism (French Cedetim); represents the 'nets of resistance in all their forms' (Fédération Syndicale Unitaire); permits the 'coming together of the different resistances' in a new internationalism (Solidaires).

Concluding, although (once again) we can neither measure nor compare the degree of networking among our groups, and more in general within the GJM, we can assess that the building of transnational alliances is indeed considered as a main goal for our organizations. If various organizational models seem to be present within our sample – often with deeply rooted and long lasting traditions – beyond diversity in size, resources and age, our organizations seem to share an interest in networking that was not as explicit in previous waves of protest. From the organizational point of view, a main innovation seems indeed to be the large presence of groups that allow for group membership – that is, that are by constitution networks of organizations (or even networks of networks). What is more, many of these groups are organized at multiple territorial levels and stress transnational networking as a main organizational choice.

Which visions and practices of democracy?

The acknowledgment of a mix of similarities and differences, old traditions and innovations, local and transnational struggles leaves open some central questions for our research: which conceptions of democracy accompany the differences in issue focus, forms of action, and organizational structures? And which conceptions and practices of democracy develop in order to meet the new challenges of transnational and multiform actors?

The main purpose of our research is the analysis of models of democracy as they are elaborated 'from below'. As mentioned (see Introduction), although representative models of democracy remain dominant, they are challenged by a crisis of legitimacy as well as of efficiency: a declining use of conventional forms of political participation is accompanied by the perception of poor performances by representative democratic government. Other models of democracy (re)emerge as possible correctives for the malfunctioning of representative democracy; experiments in participatory and deliberative forms of democracy are under way within political institutions as well as by political and social actors. In this context, various conceptions of democracy co-exist, stressing different democratic qualities. A main assumption of our research is, in fact, that the general principles of democracy (representative versus participatory, majority versus deliberative, and so on) can be combined in different forms and with different balances. Accordingly, we did not aim at measuring degrees of democracy, but instead attempted to identify various models of democracy that are present, in a more or less 'pure' form, in GJM organizations. In this sense, we analyse in detail the plurality of conceptions and practices of democracy expressed by our sampled groups.

With a focus on democracy within the movement organizations, we have constructed a typology of democratic forms of internal decision making. The first dimension concerns the degree of *participation/delegation* and distinguishes groups characterized by a central role in the decision-making process of the organization of an assembly consisting of all members from all other types of organizations (with dominance of an executive, a leader or other restricted bodies). A second dimension refers to *deliberation/majority voting* and looks at the relative emphasis on decision-making methods that assign a special role to public discussion, the common good, rational arguments, and transformation of preferences. These aspects are particularly embedded and valorized by the *method of consensus*, which put a special emphasis on the decision-making process per se. Considering this dimension, we separated groups employing the method of consensus from all other organizations employing different decision-making methods (simple majority, qualified majority, mixed methods, and so on).

The typology we developed in the Demos project (see della Porta and Reiter 2006; della Porta and Mosca 2006a) crosses the two mentioned dimensions of participation (referring to degree of delegation of power, inclusiveness, and equality) and deliberation (referring to decision-making model and quality of communication). Although we kept this typology for various parts of our research, the variables we used are slightly different, reflecting the differences in the research instruments and the types of sources used.

Analysing the main documents of GJM organizations, we operationalized the two dimensions as follows. In an *associational model,* either an assembly or another decision-making body is composed of delegates. Decisions are taken by majority vote. When, according to the selected documents, delegates instead make decisions on a consensual basis, we speak of *deliberative representation.* When decisions are made by an assembly that includes all members or whoever wants to participate, we have either an *assembleary* model, when decisions are taken by majority, or *deliberative participation,* if consensus and communicative processes based on reason are mentioned as important values in the documents.

Table 1.8 Typology of democratic internal decision-making according to fundamental documents and interviews

		Delegation of power	
		High	Low
Consensus	Low	Associational model Documents: 45.5% Interviews: 22.8%	Assembleary model Documents: 27.0% Interviews: 14.9%
	High	Deliberative representation Documents: 12.5% Interviews: 22.8%	Deliberative participation Documents: 15.0% Interviews: 39.6%

Note: valid cases for documents 212; for interviews 184.

As we can see in Table 1.8, slightly fewer than half of our sampled organizations support an associational conception of internal decision making. This means that – at least formally – a model based upon delegation and the majority principle is quite widespread. Here, the typical form of internal accountability is representative: the assembly consists of delegates and executive committees with an important role in organizational decisions, and the decision-making system stresses majority principles: preferences are aggregated either by pure majority or by bargaining. To a certain extent, this is an expected result: the presence in the GJM of well established, large and resourceful organizations such as parties, unions and third-sector associations has often been noted. In this sense our results push for a (not yet developed) reflection on the conditions for and consequences of the presence of large numbers of associations in common campaigns and networks.

However, this is only part of the picture. We classified 27 per cent of the organizations as assembleary, since in the documents we analysed they stressed the role of the assembly in a decision-making process that remains tied to aggregative methods such as voting or bargaining. The participatory elements are emphasized via the important role attributed to the assembly and its inclusiveness, but consensus is not mentioned as a principle nor used as a decision-making method. The attempts to build direct models of democracy are therefore well alive.

In an additional one-quarter (27.5%) of the organizations, the deliberative element comes to the fore. In these groups, consensus and/or deliberative democracy are explicitly mentioned as organizational values, and/or consensus is used in the decision-making process in the assembly or in the executive committee. We can distinguish between the 12.5 per cent of organizations that apply consensus within an associational type (deliberative representation) and the 15.0 per cent applying it within an assembleary model (deliberative participation). This stress on elements of discursive quality is a most innovative contribution to conceptions of democracy in social movements.

Acknowledging that constitutions and written documents are not always followed in everyday activities – praxes are often different from norms – as well as the difficulty of finding written documents for smaller and grass-roots organizations, we have complemented the information obtained on organizational ideology with interviews on organizational functioning, as perceived and reported by their speakers (see Introduction). In this part, we operationalized the dimension of *participation/delegation* by distinguishing groups characterized by a central role of the assembly in the organization's decision-making process from all other types of organizations. On the dimension *deliberation/majority voting*, we separated groups employing consensus from organizations employing different decisional methods (simple majority, qualified majority, mixed methods, and so on).[2] Almost one-quarter fall in the deliberative representative category, where the principle of consensus is mixed with the principle of delegation and about the same percentage adopts an associational model based on majoritarian vote and delegation. As many as 39.6 per cent of the groups bridge a consensual decision-making method with the principle of participation (refusal of delegation to an executive committee), while 15 per cent of the selected organizations mix the principle of delegation with the majoritarian principle (assembleary model).[3]

Comparing the results in these two parts of our research, we note that interviewees tend to stress consensus more than the organizational documents do. This can be explained in different ways: respondents might be more updated and accurate in describing the actual decision making in their groups, or they may want to give a better image of the process in their organizations. Additionally, for the interviews we had to adjust the sampling in order to make up for the organizations that for various reasons we could not interview. Whatever the explanation, norms of consensus appear as very much supported by the movement organizations. This result also confirms the normative relevance that social movement organizations give to internal decision making as incarnating their visions of democracy, as well as their availability in arguing the advantages of various models.

A global justice movement? Some conclusions

These are all issues to which we shall return in the following chapters when, first, investigating more in depth the meaning of the different conceptions of participation and consensus as well as some additional dimension of democracy; and second, looking at how values, repertoires of action, and organizational structures are linked to conceptions of democracy.

For the moment, we can return to our initial questions, summarizing at the same time the evidence presented in this chapter on our organizational population (see Table 1.9). A first main question was, to which extent can we speak of *a* global justice movement, in singular. The data presented on values, organizations, and actions seem to allow a positive answer, although with some qualifications. First, our sampled organizations display not only a high degree of subjective identification with the movement, but also a certain convergence on the definition of global justice and democracy from below as broker frames, bridging the specific issues that remain at the core of our organizations' concerns. Additionally, the participation in common campaigns does not seem an ad hoc, sporadic experience, but a repeated (and consciously advocated) pattern. Finally, networks and networking (although of a flexible type) acquire a positive meaning, being emphasized as part and parcel of the organizational identity.

A second question was, to what extent is this movement *global*? Here, our evidence points to the multilevel nature of the movement, in which the global dimension acquires more relevance. First, the definition of problems is often presented as global, as is the reference for one own identity. Second, cosmopolitan identities grow in the transnational networks of different types, to which most of our organizations are proud to belong. Third, action repertoires are presented not only

Table 1.9   A global social movement: A summary

	A movement?	*Global?*	*New?*
Frames	Bridging themes	Multilevel	Cross-issues, but not ideological
Repertoire	Intense participation	Eventful transnational protest	Constructing alternatives
Organizational net	Networking diversities	Multilevel networks	New networks

as varied, but also as modulated to target various territorial levels of governance.

The third question was, what is *new* in this movement? Without wanting to reopen an old debate on the fundamental newness of the social movement, and remaining (more pragmatically) bound to an empirical concern with specific characteristics, we can first of all single out the presence of a multi-issue discourse, albeit one that rejects the 'big ideologies' for a dialogic search for solutions to emerging (global) problems. At the level of repertoires of action, beyond the combination of protest and lobbying, the focus on information as well as the practice of alternatives is resonant with the refusal of 'taking power'. At the organizational level, the flexible networking of many and different groups brings about experimentation with not only participatory, but also deliberative models of democracy.

Notes

1. The 'public good' is also mentioned by the Turin and the Abruzzo Social Forums.
2. In more than half of the cases, the most important decision-making functions are delegated to a monocratic body (11%) or to a collective body like an executive committee (46%). Around one-quarter of the groups leave these powers to the assembly, and one-tenth attribute them to other bodies or distribute them among multiple bodies; in the remaining 4 per cent, thematic groups function as important decision-making bodies. However, around two-thirds of our groups have an executive committee. In most cases these committees are elected by the general assembly/congress or by assemblies of local groups/affiliates. As for the decision-making method of the main decisional body, slightly fewer than half of our groups declare using only a consensual method (46%); the other half (54%) use a majoritarian (simple majority and qualified majority) sometimes mixed with consensus.
3. The distribution does not change much if we select only those organizations that were present in both Work Packages. Worth mentioning are a small increase in the associational model (26.3%) and a decrease in the deliberative participatory model (32.2%).

2
Participatory Traditions within the Global Justice Movement

Herbert Reiter

Introduction

More or less explicitly, social movements express a fundamental critique of conventional politics, affirming the legitimacy (if not the primacy) of alternatives to representative models of democracy. Their ideas resonate with 'an ancient element of democratic theory that calls for an organisation of collective decision making referred to in varying ways as classical, populist, communitarian, strong, grass-roots, or direct democracy against a democratic practice in contemporary democracies labelled as realist, liberal, elite, republican, or representative democracy' (Kitschelt 1993, p. 15). In this context, direct participation plays a key role both as a value and as a practice.

At least since the 1960s, social movement groups have also tried to put these ideas into practice in their internal organization, not only for ideological reasons but also for the strategic value to be found in participatory democratic decision making (Polletta 2002). Dominant features of the various models advanced included the limitation of delegation and the direct participation of all members in internal decision making. This constituted a clear departure from the organizational forms practised by institutional political actors, including the Old Left institutional allies of new social movements. However, the Global Justice Movement has been described as a 'movement of movements', characterized by networking between genuinely new global groups and organizations stemming from previous waves of mobilizations, including new social movement and Old Left organizations (della Porta 2007c). Therefore, it can be assumed that within the GJM different participatory traditions coexist, concerning both values and internal practices.

In the following, I will explore these different traditions and discuss their impact on networking within the GJM, as well as on relationships of GJM organizations with state institutions. Based in particular on a qualitative and quantitative analysis of fundamental documents of organizations active in the social forum process, participation will be discussed as a value and as an internal practice of GJM organizations. The first part of the chapter is dedicated to the connection between participatory values and the degree of delegation in the internal decision making of the sampled organizations. The second part explores the various participatory traditions present within the GJM, looking at both cultural and organizational factors. The third part is dedicated to the impact of participatory values and degree of delegation in internal decision making on networking among GJM organizations, and on the relations of these organizations with state institutions. Our findings indicate that participatory values facilitate collaboration and networking among movement groups within the GJM, while the degree of internal delegation emerges as more significant in shaping relations with state institutions.

Participatory values and organizational structure

The data collected in the framework of the DEMOS project – in particular the analysis of fundamental documents (constitutions, mission statements, programs, annual reports, and so on) of 244 organizations active in the social forum process – allow us to look at participation from two angles: the explicit reference to participation as an internal principle or as a general democratic value, and the presence of an organizational structure characterized by a low degree of delegation in internal decision-making processes. We consider the combination of participatory values and degree of delegation as an indicator for a specific participatory tradition. The following section discusses the connection between the two dimensions.

In the fundamental documents we analysed and coded, the 244 sampled organizations (from France, Germany, Italy, Switzerland, the United Kingdom, and the transnational level) make frequent references to participatory values: 27.9 per cent explicitly mention participatory democracy as a general principle of internal debate and decision making, and 51.2 per cent explicitly refer to participation as a general democratic value.[1] More than 90 per cent of the organizations mentioning the internal principle also refer to the democratic value. For the following, we distinguish among the 113 groups that make no reference to participation as a value in their fundamental documents, the 63 groups that mention participation only as a general democratic value, and the 68 organizations that also or exclusively refer to participation as an internal principle.

In most cases, the analysed documents contained detailed enough information about the organizational structure of the sampled organizations to allow a distinction among four degrees of delegation in internal decision making (valid cases = 200). High delegation (25 per cent of valid cases) is characterized by a traditional organizational structure, with an assembly of delegates meeting less than once a year and an executive committee holding strong decision-making powers. Medium-high delegation (33%) is distinguished from the former model by more innovative features such as frequent assembly meetings or mandated delegation. Medium-low delegation (26.5%) combines an assembly of all members or whoever wants to participate with the presence of a strong executive committee. Organizations with an assembly of all members or whoever wants to participate and a weak executive committee with only co-ordinating powers were defined as low delegation (15.5%).[2]

Considering participatory values and degree of internal delegation separately, no uniform results emerge for factors that social movement studies have linked to organizational values, for instance political opportunities or a group's size or age. Concerning the country of origin of the sampled organizations, no clearly identifiable connection between participatory values or degree of internal delegation and the characteristics of political opportunities emerges (see also Chapter 3 in this volume).[3]

Organizational size and age, however, have different effects on participatory values and degree of internal delegation. As far as the latter is concerned, our data seem to confirm the 'iron law of oligarchy' (Michels 1959). As discussed elsewhere in this volume (see Chapter 6), larger movement organizations may find it harder than smaller ones to ensure that all members have the opportunity for full participation. In particular, effective decision making may not seem possible without a certain degree of delegation. In fact, for the sampled organizations, delegation in internal decision making is strongly correlated with number of individual members (Cramer's $V = 0.385^{***}$), and in a linear way: the more members an organization has, the more likely it is to show higher degrees of internal delegation. For participatory values, however, results are not significant but give a first indication for the presence of various participatory traditions within the GJM. The highest percentages for the mentioning of participatory values are in fact to be found among both relatively small groups (between 101 and 1000 members) and very large organizations (more than 100 000 members).

Apart from the size of an organization, its age has also been connected with oligarchy in movement organizations (Rucht 1999). In fact, an organizational model with low degrees of internal delegation is important among those sampled organizations that were founded in periods of high movement mobilization, between 1968 and 1989 and the year 2000 and after, respectively. However, the dominant models in the two periods were different: whereas 45 per cent of the organizations founded between 1969 and 1989 combine an assembly of all members with a strong executive committee, 43 per cent of those founded in the year 2000 and after feature an executive with only co-ordinating functions alongside an assembly of all members. Before 1968 and between 1990 and 1999, organizational models with high degrees of internal delegation dominate. The data on participatory values lead to similar results. The mentioning of participation also as an internal principle sees two significant increases, first for the period 1969 to 1989 and then for the years 2000 and after. In contrast, the mentioning of participation only as a general democratic value experiences a sharp drop for 1990 to 1999, before reaching the highest percentage for 2000 and after.

In the following, however, we are more interested in investigating the connection between participatory values and degree of internal delegation than in discussing both aspects separately. Crossing the mentioning of participatory values with the degree of delegation in internal decision making (see Table 2.1) evidences in fact a statistically significant correlation (Cramer's $V = 0.181^*$). The mentioning of participation increases from high delegation, through the intermediate categories, to low delegation. Above all, compared with the other categories, twice as many organizations with a low degree of delegation mention participation as an internal principle. An organizational structure with low delegation in internal decision making can therefore be seen as an expression of participatory values, or at least as highly related with them. However, almost half of the organizations with low and almost two-thirds of those with medium-low degrees of internal delegation do not mention participatory democracy as an internal principle. At the same time, a traditional organizational structure does not preclude explicit references to participatory values, also as an internal principle.

These results cannot be satisfactorily explained by the tendency for more informal groups not to produce the kind of documents containing references to organizational values.[4] Instead, the data seem to indicate the presence of different participatory traditions within the GJM,

Table 2.1   Delegation in internal decision making by mentioning of participatory values

Delegation in internal decision making	Participation			Total **N**
	Not mentioned	Only general democratic value	Also internal principle	
High delegation	56.0%	22.0%	22.0%	50
Medium-high delegation	47.0%	24.2%	28.8%	66
Medium-low delegation	41.5%	30.2%	28.3%	53
Low delegation	22.6%	22.6%	54.8%	31
Total	44.0% (88)	25.0% (50)	31.0% (62)	200

with participatory values connected with both low and high degrees of internal delegation. Participation as an internal principle or a general democratic value is in fact only weakly or not at all correlated with organizational features such as presence of a constitution or formalization of membership. An exception is constituted by the powers attributed to the assembly, showing a strong correlation between participation as an internal principle and definition of the assembly as the main decision-making body (Cramer's $V = 0.277^{***}$). Further, this correlation is particularly strong for organizations with medium-high and high degrees of internal delegation (0.383^{***}) and virtually disappears for those with medium-low and low delegation. Some contradictory results for other organizational features further confirm the presence of different participatory traditions within the GJM. Organizations that mention participatory values, for instance, score higher than average for both the presence of an executive committee and its explicit rejection.

It comes as no surprise that organizations with high degrees of delegation also make explicit references to participatory values. Participation of their members is in fact important if not fundamental for any social movement organization, regardless of degree of delegation in decision making. References to this importance can be found in numerous documents of the sampled organizations. In the part of the 'about us' section of its Web site dedicated to internal democracy, for instance, Amnesty International France (medium-high delegation) affirms that 'the members are the heart of the movement's life and participate in all its instances and decision making' (Amnesty France 2008). Similar statements can also be found at the transnational level. Our World is not for sale affirms in the 'about us' section of its Web site: 'The active participation of OWINFS members is what drives our collective work forward' (OWINFS 2008).

The constitutions of some organizations (for example, the Italian gay/lesbian association Arcigay, characterized by high delegation, or the German section of Pax Christi, with medium-high delegation) even affirm a duty of members to participate, while for Indymedia (low delegation), a prerequisite for participation in the decision-making processes of each local group is the contribution of an individual's labour to the group.[5] The fundamental documents of other organizations contain explicit references to the necessity to actively solicit the participation of members, regardless of whether they are of high delegation (for example, the Italian communist party Rifondazione comunista), medium-high delegation (for example, the Italian new media association Isole nella rete), medium-low delegation (for example, the British ecologist organization Friends of the Earth), or low delegation (for example, the Italian new global network Rete Lilliput).[6]

Profound differences, however, emerge in the weight that groups attribute to the individual on the one side and the organization on the other in the implementation of participatory democracy. The Italian traditional left-wing trade union confederation CGIL promises the realization of an individual's aspiration to be a protagonist and to participate through membership in the organization (CGIL 2004). The French Coordination des intermittents et précaires d'Ile de France instead describes itself as a 'horizontal organization based on direct democracy, the self discipline and the individual responsibility of each of its members' (Coordination 2003). Some organizations like the British autonomous group Wombles explicitly declare that they are not membership organizations. According to the 'Background' document on their Web site, no one has to bear allegiance to the Wombles, but people are encouraged to participate on a non-hierarchical basis (Wombles 2008). Religiously inspired organizations have a conception of participation as a vocation radiating beyond the organization. In its 'about us' section, Pax Christi UK affirms: 'The impact of Pax Christi primarily depends on how its members embody these ideals in their own lives' (Pax Christi UK 2008).

In conclusion, in the case of GJMOs, we are in the presence of various participatory traditions, with some groups connecting participation as an also individual value with high and others with low degrees of delegation. Paying attention to both cultural and organizational factors, the following section is dedicated to an exploration of these different participatory traditions.

Exploring the different participatory traditions within the GJM

I explore the differences in participatory traditions by looking at both cultural and organizational factors, concentrating for the first on the movement area and for the second on the field of organization to which the sampled groups can be attributed. Concerning movement area, we distinguish among Old Left organizations, New Left/anarchist/autonomous groups, groups working on new social movement themes, solidarity/human rights/peace organizations, and groups concentrating on specific new global themes. Concerning organizational fields, we distinguish among trade unions, parties/party youth organizations/party foundations, NGOs/formal SMOs, co-operatives, grass-roots SMOs, and 'modern' networks (see Chapter 1 in this volume). Statistically, participatory values emerge as far less correlated than degree of delegation with both movement area and organizational field. As a qualitative reading of the fundamental documents of the sampled organizations confirms, these results mirror the presence within the GJM of different participatory traditions, with the value of (also internal) participation connected with both low and high degrees of internal delegation.

Participatory values and practices in the various movement areas of the GJM

Concerning organizational age and size, the various movement areas to which the sampled organizations can be attributed are characterized by significant differences.[7] Old Left organizations were predominantly founded before 1968 and tend to have more than 100 000 individual members. Most New Left, anarchist, or autonomous groups were founded between 1969 and 1989 and are more likely to have between 100 and 1000 members. Most new social movement groups were founded in the same period, but tend to have a larger membership (1000–10 000 members). Solidarity, peace, or human rights organizations were predominantly founded between 1990 and 1999 (a considerable number, however, also before 1968 or between 1969 and 1989) and tend to have between 1000 and 10 000 members. Finally, new global groups were founded in the years 2000 and after, and are mostly small (with up to 100 individual members).

Crossing movement area with the mentioning of participatory values gives no significant results, while a strong correlation exists with the degree of delegation in internal decision making (see Table 2.2). A clear correspondence between mentioned values and practices exists for solidarity, peace, or human rights organizations: they mention participatory values less than all other groups and show a clear preference for organizational structures with high degrees of internal delegation. However, the groups of the two movement areas that most frequently make references to participation (both as only a general and as also an internal value) show quite different preferences as far as the degree of internal delegation is concerned: almost 85 per cent of Old Left groups are characterized by high or medium-high delegation, while 52 per cent of new social movement groups follow an organizational model with medium-low or low degrees of delegation. New Left, anarchist, or autonomous organizations and new global groups have above average mentions only for participation as an internal value, while for participation as a general value they remain at a low level similar to solidarity, peace, or human rights organizations. The groups from both movement areas translate their participatory values into low degrees of internal delegation, although with one difference: among New Left, anarchist, or autonomous groups, a model with medium-low delegation dominates, while new global groups show a preference for low delegation.

A qualitative reading of fundamental documents of the sampled organizations allows a closer discussion of the different participatory traditions that these results indicate for the various movement areas. A combination of participatory values with a traditional organizational structure is particularly frequent for organizations of the Old Left. Historically, in fact, the mobilization and the contributions of their members were of paramount importance for left-wing organizations (Bartolini 2000, pp. 263ff.). The Old Left organizations active in the social forum process responded to the progressive crisis of membership participation in recent decades not with an abandonment of participatory values, but with their continuous affirmation. In Article 6 of its constitution, for instance, the Italian left-wing trade union confederation CGIL underlines 'the guarantee of the highest participation of all members, personally or through delegates' as one of the cardinal points on which the democratic life of the organization rests (CGIL 2006).

Table 2.2 Movement area by mentioning of participation as a value and degree of delegation in internal decision making

Movement area	Old Left	New Left/ anarchist/ autonomous	New social movement themes	Solidarity/peace/ human rights	New global themes	Total
Participation (Cramer's V = n.s.)						
Not mentioned	31.3%	44.8%	34.5%	60.0%	45.0%	46.3%
Only as general value	34.4%	24.1%	27.6%	22.9%	23.8%	25.4%
Also as internal value	34.4%	31.0%	37.9%	17.1%	31.3%	28.3%
Total N	32	29	29	70	80	238
Degree of delegation in internal decision making (Cramer's V = 0.297***)						
High delegation	35.5%	8.0%	24.0%	27.0%	19.6%	23.6%
Medium–high	48.4%	28.0%	24.0%	46.0%	17.6%	33.8%
Medium–low	16.1%	52.0%	36.0%	22.2%	23.5%	27.2%
Low delegation	0.0%	12.0%	16.0%	4.8%	39.2%	15.4%
Total N	31	25	25	63	51	195

For the Old Left organizations active in the social forum process, there seems to be a conscious reappropriation of original participatory values, triggered not only by moments of crisis but also by interaction with new social movements.[8] Such processes seem particularly likely for the one-third of Old Left organizations that were founded between 1990 and 1999, among which we find many cases of traditional organizations 'refounded' in the wake of the fall of the Berlin wall, like the French Espace Marx, the Italian Rifondazione comunista, or the German Solid. A reappropriation of values is for instance explicitly stated by the Italian ARCI (the traditional cultural and recreational organization of the Italian communist party, refounded in 1994). The history of the organization presented on its Web site speaks of a 'recovery of the original values', one of them the active and conscious participation of citizens in democratic life (ARCI 2008).

In the case of Old Left organizations, however, we can also hypothesize incongruence between mentioned values and organizational model. Old Left organizations with high delegation in fact mention (both general and internal) participatory values more than Old Left organizations with medium-high or medium-low delegation, while for new social movement and especially new global groups, the reverse is true. For activists of Old Left groups, a survey conducted by the DEMOS team at the European Social Forum in Athens in May 2006 revealed incongruence between their perception of democracy in their group and their normative ideas on democracy, overwhelmingly supporting direct democracy. The same activists were the least satisfied with democracy in their own groups (Andretta and Reiter 2009).

New Left, autonomous, and anarchist organizations – with a dominant organizational model combining an assembly of all members with the presence of an executive committee – make fewer references to participatory values in their documents than do Old Left organizations, in particular to participation as a general democratic value. As mentioned above, however, they do score above average for the mentioning of participation as an internal principle. In addition, we have to consider that many autonomous or anarchist organizations use a terminology that does not contain 'participation', but other expressions like direct democracy, horizontality or self-organization. The Italian grass-roots trade union COBAS explicitly contrasts a negative conception of 'participation' with 'conflict' and 'self-organization from below' (COBAS 2002). In addition, many Trotskyite organizations follow a model of democratic centralism.[9] As far as New Left activists are concerned, our Athens survey revealed high satisfaction with democracy in their groups and low levels of incongruence with their normative ideas on democracy (ibid.).

For solidarity organizations, the less participatory attitude and the correlation between specialization, professionalization, and centralization in decision making underlined for single issue movements (Staggenborg 1988; Kriesi 1996) could be expected. Like Old Left groups with predominantly a traditional organizational structure, solidarity organizations in fact score lowest for mentions of participation, both as an internal principle and as a general democratic value. The fundamental documents of these organizations, be they laic (for example the Italian Forum terzo settore) or of religious inspiration (like the French Comité catholique contre la faim), mention participation (often connected with human rights or human dignity) above all as a general democratic value, to be realized in particular for their basis of reference. The declaration 'Justice for the Poor' of the German Brot für die Welt includes a section on 'Realizing human rights, fostering democracy and political participation' and calls for the construction of a just, participatory, and future-capable society (Brot für die Welt 2000). Similarly, the British Catholic Agency for Overseas Development underlines its aims of reducing poverty, enhancing dignity, and increasing participation (Catholic Agency 2004, p. 4), while Christian Aid has among its 'visions and values' 'to empower people to reform the systems that keep them poor' (Christian Aid 2005). In its Web site section on humanitarian aid, the Italian Consortium of Solidarity affirms: 'In the places where we intervene, ICS tries to root itself and to sustain the local democratic civil society and an idea of development and cooperation founded upon human rights, substantive democracy, active participation' (ICS 2008).

These references often go beyond a narrow conception of solidarity and/or advocacy. Similar to voluntary and community groups (see Parker et al. 2004), many solidarity organizations active in the social forum process see their activities as a significant contribution to democracy. In Article 3 of its constitution, the Italian ARCI underlines as one of its aims the promotion of voluntary work, understood as 'democratic participation in actions of solidarity and of citizenship' (ARCI 2006). The French Comité catholique contre la faim affirms to pursue 'a policy of education to development in France that incites everybody to acquire a spirit of citizen participation' (Comité catholique 2007, p. 2). References to internal participatory values can also be found in both more formal and more informal solidarity organizations.[10] In addition, similarly to what was observed for Old Left groups, some solidarity organizations explicitly point to a reappropriation of original values, triggered by the appearance of the GJM. The Italian Consortium of Solidarity speaks of the necessity 'to put again at the centre values and principles partly lost: the role of the social base, internal democracy, transparency in management, project quality, the search for coherence of behaviour' (ICS 2004).

Together with organizations from the Old Left, those working on new social movement themes most frequently refer to participatory values, the former slightly more to participation as a general democratic value, the latter slightly more to participation as an internal principle. Similarly to solidarity organizations, new social movement groups draw a close connection between participation and their core themes (Offe 1985). The French women's organization Les Pénélopes, for instance, in a contribution on the participatory budgeting in Porto Alegre on its Web site, underlines that these processes open the road for participation to the weakest groups, that is, women (Pénélopes 2001). In Article 2 of its constitution, the Italian ecologist organization Legambiente states as one of its aims: 'The promotion of citizens' participation in the defence of the environment and in the definition of their own quality of life' (Legambiente 2007).

At the same time, new social movement groups often pay close attention to internal participation (Rucht 1999). The British organization Friends of the Earth points to the importance of participatory processes not only for public planning, but also for the facilitation of group meetings. A specific guide on participation within the organization published as an internal document stresses the importance of argument rather than power of office and underlines that all those affected by a decision should have the opportunity to be involved in the decision-making process (Walsh 2001; see also Saunders 2007).

Surprisingly, organizations working on specific new global themes make fewer references to participatory values than either Old Left or new social movement groups. This may be explained by the fact that here we are dealing with often informal groups of recent formation. When found, however, references in particular to participation as an internal principle point to a conception of participation contrasting with the traditional understanding of Old Left organizations and going beyond the conception of new social movement groups. In point 7 of its document of fundamental values, the Italian Rete Lilliput underlines: '[Rete Lilliput] refuses the personalization and the professionalization of political commitment and wants to avoid being identified by the public with one or more people. As a priority it supports the direct participation of the members, limiting formulas of delegation and of representation' (Rete Lilliput 2001).

A characterizing feature of the fundamental documents of these groups is the search for coherence between internal practices and external claims. The Spanish group Otra Democracia Es Posible states: 'The collective Otra Democracia Es Posible wants to use in its internal functioning the same democratic procedures it demands for society' (Otra Democracia 2008). The Italian network Rete Lilliput particularly underlines the importance of the method: 'Why this insistence on a "process from below"?...The Rete Lilliput has been characterized in these years also by its attempt to experiment new modalities, of action as well as of organization, starting with the awareness that the method with which one acts conditions the result' (Rete Lilliput 2007a). The London Social Forum also draws a direct connection between internal organizational structure and democracy in general: 'Democratic ferments generate organisational forms that are based on solidarity, not competition, inclusion, not exclusion, horizontality, not hierarchy, participation, not marginalisation, conviviality, not protocol' (London Social Forum 2005).

Moreover, the problem of coherence between group practices and claims frequently becomes the topic of internal discussion, with voices questioning whether this coherence is effectively realized and whether it is possible to sustain a fully participatory model over time. At a meeting of Indymedia Italy in Genoa, one participant lamented: 'For now I cannot see the translation of the ideal into practice, for example concerning horizontality and the possibility for all to participate' (Indymedia Italia 2004). At a regional meeting of the Emilia-Romagna ATTAC-Italia committees, one intervention pointed out:

> If direct democracy and active participation are part of our political objectives, how can we not make our association the laboratory in which to experiment as the first these practices? In the same way as democracy is not something one gains once and for all but a difficult daily practice, we cannot think that Attac can begin and end in the structure abstractly planned by its founders two years ago. (Attac Italia 2003b)

In internal discussions of the Italian Rete Lilliput, a frequent lament concerned the burden that consequent participatory practices constitute for the individual members and the organization. A participant in a 2003 regional meeting of the network stated: 'The network has emptied itself, the remaining people are tired, worn out by the rhythms of participation, and the rules we gave ourselves; the organization that we gave ourselves in order to experiment with a model from below revealed itself to be too much of a strain' (Rete Lilliput 2005).

Notwithstanding similar and repeatedly voiced doubts, however, new global groups continued to confirm and reconfirm their participatory practices as prefigurative politics (Polletta 2002). The final document of the 2006 national assembly of the Italian Rete Lilliput again reaffirmed the participatory values and practices of the organization: 'We tried to practice the method of consensus, which in spite of its complexity permitted us to experiment with horizontality, diffuse leadership, participative methods. We have pursued the coherence between means and ends, between form and content; we have learned to reason collectively' (Rete Lilliput 2006a).

Finally, new global organizations also elaborate counter-models to existing democratic practices, combining concrete proposals for reforms with a utopian element largely absent from the documents of groups referring to other movement areas. On its Web site, the Spanish organization Otra democracia Es Posible published proposals for a reform of the national and regional constitutions, pushing for the introduction of referenda, popular legislative initiatives, and electoral recall. At its 2007 national assembly, in a debate about a shared political horizon, the Italian Rete Lilliput envisaged 'Omnicrazia', defined as power of all or diffuse power, as a possible utopia of politics 'outside' (to be understood as outside 'the system'), to develop alongside politics 'inside'. Instruments for politics 'outside' are the growth of organizations based on high degrees of internal democracy and the construction of a network of networks. As instruments for politics 'inside', Lilliput mentions various models – Agenda 21, community contracts, participative urban planning, participative budgeting, civic (electoral) lists, referenda, popular legislative initiatives, and the extension of local autonomies – but at the same time expresses criticism of 'empty' forms of participation.[11]

Concluding, in the movement areas of the GJM, different participatory traditions are present, combining references to participatory values with various degrees of internal delegation. The following section is dedicated to an analysis of the impact of organizational fields on participatory values and practices.

Participatory values and practices in the various organizational fields of the GJM

Organizational fields are closely connected with movement area. About 60 per cent of the trade unions in our sample have an Old Left and about 30 per cent a New Left background. Political parties, party youth organizations, and party foundations are similarly dominated by the Old Left, while about a quarter can be defined as ecologist and 16 per cent as New Left/anarchist/autonomous. Among NGOs/formal SMOs, about three-fifths are solidarity, peace, or human rights groups, while most co-operatives have a New Left/anarchist/autonomous background. Both grass-roots SMOs and 'modern' networks are predominantly new global organizations.

Analysing the correlation between organizational fields on the one side and the mentioning of participatory values and degree of internal delegation on the other reveals the specific impact of organizational constraints (see Table 2.3). In fact, certain organizational fields particularly mention participatory values. At the same time, the organizations of the various fields belong to different participatory traditions and combine participatory values with varying degrees of internal delegation.

Political parties, party youth organizations, or party foundations stand out for numerous references to participation, both as only a general democratic value and as also an internal principle: 31.8 per cent mention the former (average = 26.1 per cent) and 59.1 per cent mention the latter (average = 28.2 per cent). The particular character of political parties is underlined by the fact that trade unions, similarly dominated by institutionalized organizations with an Old Left background, mention participatory values far less. However, union organizations tend to be larger than parties. In addition, they were predominantly founded before 1968 or between 1969 and 1989, while political parties were predominantly established between 1990 and 1999.

The fact that 90 per cent of political parties, party youth organizations, and party foundations mention participation as a general democratic value has to be attributed to the character of these organizations and to the specific types of documents they produce. For party foundations, the favouring of political participation is one of their principal missions. The programmes of most of the parties and party youth organizations active in the social forum process contain calls for the strengthening of participatory processes in political decision making, regardless of whether they are more moderate or more radical or whether they have an Old Left or an ecologist background. The Italian moderate left youth organization Sinistra Giovanile (2005, p. 22) underlines the need to pass from representative to participative democracy, while the (post)communist Madrid section of Izquierda Unida Jovenes asks for a 'revolution in participation' (Jovenes 2004). At the 2005 congress of the Italian (post)communist party Rifondazione comunista,

Table 2.3 Organizational fields by mentioning of participation as a value and degree of delegation in internal decision making

Organizational field	Trade union	Party/party youth org./party foundation	NGO/formal SMO	Co-operative	Grass-roots SMO	'Modern' network	Total
Participation (Cramer's V = 0.220*)							
Not mentioned	54.5%	9.1%	51.6%	85.7%	58.3%	41.0%	45.6%
Only general value	22.7%	31.8%	26.3%	14.3%	16.7%	27.7%	26.1%
Also internal value	22.7%	59.1%	22.1%	0.0%	25.0%	31.3%	28.2%
Total N	22	22	95	7	12	83	241
Degree of delegation in internal decision making (Cramer's V = 0.334***)							
High delegation	33.3%	27.3%	19.5%	16.7%	14.3%	30.9%	24.7%
Medium-high	52.4%	36.4%	26.8%	0.0%	14.3%	25.5%	33.3%
Medium-low	9.5%	36.4%	37.9%	83.3%	0.0%	7.3%	26.3%
Low delegation	4.8%	0.0%	5.7%	0.0%	71.4%	36.4%	15.7%
Total N	21	22	87	6	7	55	198

secretary general Fausto Bertinotti presented the construction of participative democracy as a primary objective to be realized by entering a centre-left government coalition (Rifondazione 2005). In its 2007 programme ('To change society, invert the trend: Make of each citizen a conscious actor'), the French Green party demands the introduction of participative democracy at all levels of public decision making in order to permit everybody to participate in the elaboration of the decisions that concern him/her (Les Verts 2007). We can assume that with these programmatic positions, party organizations at least in part respond to demands advanced by civil society in general and the GJM in particular.

More than other organizational fields, political parties, party youth organizations, and party foundations mention participation also as an internal principle. The Italian Rifondazione comunista affirms in Article 7 of its constitution that leading functions express themselves in promoting the democratic participation and political activity of all members and organizing the political activity in such a way as to favour the broadest participation. In Article 8 of its constitution, Rifondazione's Spanish sister party Izquierda Unida describes its internal functioning as a new form to make politics, where the participation of all of its components is the defining practice of its organization (Izquierda 2004).

In most political parties, however, references to participatory democracy as an internal principle go hand in hand with organizational characteristics foreseeing traditional forms of delegation. In fact, more than 60 per cent of the sampled party organizations show high or medium-high degrees of delegation and none of them a low degree. According to Article 8 of Izquierda Unida's constitution, the democratic and participative functioning of the party is based on the primacy of the assemblies (at the higher territorial levels composed by delegates), guaranteeing that the ensemble of decisions goes from top to bottom (Izquierda 2004). The combination of internal participation as a value with high degrees of internal delegation is a specific characteristic of political parties. In fact, participation as an internal principle is mentioned far more by parties with an assembly of delegates than by parties with an assembly of all members. In NGOs/formal SMOs and especially in 'modern networks', to the contrary, this trend is reversed. For political party organizations we can hypothesize the same incongruence between organizational values and practices discussed above for Old Left organizations in general.

Political parties, in particular those of the Old Left, seem to stay committed to and defend a specific tradition of political participation and the organizational form in which it historically found its expression. A clear statement to this effect can be found in a document of Rifondazione comunista:

We think that, also in this phase, the party as a permanent organization of women and men that choose to constitute themselves in a political community in order to cooperate in realizing a project of society is indispensable for connecting and penetrating with a unitary project of struggle the society, the economy, the state organization, be it national or international, and that in the face of the crisis of democracy and of the nation state it continues not only to represent a space of participation but also to offer a possibility for the entry of the masses into the political arena. (Rifondazione 2002)

At least in part, this commitment can also be interpreted as a reappropriation of original values (see above).

Apart from political parties, the only organizational field with above average mentioning of participatory values are 'modern' networks, an organizational form emerging only in recent years. Our World Is Not For Sale, one of these 'modern networks', describes itself in the 'about us' section of its Web site as a loose grouping of organizations, activists, and social movements (OWINFS 2008). In fact, we can define such groups as loose networks of existing organizations that often (but not exclusively) form for the purpose of pursuing specific aims or conducting specific campaigns.

'Modern' networks have some special characteristics. Similar to grass-roots SMOs, about one-third of the sampled networks are not membership organizations, that is, they have neither formal nor informal membership. Of those that do have membership, about one-third have only collective members, automatically leading to considerable degrees of delegation – in fact, more than 50 per cent of 'modern' networks have high degrees of internal delegation – although coupled with autonomy of member organizations. Moreover, 'modern' networks are predominantly very young: 58 per cent were founded in or after the year 2000, compared with an average of 20 per cent among the sample. In addition, they are particularly numerous in the new global movement area (58 per cent; average 32 per cent).

Contrary to political parties, networks with an assembly of all members (or whoever wants to participate) mention participatory values far more than networks with an assembly of delegates. This is particularly the case for participation as an internal principle. We are clearly in the presence of a conception of participation different from that of political parties, translating participatory values into low degrees of delegation. This can also be observed in loosely structured ad hoc organizations like campaigns. The British Stop the War Coalition (2008), for instance, underlines that local groups should have regular, open, and inclusive meetings.

As an organizational form, 'modern' networks are particularly widespread at the transnational level: 60 per cent of the sampled transnational organizations are networks, compared with an average of 33 per cent. If mentions of participation as a general democratic value are particularly dominant at the transnational level, references often point to a more general commitment, including internal processes. In Point 10 of its Charter of Principles, the World Social Forum (2002) declares itself to uphold respect for the practices of real and participatory democracy. The campaign Reclaim Our UN (2005a) defines its work as an open and participatory process. In addition, specific references to internal participation are not completely absent. Peoples' Global Action (2002) speaks of the need to develop a diversity of forms of organization at different levels, all based on direct democracy.

In the classification of organizational fields, two categories (co-operatives and grass-roots SMOs) were retained despite being only very weakly represented among the sampled organizations. This decision was determined by the conviction, derived above all from a qualitative reading of the respective fundamental documents, that aggregating them with others would distort the results. For different reasons, the groups in both categories make relatively few references to participatory values. Co-operatives are predominantly economic enterprises, a fact that is reflected in their fundamental documents. Grass-roots SMOs produce relatively few documents of the kind we analysed, leading to few references to participatory values and to difficulties in classifying these groups according to the degree of delegation in internal decision making.[12] Both categories clearly favour organizational models with an assembly of all members, that is, a low degree of internal delegation. However, also because of clear legislative provisions, co-operatives feature strong executive committees, usually absent in grass-roots SMOs.

Concluding, the specific impact of organizational field on participatory traditions emerges in particular for political party organizations and for 'modern' networks, the former connected with a traditional way of 'making politics', the latter emerging with the GJM.

Participatory traditions and external relations

The following section is dedicated to the impact of the various participatory traditions and their components on the external relations of the sampled organizations. Participation as a value and degree of internal delegation in fact work differently, depending on whether we look at relations with other movement actors or with state institutions. Concerning relations with other movement actors, participatory values, regardless of degree of internal delegation, constitute a bridging element within the GJM and form a basis for collaboration and networking among 'tolerant identities' (della Porta 2005c). Instead, degree of delegation in internal decision making emerges as the more important factor for relations with local, national, and international state institutions.

Participatory traditions and relations within the GJM

A first indication for the bridging function of participatory values can be found in their connection with other democratic values present in organizations active in the GJM. The variable on participation used to this point shows a strong correlation with dummy variables on consensual method (0.409***), internal inclusiveness (Cramer's V = 0.396***), equality (0.349***), general inclusiveness (0.340***), dialogue/communication (0.263***), difference/plurality/heterogeneity (0.256***), and transparency (0.240***). Degree of delegation, in contrast, shows a strong correlation only with consensual method (0.312***) and difference/plurality/heterogeneity (0.262**). It is further related to a lesser extent with internal inclusiveness (0.226*) and transparency (0.219*), but unrelated to the other variables.

The particular importance of participatory values as a bridging element within the GJM and as a basis for collaboration and networking, regardless of the degree of internal delegation, is further underlined by the strong correlation that participation as a value shows with the basic themes on which the sampled organizations work. As explained in Chapter 1 of this volume, we aggregated the single themes mentioned in the analysed documents on the basis of bivariate correlations between them, constructing normalized additive indexes. Participatory values are strongly correlated with 'new globalism', that is, another globalization, democracy, and social justice (Cramer's V = 0.314***); with 'ecominority', that is, ecology, women' rights, and antiracism (Cramer's V = 0.330***); and with peace and nonviolence (Cramer's V = 0.294***).

Above all, an even stronger correlation exists between participatory values and an additive index of all basic themes (Cramer's V = 0.401***), further confirming their role as a bridging element within the GJM. Degree of internal delegation, to the contrary, is correlated with none of these indexes.[13]

Turning to whether or not networking with other social movement organizations is mentioned, again only participation as a value emerges as significant on the national (Cramer's V = 0.173*) and transnational levels (Cramer's V = 0.203**). However, both the mentioning of participation as a value and degree of internal delegation are correlated with the ways in which networking occurs (see Table 2.4). At the national level, organizations that do not mention participatory values tend to network more with groups working in the same thematic area, while those that mention participation only as a general value tend to network more in general. Further, the organizations mentioning participation also as an internal principle score comparatively high for networking also with organizations working on other themes. These patterns of networking remain, regardless of the degree of internal delegation. Concerning the latter, clear preferences emerge: organizations with a high degree of delegation network above all with groups working in the same thematic area. Groups with medium-high and medium-low delegation declare networking in general, while low delegation groups do so also with organizations working on different themes than they do. The results for transnational networking follow similar patterns.

In conclusion, participatory values, regardless of the degree of internal delegation, seem to be of particular importance for collaboration and networking within the GJM. This is further confirmed by information collected in another part of the DEMOS project, based on interviews with key members of organizations active in the social forum process.[14] Among others, the interviewees were asked whether their organization felt a part of the GJM. This variable is significantly correlated with the mentioning of participation as a value (Cramer's V = 0.199*) but not with degree of delegation in internal decision making.

Participatory traditions and relations with state institutions

The strategies and action repertoires that the sampled organizations claim to employ can give us first indications about their relations

Table 2.4 Mentioning of participatory values and degree of delegation by national networking

National networking	Not mentioned	Yes, in general	Yes, with orgs working in the same thematic area	Yes, also with orgs working on other themes	Total N
Participation (Cramer's V = 0.201**)					
Not mentioned	25.7%	29.2%	35.4%	9.7%	113
Only general	9.5%	42.9%	34.9%	12.7%	63
Also internal	16.2%	36.8%	20.6%	26.5%	68
Total	18.9%	34.8%	31.1%	15.2%	244
Degree of internal delegation (Cramer's V = 0.201**)					
High delegation	16.0%	26.0%	48.0%	10.0%	50
Medium-high	12.1%	48.5%	28.8%	10.6%	66
Medium-low	18.9%	41.5%	24.5%	15.1%	53
Low delegation	19.4%	32.3%	12.9%	35.5%	31
Total	16.0%	38.5%	30.0%	15.5%	200

with state institutions. Most of the objectives and functions mentioned in organizational documents – lobbying, representation of specific interests, self awareness/self help, advocacy, offer/supply of services to the constituency, spreading information/influencing mass media/raising awareness, political education of the citizens, legal protection/denunciation on the specific theme of repression – are not correlated with participatory values. Exceptions are constituted by protest/mobilization (Cramer's $V = 0.223^{**}$) and political representation (Cramer's $V = 0.201^{**}$), both connected in particular with the mentioning of participation also as an internal principle. In this case, internal participation seems to be associated with different participatory traditions: the more unconventional forms of political participation of new or newest social movement organizations as well as the New Left and the more conventional forms practised in particular by political parties of the Old Left.

Turning to degree of internal delegation, a correlation exists for a number of objectives and functions mentioned in organizational documents, all of which are pursued in particular by organizations with high and medium-high delegation: representation of specific interests (Cramer's $V = 0.305^{***}$), advocacy (0.225^*), lobbying (0.213^*), and offer of services (0.208^*). Neither protest/mobilization nor political representation is significant, but all organizations with low degrees of delegation practise the former and none the latter. As could be expected, according to a neo-institutional approach (March and Olsen 1989; Boli and Thomas 1999), most of the strategies and action repertoires that lead to a collaborative relationship with state institutions are pursued by organizations with more centralized decision-making structures.

These results seem to indicate that, differently from relations within the GJM, relations with state institutions are influenced more by organizational features than by mentioned values. In fact, collaboration with state institutions measured on the basis of interviews with representatives of the sampled institutions is at best weakly correlated with participation as a value.[15] The organizations mentioning participation also as an internal principle show a less collaborative attitude towards national and international institutions, and more of these groups refuse collaboration or remain indifferent. They show a more collaborative attitude only towards local institutions. The majority of the groups that mention participation only as a general democratic value show instead an attitude of collaboration with restrictions.

Compared to these results, the greater impact of the degree of internal delegation is evident, in particular for international and national institutions (Cramer's $V = 0.412^{***}$ and 0.413^{***}, respectively). Regarding local institutions, the impact of degree of internal delegation decreases significantly (Cramer's $V = 0.227^{*}$). In fact, while collaboration with national and international institutions is practised above all by structured organizations, small groups with low degrees of delegation also collaborate with local institutions.

An analysis of references in organizational documents to collaboration, democratic control, or refusal as characteristics of relations with local, national, and international state institutions confirms these trends. Organizations referring only to collaboration were classified as uncritical collaborators. Groups combining collaboration with either democratic control or refusal were defined as critical or selective collaborators. Democratic controllers make no references to unconditioned collaboration or refusal, while reluctant controllers or objectors either combine democratic control with refusal or explicitly refuse collaboration with state institutions (see Table 2.5).

The mentioning of participation as a value in fundamental organizational documents shows no statistically significant correlation with relations with local, national, or international state institutions. However, the groups mentioning participation only as a general democratic value are more likely to seek the role of critical or selective collaborator. In contrast, the organizations mentioning participation also as an internal principle appear more in the role of reluctant controller or objector, although without disdaining uncritical collaboration or democratic control. These results further confirm that the mentioning of participation in particular as an internal value does not lead to clear preferences in the relations with state institutions.

In fact, relations with state institutions seem less influenced by the presence of participatory values and more by the way in which these values are combined with different degrees of internal delegation. Groups with high or medium-high delegation emerge particularly as critical or selective collaborators, but also (especially medium-high delegation groups) as uncritical collaborators. For organizations with medium-low delegation, uncritical collaboration loses in importance while democratic control gains. Low delegation groups make fewer references to collaboration with state institutions than the other organizations do, but when they make them the refusal of collaboration clearly dominates.

Table 2.5 Mentioning of participatory values and degree of internal delegation by relations with local, national, or international state institutions

	Typology of relations with state institutions (including IGOs)					Total N
	Not mentioned	Uncritical collaborator	Critical or selective collaborator	Democratic controller	Reluctant controller or objector	
Participation (Cramer's V = n.s.)						
Not mentioned	48.7%	9.7%	18.6%	14.2%	8.8%	113
Only general	34.9%	9.5%	38.1%	9.5%	7.9%	63
Also internal	36.8%	10.3%	26.5%	10.3%	16.2%	68
Total	41.8%	9.8%	25.8%	11.9%	10.7%	244
Degree of internal delegation (Cramer's V = 0.213**)						
High delegation	44.0%	12.0%	28.0%	14.0%	2.0%	50
Medium-high	31.8%	16.7%	33.3%	12.1%	6.1%	66
Medium-low	35.8%	7.5%	30.2%	17.0%	9.4%	53
Low delegation	61.3%	3.2%	6.5%	6.5%	22.6%	31
Total	40.5%	11.0%	27.0%	13.0%	8.5%	200

Conclusion

For organizations active in the social forum process, a statistically significant correlation emerges between the mentioning of participatory values, in particular as an internal principle, and an organizational structure characterized by low degrees of delegation. However, a considerable number of organizations with high degrees of delegation also make references to participation in their fundamental documents, also as an internal value. In addition, participatory values and organizational features show only a weak and in some cases contradictory relation, while profound differences exist among the sampled groups concerning the role attributed to the organization for the realization of participatory values. Therefore, in the case of GJMOs, we are in the presence of various participatory traditions, with some groups connecting the value of (also internal) participation with high and others with low degrees of delegation.

The different participatory traditions present within the GJM can be connected with both the movement area and the organizational field to which an organization can be attributed. Regarding movement area, Old Left organizations active in the social forum process tend to make strong references to participation also as an internal value, but predominantly follow an organizational model with high degrees of delegation. For these organizations, there seems to be a conscious reappropriation of original values, but we can also hypothesize incongruence between mentioned values and organizational practices. Solidarity, peace, and human rights groups follow a similar organizational model but make significantly fewer references to participatory values. Similarly to the Old Left, new social movement organizations stress participation as a general and as an internal value, but they tend to translate these values into lower degrees of internal delegation. Both New Left and new global groups make an above average number of references only to participation as an internal value. Whereas the former combine an assembly of all members with a strong executive, the latter tend to avoid all forms of internal delegation. The new global movement area distinguishes itself by a strong utopian element and the confirmation of participatory practices as prefigurative politics.

Concerning organizational fields, political party organizations and 'modern' networks have a particular impact on participatory traditions. The very high number of references that political party organizations make to participation as a general democratic value must be attributed to the character of these organizations and to the specific types of documents they produce. In general, the programmes of party organizations active in the social forum process contain calls for the strengthening of participatory processes in political decision making, at least in part responding to demands advanced by civil society in general and the GJM in particular. In addition, political parties stress the value of internal participation, although usually combining it with high degrees of internal delegation, defending a specific tradition of political participation and the organizational form in which it historically found expression. 'Modern' networks, to the contrary, are bearers of a different conception of participation, translating participatory values into low degrees of delegation. Emerging with the GJM, 'modern networks' are particularly numerous at the transnational level. If at this level participation is especially mentioned as a general democratic value, references however point to a more general commitment, including internal processes.

Concerning external relations of GJMOs, a different impact emerges for participatory values and degree of internal delegation. Concerning relations with other movement actors, participatory values constitute a bridging element within the GJM. Being closely connected (regardless of the degree of internal delegation) with a cluster of other democratic values and with the basic themes on which the sampled organizations work, participation as a value forms a basis for collaboration and networking among 'tolerant identities' (della Porta 2005c). Concerning relations with local, national, and international state institutions, to the contrary, the degree of delegation in internal decision making assumes a greater importance. Whereas organizations with high degrees of internal delegation tend to follow a line of critical or selective collaboration with state institutions, groups with low degrees of internal delegation tend to show an attitude of refusal.

Notes

1. We must be aware that more formal organizations are more likely to produce the kind of documents that contain references to organizational values. In fact, our data show a statistically significant correlation between participation as a democratic value and a normalized additive index of formalization based on information on the presence of a constitution, a formally adopted program, formal membership, and so on (Cramer's $V = 0.260^*$). In general, references to participatory values can more frequently be found for organizations scoring high on the formalization index.
2. Again, it is more likely that formalized organizations produce documents containing sufficient information for a classification. Our data evidence a very strong correlation between the degree of delegation in internal decision

making and the normalized additive index on formalization (Cramer's $V = 0.401^{***}$).

3. Country of origin is significant neither for participatory values nor for degree of internal delegation, regardless of whether countries are aggregated on the basis of a north/south division or on the basis of the dominant government in the years 2001–2006 (see Chapter 7 for the latter recoding).
4. We can assume that organizations producing documents containing sufficient information for a classification according to degree of delegation also produce documents containing references to organizational values.
5. Article 8 of the constitution of Arcigay affirms: 'The members are held to participate in the associative life' (Arcigay 2007). For Pax Christi Germany, see section 4 of the preamble of the constitution: 'The members of Pax Christi are under the obligation to work personally and together with others for the construction of a new world of justice and peace' (Pax Christi Germany 1948). For Indymedia, see Point 7 of its 'Principles of Unity' (Indymedia 2001).
6. Article 7 of Rifondazione's constitution reads: 'Leading functions express themselves in: a) promoting the democratic participation and political activity of all members; ... f) organizing the political activity in a way as to favour the broadest participation' (Rifondazione 2008). In Article 17 of its constitution, Isole nella rete underlines as one of the duties of the executive committee to favour the participation of the members in the association's activities (Isole 1996). For Friends of the Earth, see Walsh (2001). Rete Lilliput continually stresses the need to prepare and conduct meetings in a participatory way, and surveys carried out at the meetings include questions on whether this objective was achieved.
7. Movement area is strongly correlated both with the year of foundation of an organization (Cramer's $V = 0.421^{***}$) and the number of individual members (Cramer's $V = 0.346^{***}$).
8. The 'reappropriation' of values by organizations can be seen as a process different from but not mutually exclusive to the 'reappropriation' of more structured organizations by their base, observed especially during periods of high mobilization (McAdam et al. 2001, p. 44). For the Italy of the 1980s, Donatella della Porta (1996) has spoken of the penetration of new social movement values in Old Left parties and unions as an effect of the double memberships of activists.
9. The British Socialist Workers Party (SWP) affirms: 'Democracy is at the heart of socialism and is central to the workings of the SWP. The SWP is a democratic centralist organisation that decides its policies through full discussion and debate among its members and then implements these policies in a united and disciplined way' (SWP 2004, p. 3).
10. The more informal Agir ensemble contre le chômage explains in its Charter: 'AC! wants to be a place of solidarity, of practice and apprenticeship of a real democracy' (Agir 2002). In its 'Projet associatif', the more formal Artisans du Monde dedicates a section to the participatory democracy it is trying to create internally, starting at the local level, as a necessary complementary feature to its representative structure (Artisans 2005, pp. 32ff.).
11. See Rete Lilliput 2007b. The minutes of the fourth national assembly in 2006 (Parte II. Sessioni tematiche) contain 'A parenthesis on the subject of participation': 'Participation has a sense if it is participation in the decision

making process. There is a fundamental difference between participation and the construction of consensus, even if professionals of participation (a few good recycled people – and recycling is not a bad thing, it depends on how you do it – that conduct Agenda 21, territorial pacts, strategic plans, etc.) when they speak about participation very often mean – at least judging from the things that they do – nothing else but "construction of consensus". That a public administration sees to and wants to see to the construction of consensus is a good and right thing, it is not a negative aspect, not to be criticized, to the contrary, it is necessary that they do this, but it is something else than participation' (Rete Lilliput 2006b, p. 19). In spring 2008, Rete Lilliput organized a seminar on forms of political participation under the title 'Acting another politics – constructing and practicing democracy' (see Rete Lilliput 2008a).

12. The classification of one grass-roots SMO as high delegation is explained by the fact that the analysed documents did not mention an assembly but another decision-making body. The group in question, however, defines itself as an 'open collective' (Schnews, 'about us' section of the Web site).

13. Neither participatory values nor degree of internal delegation is correlated with the index 'critical sustainability', that is, references to sustainability, solidarity with the third world, critical consumerism, and ethical finance. The same is true for the more ideological themes like anti-capitalism, communism, anarchism, autonomy/antagonism, or socialism.

14. Of the 244 organizations whose fundamental documents were analysed, 160 were also included in the part of the DEMOS project based on interviews.

15. Collaboration with local and international institutions is not significant, whereas for collaboration with national institutions the Cramer's V is 0.203*.

3
Consensus in Movements

Donatella della Porta

Social movements, conflict, and consensus: An introduction

> We have approved unanimously that the constitution of ATTAC-Spain should be based on a consensual basis. (ATTAC Spain 2001)

> Our aim is to take decisions that reach the maximum consensus. (RCADE 2001)

> All Independent Media Centers…shall organize themselves collectively and be committed to the principle of consensus decision making. (Indymedia 2002)

> The Turin Social Forum will experiment with an organizational path that favors participation, reaching consensus and achieving largely shared decisions. (Torino Social Forum 2008)

Like these social movement organizations, many others groups linked to the Global Justice Movement mention consensus as a main organizational value. Although now quite widespread cross-nationally, consensus has not traditionally been a main catchword for social movement organizations, nor for political organizations in general. Similarly, consensus as a concept has not been relevant for social movement studies, which have stressed *conflict* as the dynamic element of our societies. The 'European tradition' in social movement studies has looked at new social movements as potential carriers of a new central conflict in our post-industrial societies, or at least of an emerging constellation of conflicts. In the 'American tradition', the resource mobilization approach reacted to a then dominant conception of conflicts as pathologies. In his influential book *Social Conflicts and Social Movements*, Anthony Oberschall (1973) defined social movements as the main carriers of societal conflicts. In *Democracy and Disorder*, Sidney Tarrow (1989) forcefully pointed to the relevant and positive role of unconventional forms of political participation in democratic processes.

Not by chance, *Social Movements, Conflicts and Change*, one of the first book series to put social movements at the centre of attention, linked the concepts of social movements and conflict. From Michael Lipsky (1967) to Charles Tilly (1978), the first systematic works on social movements developed from traditions of research that stressed conflicts of power, both in society and in politics. In fact, a widely accepted definition of social movements introduced conflict as a central element in their conceptualization:

> Social movement actors are engaged in political and/or cultural conflicts, meant to promote or oppose social change. By conflict we mean an oppositional relationship between actors who seek control of the same stake – be it political, economic, or cultural power – and in the process make negative claims on each other – i.e., demands which, if realized, would damage the interests of the other actors. (della Porta and Diani 2006, p. 21)

In the introduction to the same book, the word 'conflict' is mentioned 59 times, compared with five for the other term I will discuss in this chapter: 'consensus'.

Nevertheless, if the presence of conflicts is certainly not denied, especially since the 1990s the conception of politics as an arena for the expression of conflicts has been challenged (or at least balanced) by an emerging attention to the development of political arenas as spaces for consensus building. In political theory, a focus on consensus emerged within the debate on *deliberative democracy* – stressing in particular the importance of the quality of communication for reaching consensual definitions of the public good in democratic processes (see della Porta 2005a and 2005b; also Chapter 1 and Conclusions in this volume). Some proponents of the normative deliberative vision of democracy have seen social movements and similar associations as central arenas for the development of these consensual processes (Mansbridge 1996; Cohen 1989; Dryzek 2000; Offe 1997).

Again in normative theory, but also in the empirical research on institutional participation of non-institutional actors in democratic decision making, attention to consensus developed especially within the study of civil society. A core meaning in the definition of civil society refers, in fact, to ruling governed societies based upon the consent of individuals rather than coercion (Kaldor 2003, p. 1). In this vision, civility implies respect for others, politeness and the acceptance of strangers (Keane 2003). In many reflections on contemporary societies, civil society is referred to as capable of addressing the tensions between particularism and universalism, plurality and connectedness, diversity and solidarity. Civil society is 'a solidarity sphere in which a certain kind of universalizing community comes gradually to be defined and to some degrees enforced' (Alexander 1998, p. 7). In social movement studies, concepts such as 'free spaces' point at the role of movements in constituting open arenas where public issues are addressed (Evans and Boyte 1992).

In the GJM, deliberative practices have indeed attracted a more or less explicit interest. Within this conception, politics is a space for the construction of common identities that would overcome conflicts of interest, and discourse is a way of addressing even the most divisive issues through the development of mutual understanding about the public good.

The tension between conflict and consensus can be addressed by a conceptualization of various arenas for politics: consensual ones, where relatively minor conflicts among potentially compatible actors are addressed through discourse and the search for consensus; and conflictual ones, where conventional and unconventional forms of political participation are used in a power struggle. This seems to be the view of two of the main proponents of the concept of civil society, who stated, 'social movements construe the cultural models, norms and institutions of civil society as the main stakes of social conflicts' (Cohen and Arato 1992, p. 523).

However, this is no easy solution. In general, although it is to a certain extent normal to have different visions for internal and external democracy, the concept of politics as a space for mutual understanding is in inherent tension with the view of politics as conflict for power. Second, the borders between the two 'arenas of politics' are not so easy to draw. This is all the more true for a 'movement of movements', where networking and dialogue among diverse and plural actors is stated normatively, but where organizational loyalties nevertheless persist. With their strong profile and legacy from the past, large, old, formal, well-structured organizations are also part and parcel of the movement. As we will see, in fact, different conceptions are present within the Global

Justice Movement Organizations (GJMOs), bridging 'consensus' with varying organizational values and practices.

In what follows I shall address this tension between conceptions of conflicts and consensus indirectly, looking at the way in which consensus is defined and addressed by GJMOs. In this endeavour, I rely upon qualitative and quantitative databases constructed from the fundamental documents of 244 social movement organizations. First, I will describe some main democratic values that are often mentioned in the documents of those organizations (section two). In the subsequent sections I aim at *explaining* the consensual conceptions of democracy in both (different) epistemological meanings of social science explanation. Triangulating methods, I look at the quantitative data for statistical associations between the mentions of some democratic values (including consensus) by GJMOs and independent variables referring to organizational resources and cultural norms (third section). Within an interpretative perspective, I also highlight the different meanings of consensus for different types of actors (fourth section).

Consensus as a multidimensional concept

In the Global Justice Movement, references to consensus have been seen as belonging to a search for innovative models of decision making aimed at overcoming the limits of 'assemblearism' as well as delegation. In the social forum process, emerging models 'combine limited and controlled recourse to delegation with consensus-based instruments appealing to dialogue, to the transparency of the communicative process and to reaching the greatest possible consensus' (della Porta et al. 2006, p. 30).

Our research indicates that consensus is mentioned by several (about one-quarter) and diverse organizations involved in the GJM. Already proposed within the student movement and taken up later with more conviction by the feminist movement, consensual methods have been considered as inefficient, slowing down decision making to the point of jeopardizing action. Many global justice groups revived the consensus model but developed new, more or less formalized rules to help in overcoming the hurdles to decision making created by differences of opinion or the manipulation of the process by a few individuals.

Our qualitative as well as quantitative analysis of the organizational values on democratic issues indicates a considerable focus on consensus as well as on some 'bridged' concepts. In our analysis of the organizational documents, we have coded references to democratic values, distinguishing values mentioned when addressing the internal functioning of our organizations from general democratic values. Additionally, we have analysed in depth the symbolic contexts in which these values were mentioned.

In general, the issue of democracy emerges as very relevant for our GJMOs: most of the organizations we have sampled make reference to democratic values in their fundamental documents. Our quantitative data indicates that three sets of values are often mentioned in the democratic conceptions of the Global Justice Movement organizations we have analysed (Table 3.1). As we will see in this section, many of these values resonate with both normative theorists and empirical researchers associated with the above-mentioned conceptions of participatory democracy, deliberative democracy, and civil society.

Table 3.1 Internal and general democratic values (% of yes) No. of cases = 244

Internal Values	% of yes	External Values	% of yes
Consensual method	17.2	Difference/plurality/ heterogeneity	47.1
Deliberative democracy	7.0	Dialogue/communication	31.6
		Transparency	23.8
Participatory democracy	27.9	Participation	51.2
Inclusiveness	20.9	Inclusiveness	25.8
Explicit critique of delegation/representation	11.1	Equality	34.0
Non-hierarchical decision-making	16.0		
Limitation of delegation	6.6	Representation	6.1
Any of the three values mentioned above (index of critique of delegation)	23.4		
Rotation principle	6.6		
Mandate delegation	6.1		
Autonomy of member organizations*	33.1	Autonomy (group; cultural)	18.9
Autonomy of the territorial levels**	38.5	Individual liberty/ autonomy	21.7
Any of the two values mentioned above (index of organizational autonomy)	39.8	*Any of the two values mentioned above (index of individual or cultural autonomy)*	32.4

Notes: * Variable is not applicable for 114 (46.7%) groups, which do not mention organizations as members. ** Variable is not applicable for 62 (25.4%) groups, which do not mention territorial levels of their organization.

A first set of values points at some *deliberative* qualities of the GJM as open spaces. In normative conceptions of deliberative democracy, *consensus* plays a key role, as decisions are reached by convincing others of one's own argument. In contrast with majoritarian democracy, where decisions are legitimized by voting, decisions must be approvable by all participants. As mentioned (see Introduction to this volume), the deliberative conception of democracy includes norms of equality, inclusiveness, plurality of values, high-quality discourse, and transparency. In addition, the conception of civil society has a *discursive* dimension: 'To the degree this solidarity community exists, it is exhibited by "public opinion", possesses its own cultural codes and narratives in a democratic idiom, is patterned by a set of peculiar institutions, most notably legal and journalistic ones, and is visible in historically distinctive sets of interactional practices like civility, equality, criticism and respect' (Alexander 1998, p. 7). As an internal value, the consensual method is mentioned by 17 per cent of our groups, and deliberative democracy by 7 per cent. Looking at general democratic values, references to plurality, difference, and heterogeneity have been highlighted as important democratic elements in the documents of as much as half of our sample, with a value very near to that of the reference to (more traditional) participation.

Among the groups most committed to experimentation with *consensual methods*, specific rules are developed in horizontal communication and conflict management: 'consensus tools' include 'good facilitation, various hand signals, go-rounds and the breaking up into small and larger sized groups. These methods should be explained by the facilitator at the start of each discussion, but if you wish to know more about how we are using them please contact members of the process group at this gathering' (Dissent! – A Network of Resistance against the G8). Facilitators or moderators are used (for instance, for the Italian Rete Lilliput or the British Rising Tide), with the aim of including all points of view in the discussion as well as implementing rules for good discussion, going from the (limited) time allocated to each speaker to the maintenance of a constructive climate. The method of consensus:

> stipulates that in the course of discussion the degree of agreement of the group's various members on a specific question, which must be presented clearly and explicitly, must be assessed. Confrontation is continued, working on the possibility of reconciling differing opinions, based on an incremental model, whereby a decision can always be brought back into discussion so as to satisfy the widest possible

number of people. The consensus method invites everyone to communicate the reasons for any disagreement, clarifying whether they will be prepared to uphold the decision eventually taken without exiting the group. The consensus method thus builds 'agreement within disagreement', since any particular disagreement is always set within a framework of more general agreement, based on respect and reciprocal trust. (della Porta et al. 2006, pp. 53–4)

Supporting this type of conception, in its 'Criteri di fondo condivisi' (2002) Rete Lilliput defines the 'method of consensus' as a process in which, if a proposal does not receive total consensus from all participants, further discussion ensues in order to find a compromise with those who disagree. If disagreements persist and involve a numerically large minority, the project is not approved (Tecchio, quoted in Veltri 2003, p. 14). Similarly, for Dissent!:

Consensus normally works around a proposal, which, hopefully is submitted beforehand so that people have time to consider it. The proposal is presented and any concerns are discussed. The proposal is then amended until a consensus is reached. At the heart of this process are principles that include trust, respect, recognition that everyone has the right to be heard and to contribute (i.e. equal access to power), a unity of purpose and commitment to that purpose and a commitment to the principle of co-operation. At these gatherings we seek to reach consensus on most issues, although this is not always possible and often there is no need to reach 'one decision' at the end of a useful discussion. (Dissent! 2008)

In the same vein, the Spanish net Espacio Alternativo (2008) defines the rules for good communication thus:

In this direction, the following criteria are to be met: 1) trying to develop good debates on which are the real differences, if any; 2) signalling what these differences are; 3) knowing how widespread a certain position is in the member organizations; 4) spreading information about them through the communication instruments of the federation; 5) respecting the rights of individuals and collectives to disagree on specific points, in words as well as in deeds.

Attention to consensus methods as a way to improve communication resonates with the widespread idea of the movement as building public spaces for dialogue and (good) communication. This is illustrated for instance by the Spanish Derechos para Tod@s (s/d), which stresses:

> our goal is to contribute to the spreading of debates, not by narrowing spaces, but by opening them to all those who are critical of this glob-alization that causes exploitation, repression and/or exclusion... No alternative to the current system can be regarded as the 'true' one. That is, we want to set up a space to reflect and to fight for a social and civil transformation. (Jiménez and Calle 2006, p. 278)

Attention to consensus building and debate as being valuable per se is reflected in the conception of the organization as an arena. In its self-presentation, ATTAC Germany states that the organization is 'a place, where political processes of learning and experiences are made possi-ble; in which the various streams of progressive politics discuss with each other, in order to find a common capacity of action together' (ATTAC Germany 2001). The Foro Social de Palencia (2008) presents itself as a 'permanent space for encounters, debates and support for col-lective action', where 'decisions are made by consensus'. In fact, the pluralist nature of the forum is positively assessed in its definition as 'a meeting place of different visions and positions with some common denominator, not an organization that has to reach a unique position'.

Mechanisms of national and transnational diffusion certainly helped in spreading the values of consensual decision making. The 'Zapatistas experience' is often mentioned as a source of inspiration. The founding assembly of ATTAC Italy, held in Bologna in June 2001 (about 2000 par-ticipants), 'created a provisional directory but as far as the drawing up of a constitution was concerned decided on a "zapatist consultation"' (Reiter 2006, p. 255). Similarly, the mentioning of consensus in the con-stitution of the World Social Forum reverberated in most regional and local forums stressing consensus as a main organizational principle – for example, all Sicilian Social Forums state that decisions have to be taken by '*massima condivisione*' (maximal level of sharing) (Piazza and Barbagallo 2003). In March 2001, the Genoa Social Forum stressed the value of the consensual method, seen as 'a way to work on what we have in common and continue to discuss what divides us.... So that all can feel the decisions taken as their own, although with different degrees of satisfaction' (quoted in Fruci 2003, p. 189). Transnational campaigns and social forums also helped to support mutual learning about the techniques that facilitate consensual decision making. So, for instance, in international meetings, the Italian metalworkers' union

FIOM became acquainted with, and started to appreciate, the use of facilitators (Reiter 2006, p. 249).

At the national level, social movement organizations often refer to specific documents written by groups and individuals promoting the method of consensus by formulating specific rules of communication. For instance, Indymedia Italy refers to a document written on the occasion of the assembly of the organization involved in fair trade (the Carta Italiana dei Criteri del Commercio Equo e Solidale, Italian Charter for the Criteria for fair and solidarity trade; http://italy.indymedia.org). Often, the most committed organizations also offer training. Among them, the British Dissent! network (2004a) organizes, at the local level, '3 or 4 days of community work, building, community empowerment projects, dance training, consensus training. The goal is to introduce principles and leave the community with tools, skills and energy to continue projects'.

A second set of values reported in the fundamental documents of our organizations revolves around *participation*, a fundamental component of social movements' conception of democracy that takes on new meaning in the GJM (see also Chapter 2). In normative theory, beyond the traditional reflections of participatory democracy (Pateman 1970), some normative conceptions of deliberative democracy support participatory visions, as deliberation is said to require 'some forms of apparent equality among citizens' (Cohen 1989, p. 18) and must exclude power – deriving from coercion, but also an unequal weighting of participants as representatives of organizations of different sizes or influence. In what is described as a 'utopian version', the concept of civil society is also linked to the notion of participation: 'It is a definition that presupposes a state or rule of law but insists not only on restraints on state power but on a redistribution of power. It is a radicalization of democracy and an extension of participation and autonomy' (Kaldor 2003, p. 8).

As for the values on internal democracy, participation is still a main component of the GJMOs' vision, mentioned by one-third of the organizations as an internal value and by more than half as a general value. This applies not only to the pure forms of social movement organizations; trade unions and left-wing political parties also refer to participation as a founding principle. However, additional values emerge that specify (and differentiate among) the conceptions of participatory democracy. References to limits to delegation, the rotation principle, mandated delegation, and criticism of delegation as internal organizational values are present although not dominant (each mentioned by between 6 and 11 per cent of our groups). Non-hierarchical decision making is often mentioned (16 per cent), and inclusiveness is even more frequently mentioned (21 per cent and 26 per cent). If we group the positive responses on critique of delegation, limitation of delegation, non-hierarchical decision making, and mandated delegation into an index of non-hierarchical decision making, 23.4 per cent have positive scores. Significantly, representative values are mentioned by only 6 per cent of our organizations.

A third set of values can be described under the label of autonomy, resonating with those put forward in normative theories of civil society, as the notion of civil society links consensus to values of autonomy. In Cohen and Arato's words, 'The legitimating principles of democracy and rights are compatible only with a model of civil society that institutionalizes democratic communication in a multiplicity of publics and defends the conditions of individual autonomy by liberating the intimate sphere from all traditional as well as modern forms of inequality and unfreedom' (1991, p. 455). In our database, the autonomy of member organizations (33%) and local chapters (38.5%) is frequently invoked. As for the general values, if we combine mentions of cultural and individual autonomy, these add up to 39.8 per cent of the sampled organizations.

Explaining consensus: Structures and cultures

Social movement studies have traditionally linked organizational structure and values to political opportunities. Among the institutional variables considered as relevant for social movements are the territorial division of competences and the functional division of power (Kriesi 1995; Kriesi et al. 1995; Rucht 1994, 1996). Territorial centralization and functional concentration of power reduce institutional channels for challengers, producing more radical visions of alternative, participatory forms of democracy; and vice versa. Decentralized states should facilitate decentralized movement organizations, which are also more horizontal; in reverse, strong states tend to feature more bureaucratic movement organizations.

Comparing France, West Germany, and the United States, Dieter Rucht (1996, p. 198) found that in the two federal states, USA and Germany, the grass-roots level of the movements was much stronger than in more centralized France; at the same time, however, there was also a very strong interest group type of social movement structure. In parallel, inclusive cultural traditions should spill over from institutions to civil society organizations. However, relations might be more complicated. In fact, as Rucht himself argues (1996, p. 192), 'In the long run, this [decentralisation] encourages the formalisation of centralised and professional interest groups within the movement (and movement parties)', while 'strong executive power structures in a given political system tend to induce a fundamental critique of bureaucratic and hierarchical political forms, which is then reflected in the movements' emphasis on informal and decentralised structures'. This means that in federal states we have both professional and grass-roots organizational structures, with more space for participation overall. Similarly, more inclusive states, opening channels of participation, have favoured the development of large, well-structured, and formalized associations. At the same time, however, smaller groups have contested the institutionalization and moderation of those associations, experimenting with alternative organizational models.

Our cross-national analysis indicates, in fact, that different democratic values are indeed present in all analysed countries and at the transnational level, without any clearly identifiable connection with the characteristics of political opportunities. References to internal participation are more widespread among the more highly-mobilized Italian (51.2%) and Spanish (35.1%) organizations, but also among the Swiss (40%). References to inclusiveness are especially frequent in consensual Switzerland (42.9%) but also in majoritarian Great Britain (34.2%). Critique of delegation is more frequent in centralized France (28.1%) and Great Britain (31.6%), but also in decentralized Spain (21.6%). Consensual methods are often mentioned in Spain (35.1%) and in Germany (22.6%). Values of external inclusivity, difference/plurality/heterogeneity as well as dialogue/communication and transparency are much more frequently addressed in Switzerland and at the transnational level. Participation as a general value is to be found more often in the fundamental documents by Italian and Swiss organizations, as is equality (the latter also by the British groups).

Although some of these results might be linked to our sampling strategy, our background knowledge on the GJM in the various countries points at its internal heterogeneity, in each and every one of our selected countries. At any rate, in order to understand the differences in terms of emphasis on different values, we must turn to some characteristics of the organizations themselves. In line with the main hypotheses in social movement and organizational studies presented in the introduction to this volume, I shall look at organizational resources as well as cultural ones. In each of the next two paragraphs, I shall present some general hypotheses and test them by crossing some selected values with indicators of organizational structure and norms.

Democratic visions, consensus and organizational structures

[The network] favors fast and complete circulation of information, in order to allow for the construction of processes based upon consensus, giving everyone the possibility to intervene and express both agreement and disagreement; it applies criteria of constant verification on the organizational modes, the work done and the allocated tasks (if any). If there are roles of speaker, referent, coordinator or others, these must be constrained by temporal limits, defined by the duration of the initiative/campaign and/or by rotational criteria. (Rete Lilliput 2008b)

In this way, the Italian Rete Lilliput links the method of consensus to some specific organizational characteristics – in particular a participatory structure, with limits to delegation and an emphasis on broad and equal involvement of all members. Consensual decision making, as well as related democratic values, have been seen as influenced by some characteristics of the organizational structure. More broadly, organizational structure has been linked to conceptions and practices of democracy: either organizational structures constrain the conceptions of democracy or, in reverse, values orient the choice of organizational models.

In the social science literature, we can find some explanatory hypotheses that specify this relationship. Mansbridge (2003) has suggested that a decision-making model based on consensus is especially advantageous for organizations without other legitimate tools for convincing members to act collectively. More informal organizations (such as Earth First) seem more able to promote good communication than those that are more hierarchically organized (such as Friends of the Earth) (Whitworth 2003). As for the Global Justice Movement, the emphasis on consensus seems greater in decentralized networks such as Rete Lilliput (Veltri 2003) than in more centralized ones, such as ATTAC-Italia (Finelli 2003). In addition, transnational networks (counter-summits or social forums) seem particularly sensitive to deliberative values and more able to integrate different organizations through the construction of master frames (della Porta et al. 2006; Andretta 2005a). Mobilization in specific campaigns at the national or local level (against the war, in favour of immigrants' rights, or on labour issues) often includes moments of negotiation between representatives of social movement organizations (Andretta 2005b).

We can define organizational structures in terms of amount of resources (as indicated by size of membership, presence of paid staff, size of budget) as well as by organizational model (as indicated by degree of formalization,[1] presence of an executive, and relevance of the assembly). Looking at the interaction between organizational characteristics and democratic values (and leaving aside the participatory values already analysed in the previous chapter), we note a low overall impact of organizational structures on expressed democratic values (selected results in Table 3.2) – even though, when associations emerge, they often (but not always) tend to confirm our expectations. First of all, looking at organizational resources, in line with our expectations, *consensual methods* are more often mentioned by smaller organizations with lower budgets and no paid staff (32 per cent for groups with up to 100 members and 25 per cent for those with between 100 and 1000, but only around 9 per cent for those with more than 1000 members). Critiques of delegation and non-hierarchical principles are more often stressed by organizations with fewer than 1000 members and a low budget (30 per cent of organizations with no budget mention those principles, compared with only 8.3 per cent of those with a budget of more than 500 000 euros). The same variables, however, have no or little impact on mentions of the other values, which in some cases tend to increase with organizational resources. Mentions of the autonomy of local chapters and organizational members is related with the size of individual membership (62 per cent of the organizations mentioning this value in their documents have more than 1000 individual members) and territorial levels covered (68.7 per cent have three or four territorial levels). Similarly, autonomy is more often mentioned by groups with larger individual membership and multilevel organizations (59.5 per cent with three or four levels).

The index of formalization is positively associated with mentions of such values as equality, and autonomy of chapter and member organization, as well as with critique of delegation. An explicit rejection of the executive increases the chances that such values as consensus, internal inclusion, equality, and horizontality are mentioned. In parallel, the relevance of the assembly is positively associated with mentions of consensus, dialogue, and horizontality.

To summarize, while most associations go in the expected directions, it seems that many general values are only indirectly linked to organizational characteristics. These values seem to be either very general (participation, inclusiveness) or endowed with multiple meanings (equality, individual and collective autonomy) and are, in fact, spread across groups with different organizational structures and

Table 3.2 Association between selected organizational values and organizational structure (Cramer's V) (selected results)

	Consensus or deliberation as value	Dialogue	Difference/ heterogeneity/ plurality	Internal inclusiveness	Equality	Critique of delegation/non hierarchical decision making	Individual/coll. Cultural autonomy	Autonomous chapters/member organizations
Size (individual members)	n.s.	n.s.	n.s.	n.s.	n.s.	n.s.	n.s.	n.s.
Paid staff	0.151* (no)	n.s.	n.s.	n.s.	n.s.	0.174*	n.s.	n.s.
Budget	0.212* (<10000)	n.s.	0.156°	0.190* (<10000)	n.s.	n.s.	n.s.	n.s.
Degree of formalization	n.s.	n.s.	n.s.	n.s.	0.256°	0.254°	n.s.	0.260°
Presence of an executive	0.277*** (rejected)	n.s.	n.s.	167* (rejected)	0.178* (yes or rejected)	0.368*** (rejected)	n.s.	n.s.
Relevance of the assembly	0.239*** (+assembleary)	0.139° (+assembleary)	n.s.	n.s.	n.s.	0.150° (+assembleary)	n.s.	n.s.

Notes: level of significance: *** significant at 0.001 level; ** significant at 0.01; * significant at 0.05; ° significant at 0.10 level; n.s. = non significant.

resources. In contrast, the critique of delegation and the appeal to consensual values seem more frequent for smaller and more participatory
groups. However, structural organizational characteristics are not very
strong in explaining the references to democratic values.

Consensus, themes, identities

> Inclusiveness also implies creative methods for constructing meet-
> ings. All too often we become victims of our own self-imposed
> agendas, of our self-imposed time constraints, of our self-imposed
> procedural routines. This does not mean that agendas or proce-
> dures are unimportant. Rather, it means that we should consider
> them flexibly, as our creations that we can change according to
> our needs, not as our gods ruling our lives. All too often we react
> with stereotypical programmes or short-cuts at the first impasse, so
> as 'to save time'.... The practices of consensus-seeking strengthen
> bonds, trust, communication and understanding. On the other hand,
> decision-making based on voting creates power blocks, power games,
> and hegemonic strategies, excluded and included, hierarchies, thus
> reproducing the same kind of social relations we are opposing. This
> productivist mentality is the same as our managers and our bosses,
> all so focused on 'results', forgetting the life process that goes into
> producing those results, hiding the voices excluded for the sake of
> results, and so excluding different results that would be possible if
> those voices were included. We have a chance to redefine for our-
> selves what democracy is, and make it a living example for others.
> (London Social Forum 2003)

For the London Social Forum, the use of the method of consensus
is linked to the group's self definition, reflecting in particular the
preference for prefigurative politics over effectiveness. The search for
consensus certainly requires the investment of much time and energy
debating different options in terms of their practical effects, but also has
ethical implications. For example, within Rete Lilliput, which openly
advocated the consensus method, proposals were made to introduce
restricted delegation for precise mandates or majority voting on certain issues, limiting consensus to fundamental decisions in the name of
efficiency. However, the proposals were defeated on the basis of a (normative) statement about 'the validity of the consensus method which
is said to have permitted ("even in its complexity") to experiment with
horizontality, diffuse leadership and participative methods' (Reiter 2006,
p. 262). As the group stated, 'We have pursued the coherence between

means and ends, between form and content; we have learned to reason collectively.' Privileging consensus, Rete Lilliput renounced the writing of a document on 'the world we want', stating 'we agree that we all dream of a different world, but it is not at all clear that we all want the same things; we are not able to write a document on which consensus can be reached; it does not make sense to freeze in a written document the idea of the world we want, the challenge is to work together in order to invent and construct the alternative' (quoted in Reiter 2006, p. 263).

That the ideology of a movement affects its view of democracy can be seen as a truism. Nevertheless, the relationship between internal decision making and general values has long been neglected in empirical research and theorizing. The resource mobilization approach emphasized the instrumental role of institutionalization for the achievement of movement goals, and only limited attention has been given to how cultural processes influence internal organizational structures (Minkoff 2001). As has been noted, 'the spirit of Michels infuses resource mobilisation arguments through a sort of syllogism: organisations are resources; effective organisations are hierarchies, therefore, hierarchical organisations are valuable resources for movements' (Clemens and Minkoff 2004, p. 156; see also Gamson 1990). Indeed, only recently have organizational forms been analysed in relation to the cultural meaning that activists assign to them. Organizational forms have in fact been described as part of a broader social movement repertoire (Clemens 1993). Normatively oriented, organizations may have a 'prefigurative' function, embedding the kind of social relations that activists would like to see in the world outside (Breines 1989).

If organizational values are not just means but also ends in themselves (Polletta 2002), the question of which values are linked with which vision of democracy acquires relevance. This subject has been addressed in previous studies by looking at the relations between individual values and organizational values (see della Porta 2005c on tolerant identities; Gundelach 1989 on anti-hierarchical values); democratic values and other values at the organizational level (for example, Katsiaficas 1997 on autonomous values); organizational values and general cultural values (for example, Eber 1999 on values of social responsibility). Multi-issue SMOs have been found to invest more in the development of and member participation in channels of communication (Faber and McCarthy 2001). Environmentalists focused on social justice elaborate a particular view of democracy stressing fair democratic procedures, inclusion, and equal treatment (Salazar and Alper 2002).

In the GJM, consensual decision making has been seen as resonant with values such as non-violence and respect for minorities (Veltri 2003). In addition, research on the decision-making processes of international protest events (such as counter-summits), involving many and different groups, indicated that consensual decision making allowed for the development of a master frame connecting the various meanings given to the protest, and culturally integrating the various organizations (della Porta et al. 2006; Andretta 2005a; Mosca 2005). Conversely, single-issue movements seem to be less oriented to participation: degrees of specialization, centralization, and professionalization tend to co-vary (Staggenborg 1988; Kriesi 1996). Prefigurative conceptions of politics (as expressed in the search for intrinsically rewarding forms of action, such as happenings) favour inclusionary organizing, consensual decision making, interpersonal collective bonds, and personal belonging (Podilchak 1998).

In our research, we have different indicators that allow us to control for the effects of culture on the three mentioned sets of democratic values. First of all, the hypothesis that democratic concerns are higher for multi-issue organizations is confirmed by our data. Crossing democratic values with an additive index of the mentioned themes (see Chapter 1), we have high and significant correlation coefficients.[2]

Additionally, democratic values are linked to movement area, which we operationalized by distinguishing Old Left, New Left, and anarchist/autonomous groups; new social movements; solidarity movements; and new global movements (see Chapter 1). Crossing democratic values with movement area (Table 3.3), the use of consensus emerges as especially widespread among new global organizations (28.8 per cent, compared with between 15 and 18 per cent in the other areas). Dialogue is stressed especially by new social movement and new global organizations, while equality is more often mentioned in Old Left, New Left/anarchist/autonomous groups, and new social movement organizations. Values of autonomy are especially present in the documents of New Left/anarchist and autonomous groups. The new global organizations also stress more than the others anti-hierarchical values, participation, and inclusiveness as an external value (together with the New Left and new social movements). In contrast, references to participatory democracy as well as transparency are more frequent among the new social movements (but also the Old Left), as are internal values of individual and collective autonomy, equality, and inclusiveness (also by the New Left and, for inclusiveness, the Old Left). The Old Left mentions more often representative democracy.

Table 3.3 Mentions of democratic values by movement area (% of yes)

	Consensus	Dialogue	Difference/ heterogeneity/ plurality	Internal inclusiveness	Equality	Critique of delegation and non-hier. (index)	Individual/coll. cultural autonomy	Autonomous chapters/member organizations
Old Left	18.8	21.9	56.3	21.9	43.8	15.6	21.9	46.7
New Left/anarchism/ autonomy	17.9	32.1	50.0	39.3	50.0	46.4	57.1	60.0
NSM	17.9	42.9	50.0	25.0	42.9	28.6	46.4	52.2
Solidarity/peace/ human rights	15.7	22.9	37.1	12.9	25.7	10.0	22.9	30.9
New Global	28.8	38.8	50.0	21.3	27.5	28.8	31.6	34.4
Other	0.0	33.3	50.0	0.0	50.0	0.0	33.3	50.0
Total	20.5	31.6	47.1	20.9	34.4	16.7	32.4	40.3
Cramer's V	n.s.	n.s.	n.s.	206°	201°	0.273***	0.247**	210°

Note: level of significance: *** significant at 0.001 level; ** significant at 0.01; * significant at 0.05; ° significant at 0.10; n.s. = non significant.

These associations are in part reflected in the organizational population to which a group belongs. Here, we distinguished in particular among parties, unions, co-operatives, NGOs, informal SMOs, formal SMOs, and new networks (see Chapter 1). Crossing these with organizational formulas, we noted that modern networks linked to the GJM more often emphasize values such as participation, inclusiveness, and horizontal decision making (in the latter case, together with grass-roots SMOs and unions), as well as consensus (with grass-roots and more formal SMOs), transparency, heterogeneity, and dialogue (with parties and formal SMOs). Additionally, references to all mentioned themes (with the exception of critiques of delegation) are associated with mentions of multiple themes.

Compatible results emerge if we look at the organizational generations, as coded based on year of foundation. Research on different types of political organizations has stressed their tendency to remain influenced by the specific conditions in which they were created as well as the choices made at the very beginning of their existence. Clientelistic structures tend to survive in political parties that had to distribute individual incentives when they emerged (Shefter 1977), and left-wing parties tend to reproduce the democratic centralism they had chosen when they were founded (Panebianco 1982). Similarly, social movement organizations – notwithstanding much lower rates of survival – tend to maintain, when they do survive, some of the characteristics they developed at their founding. Despite processes of institutionalization, for example, Italian women's organizations in the 1980s and 1990s maintained a reliance upon the affinity groups and small size structures characterizing the consciousness-raising groups that had been so important in the 1970s phase of high mobilization (della Porta 1995). Similarly, the autonomous squatted youth centres, although becoming more efficient in selling cultural products and more open to collaborative interactions with local institutions, maintained a concern for autonomy, often expressed in the refusal to occupy spaces officially allocated to them and a preference for illegally squatted spaces (ibid.).

A characteristic of the GJM is its capacity to remobilize organizations that had emerged in previous cycles of protest. Looking at year of foundation, we might note that organizations founded after 2000 refer more often to consensus (27.9 per cent, compared with 6.1 per cent of groups founded before 1968, 8 per cent of those founded between 1969 and 1989, 18.8 per cent of those founded between 1990 and 1999) as well as some linked general values as difference/plurality/heterogeneity, dialogue/communication. These newer groups also seem more sensitive to participatory values, citing more often than the other organizations values such as internal participation (36.8, compared with 18.2 for those founded before 1968), participation as a general value (66.2 per cent compared with 42.4 per cent for those founded before 1968), inclusiveness (both as value mentioned in relations to the internal life of the organization and as more general value), and critique of delegation (30.9 per cent against 12.1 per cent for those founded before 1968). In reverse, references to individual and cultural autonomy are slightly more present in older organizations (1969–89), and mentions of individual and collective autonomy as well as equality and transparency seem quite stable.

Understanding conceptions of consensus

Consensus: Majority which emanates without vote or with a widely majority vote. . . . If a large majority does not emerge (a minimum of 75%), the debate continues. (AC!, Charte 2002)

People can object to proposals or block consensus being reached. Major decisions are only made when everyone is in agreement. This means lots of talking! Hand signals are used to communicate with the facilitator and other people in the meeting when you are not speaking. (Dissent! 2004b)

The selected quotes accurately represent the growing interest in 'consensus' that characterizes many GJMOs, but also the different meanings given to the term within different traditions. While the statistical analysis allows us to identify some associations between references to consensus and other characteristics of our organizations, the qualitative analysis of our documents allows for a better understanding of the relations between democratic values and other organizational characteristics by pointing at the diverse meanings that consensus has for various organizations, as this emerging value is bridged with previous organizational cultures. I distinguish in particular between plural and communitarian conceptions of consensus, each connected to different traditions.

The first is a *plural conception of consensus through high-quality dialogue*. This is a most innovative understanding of the method of consensus, which often characterizes network organizations. As in many social forums, consensus is considered here to be 'functional for safeguarding the unitary-plural nature of the movement as well as members' demands for individual protagonism' (Fruci 2003, p. 169). In networks and campaigns, the consensual method is advocated as allowing for working on what unites, notwithstanding the differences. The Spanish Espacio alternativo (2008) considers that 'the method for clarifying differences has to be consensus and large agreement on the basis of achieving unity beyond these differences. We therefore consider that...we have to continue our debate until we agree on the themes, trying to reach consensus and common positions. If they are not possible, our public communication would ensure knowledge of agreements and differences'.[3] The transnational network Our World is Not for Sale also explicitly links the consensus method to networking:

> OWINFS works to develop and link campaigns around the world toward the end of reshaping the corporate-dominated trade agenda to support human rights, environmental sustainability and democratic principles. OWINFS acts as a 'hub' for social movements and NGOs working on globalization issues who are interested in sharing analysis and coordinating action efforts internationally. The active participation of OWINFS members is what drives our collective work forward. We coordinate efforts on conference calls and make decisions by consensus. There is no formal network 'staff' – rather member groups volunteer to carry out agreed upon tasks. A strength of the network is that individual movements and organizations can work together where it is strategic and helps advance their initiatives, and are free to dedicate as much or as little time to the network as makes sense for them in order to meet their objectives. (OWINFS 2008)

In this sense, in organizational networks, consensual principles are presented as resonating with a respect for the *autonomy* of the individual organizations that are part of the federation. Dissent! (2008) explains the ways in which the group made decisions as follows:

> The previous Dissent! gathering reached consensus that: (1) The Dissent! Network holds bi-monthly gatherings. The Gatherings are the only Network decision making body – email lists and web discussion forums are not where Network decisions are made! Local groups are autonomous from one another and are able to take any form of action they choose. Local Dissent! Network groups should not speak for the whole network. (2) Local groups should also consider, however, that the actions which they take will actually reflect on the

network as a whole. The Dissent! Network is therefore primarily a networking tool. (Dissent! 2008)

Consensual decisions seem all the more necessary when organizations emphasize *internal diversity*. This is the case, for instance, for ATTAC Italia, which in its Charter of Intent stipulates that it 'wants to be a democratic and open association, transversal and as much as possible pluralistic, composed of diverse individuals and social forces.... it wants to contribute to the renovation of democratic political participation and favours the development of new organizational forms of civil society' (Reiter 2006, p. 255). As its national assembly stated, 'We want to continue to build shared associational forms, based on participation and the consensual method, fit for letting diversities meet and work together and develop democratic decisional practices. Because we consider democracy as the most important element of the common good and we want, all together, to re-appropriate it' (ATTAC Italia 2007).

Participation and the method of consensus are, in this sense, considered as the main expressions of democracy 'as a common good'. In particular, but not only, for networks, consensus resonates in fact with an emphasis on the *respect for differences*, bridged with calls for *inclusiveness*, within the conception of the organization as an open space – a metaphor often used by our groups. For instance, the Turin Social Forum (2008) states that:

> the TSF wants to be an open place in which even the individuals, as well as the organized actors, can meet and work together; a space in which internal differences are accepted and given a positive value, and not considered as an instrument to be used in order to acquire increased visibility and impose working methods; a space in which there should be no place for hegemony and instead the search for a sufficient degree of maturation and consensus is the guiding principle for each initiative.[4]

Another vision can be identified as a *communitarian conception of consensus as collective agreement*. This conception is expressed by groups with a deeply rooted 'assembleary' tradition. For instance, the British Wombles declared:

> We have no formal membership; all meetings are weekly & open to anyone who wishes to attend. These meetings are where any & all decisions concerning the group are made. The politics we espouse

are those we wish to live by – self-organisation, autonomy, direct democracy & direct action against the forces of coercion and control. ... As such, no individual can speak on behalf of the Wombles as all group & all decisions are made collectively based on consensus. (Wombles 2004)

Similarly, among the Italian Disobbedienti, in case of disagreement in its management council regarding decisions under discussion, these decisions are frozen and set aside, pending resumption at a later date (della Porta et al. 2006, p. 53).

In this area, consensus resonates with *anti-authoritarian, horizontal relations*. According to Indymedia Italy (2002),

All IMCs (Independent Media Centers) recognize the importance of the methods (used) for promoting social change and are committed to the development of non-hierarchical and anti-authoritarian relations, as far as both interpersonal and group dynamics are concerned. Therefore, [they are committed] to organize collectively and adopt, in order to make decisions, the method of consensus, that develops in a participatory, horizontal and transparent way.

In this vision, consensus is presented as part of a more complex, anti-hierarchical framework. Alternativa Antimilitarista-MOC, a group that declares making decisions by consensus within general assemblies, defines 'a process in which we attempt to reach the most satisfactory agreement for all members'. Consensus is mentioned here as part and parcel of a horizontal conception of democracy:

we promote forms of horizontal organization by taking our decisions by consensus, since our very functioning challenges hierarchical structures, in the attempt to overcome all possible leadership. We promote rotation and the capacity of all group members so that they can get involved in the activities they wish to perform. There is no 'charge' that gives any individual more power. (Alternativa Antimilitarista-MOC 2004)

Consensual methods should help in avoiding the creation of power relations. Thus, Indymedia presents itself as a 'platform for your news and background information on political and social issues. In order to avoid the development of positions of power, the members of the moderation committee rotate and the committee decides on the basis of consensus'

(Was ist Indymedia?/Grundsätze). The French Réseau Intergalactique, which developed around the construction of a self-managed space at the anti-G8 summit in Evian, states in its Charter, 'there is no dominant voice. It is what we call a horizontal way of functioning: there is no small group that decides. Thus, there is not on the one side thinking heads and on the other side small hands and feet. The aim is to facilitate the integration of each in the discussion and decision-making.'

Consensual methods are also adopted within a prefigurative vision of organizational life. They are linked to the aim of realizing social changes not only though political decisions, but through deep transformations in everyday life and individual attitudes. For 'it is impossible to realize a social transformation through merely political decisions. The activities have to relate to the needs and desires of the people, so that anti-militarism can bring about life alternatives and a struggle in positive way. This would develop by consensus, understood as a process that aims at reaching the agreement which is most satisfactory for all' (ibid.).

Summarizing

If social movements have traditionally been considered as conflictual actors and social movement studies have traditionally linked movements and conflict, growing interest has recently focused in both arenas on what could be considered the opposite of conflict: consensus. This attention resonates with concepts such as civil society and deliberative democracy, which have become increasingly relevant in social and political theory. Even though conflict is used to refer to the relations between social movements and their external opponents and consensus to refer to relations inside the movement, there is nevertheless an inherent tension between the two concepts, as they tend to construct different visions of politics as, respectively, antagonistic and the realm of power struggle, or, alternatively, deliberative and oriented to dialogue. In the first conception, conflicts are perceived as irreconcilable: the political debate is characterized by a struggle between hegemonic and counter-hegemonic discourses, and no common good in this sense exists. In the second, conflicts can be solved through dialogue: discourses (or at least good communication) help in the emergence of a shared understanding of the common good – and democracy is indeed conceived as the most important common good. Open in political theory (with the critique of the Habermasian conception of deliberation) and in social theory (with the critique of a 'neoliberal' vision of the civil society), this debate resonates not only within social movement studies, but also in social movement organizations themselves.

The results of our research indicate, in fact, that references to consensus emerged in the Global Justice Movement, presented as a new value, especially by recently created organizations. Travelling from the Zapatistas Sierra Lacandona to Europe, consensus values (and the method of consensus, often written in capital letters in the documents of the one-fifth of our organizations that mention it) tended to be linked to other values resonant within the social movement tradition. In the documents of our organizations (as, significantly, in theories on deliberative democracy and civil society), consensus is bridged to values such as pluralism, dialogue, inclusiveness, horizontality, participation, and transparency.

We also saw, however, that the mentioning of consensus, as well as other values, tended to vary. Regarding structural characteristics, we found more frequent references to consensus in organizations with smaller memberships and budgets, as well as no paid staff and more reliance on the assembly. In line with expectations, consensual methods are mentioned more often by smaller organizations, confirming the prediction that the smaller the size, the easier the communication. There is also some coherence between the search for consensus and horizontal organizational forms, as indicated by the explicit rejection of an executive and the high value given to the assembly. Similar paths also hold for the explanation of related values such as the critique of delegation.

However, the explanatory capacity of these organizational elements varied for the assorted democratic values – with some values (for example, inclusiveness, dialogue, equality) appearing widespread across different organizational forms. Instead, more explanatory power is seen in the reference to various themes that appear as relevant in the GJM. Social movement organizations can be defined, in fact, as arenas for the elaboration of values. Significantly, the democratic values that are mentioned are particularly associated with references to alter-globalist issues, while anti-capitalism and traditional left-wing themes have much less explanatory capacity. References to consensus are more frequent in networks, in line with the expectation that this form of organization requires more attention to the development of agreement among the various nodes of the network.

In particular, confirming some hypotheses that have emerged in the social science literature, consensual values (as well as other related values) are particularly widespread in the organizations that were founded during the newest wave of protest on global issues, that adopted the most recent organizational forms (such as networks), or that praised horizontal linkages, as well as among the more multi-issue organizations. More in general, attention to democracy seems to be higher in more recent organizations, that is, those emerging within the GJM and reflecting its concern with democracy from below. References to consensus as a democratic value seem to be especially frequent in organizations that were more recently founded, and in new types of networks. Moreover, transnational social movement organizations, with their need to develop communication across different cultures, pay special attention to inclusiveness and assign a very positive value to difference.

Using a more in-depth qualitative analysis of our documents, however, we observed that consensus has acquired different meanings when meeting different organizational cultures. In particular, we can single out a conception of consensus that developed mainly in network organizations, characterized by wide heterogeneity. Here, good communication is perceived as all the more relevant in order to improve dialogue among diverse actors. In a different, horizontal tradition, the method of consensus is coupled with an assembleary tradition. Here, assembleary collective decision making through consensus is a way to form the collective identity of the group.

Common to our organizations is an emphasis on the construction of open spaces, for high-quality dialogue between many and diverse actors. If social movements have traditionally been seen as aiming at building public spaces, there are some recent innovations in the GJM that deserve attention. In particular, traditional conceptions of participation are intertwined with conceptions of deliberation, which meet those values of openness, inclusiveness, plurality, dialogue, good communication, autonomy, and consensus that resonate with conceptions of public spaces. Although with different meanings, consensus is particularly relevant as a normative base for the creation of public spaces. In fact, organizational forms such as the social forum present themselves as spaces open to the encounter of diverse actors and value a dialogue oriented to the exchange of knowledge as well as reciprocal understanding.

Notes

1. We have calculated an additive index of formalization that includes the presence of a constitution, a document of fundamental values, a formally adopted program, formal membership, and membership cards. The index is normalized by the number of variables included and varies from 0 to 1.

2. ETA for association of the additive index is 0.351* for consensus; 0.365*** for difference/plurality/heterogeneity; 0.367 for internal inclusiveness; 0.563*** for equality; 0.321 for autonomy of chapters and member organizations; 0.193*** for individual and collective autonomy.
3. Rete Lilliput developed a sophisticated system of consensual online decision making oriented towards the implementation of 'Lilliputian thinking of "acting on what unites us and research on what divides us"'. In this conception, the valorization and involvement of each individual member is mentioned, together with consensual attitudes. In its presentation of 'Democrazia a bolle' (based on online deliberation, with each member expressing positions from consensus to conditional agreement, constructive disagreement, and dissent), Lilliput states, 'We tried to design a method which could be used directly by all Lilliputians in order to participate in the writing of these documents. In other words: * the documents can originate in any node of the net; * all mechanisms used in order to manage the documents are simple and transparent' (Il metodo a bolle).
4. The minutes of the seminar 'Quale futuro' mention the intervention by an activist who stressed that 'the TSF made the strongest effort in order to be inclusive: it practiced the method of consensus, it gave representativeness to all sides; it never decided through a majority vote'.

4
Social Movements and Multilevel Governance: The External Dimension of Democracy

Donatella della Porta

Social movements and multilevel governance: An introduction

Social movement organizations have traditionally intervened in 'normal' politics, exploiting political opportunities and struggling for changes in politics, policies, and (sometimes) the polity. Not only 'old' but also 'new' social movements have allied with political parties, even funding new ones or at least giving them new energies.

Especially since the 1990s, however, a depoliticization of social movements has been noted, and images of 'anti-political' or populistic movements, or at least single-issue ones, have emerged. Social movements in general, and the Global Justice Movement in particular, have been stigmatized in political debates and political sciences as anti-political, or at a minimum populistic actors. Activists tend to define themselves as anti-institutional, stressing an alternative vision of politics 'from below'. While the labour movement has traditionally had strong ties with the party systems and new social movements brought about new parties, the most recent movements have been defined as more interested in changes in everyday life than in political transformation, of either a revolutionary or a reformist nature.

Inspired by new social movements and the movement for democracy in Eastern Europe (Mitzal 2001), the return of the concept of civil society expresses a 'concern about personal autonomy, self organization, private space' (Kaldor 2003, pp. 2, 4). In fact, the civil society literature has stressed the autonomy of the social from the political, even if, in most cases, it goes with a reflection upon the specific (and politically implemented) rights that are necessary for the full development of a democratic civil society. A global civil society has been defined as stemming from the taming process of the social movements of the pre-1989 period as well as the decline of old civic associations (such as unions) and the transformation of the former into NGOs: professionalized, institutionalized and organized around particular causes (Kaldor 2003).

However, recent waves of protest on global issues have also been interpreted as reflecting a 'return to politics' at the national level, as well as the 'politicization' of a supranational level of governance, which had traditionally been conceived (if considered) as highly technical and legitimated 'by the output' (della Porta 2009). In fact, in various ways, International Governmental Organizations (IGOs) have provided opportunities for the development of transnational networks of protest and global frames, acting, as Sidney Tarrow (2005) suggested, as a coral reef for movements beyond borders (see also della Porta and Caiani 2009). While some (especially the International Financiary Institutions such as the World Bank, International Monetary Fund and World Trade Organization) have been seen as main targets for protest, others, however contested, have also offered some discursive and political opportunities for access by social movement organizations.

A most discussed and studied case for the latter is the EU. In their search for complementary sources of consent that could allow them to face the challenges of weak electoral accountability and the erosion of 'legitimacy by output', European institutions began to discuss various ways to involve citizens in decision making. Among others, the White Paper on European Governance (European Commission 2001) recognizes the principle of participation by means of open consultation with citizens and their associations as one of its fundamental pillars. This attention to the civil society corresponds to a more general development in the legitimation strategies of the EU, defined as a 'fragmented democracy split between government *by* and *of* the people at the national level, and governance *for* and *with* the people at the EU level' (Schmidt 2006, p. 9). Government *with* the people has been advocated in the consultation of civil society organizations and even in contracting-out services and material support for their activities (Ruzza 2004; Balme and Chabanet 2008).

As we will see in this chapter, however, in our research GJM organizations did not emerge as anti-political: to the contrary, they claimed a 'political nature' and, additionally, participated in multiple and complex relations with institutions of multilevel governance. Protest is only a part of their activity, considered as undoubtedly important but often ineffective unless accompanied by more direct interactions with

government and public administrations. Social movement organizations address representative democracy: they not only struggle against,
but often also collaborate with representative institutions. In trying
to influence institutional decisions, our GJMOs in fact use a variety
of strategies and reveal diverse attitudes towards institutional politics.
Moreover, these interactions emerge as increasingly multilevel as many
organizations refer to interactions with representative institutions at the
local, national, or international level. Although formally closed to actors
from below – not directly accountable to an electorate and rarely called
to account in the public sphere – many international institutions appear
not only to attract protest, but also to open channels of interactions with
civil society organizations.

In what follows, I first attempt to qualify these interactions according
to both the organizational ideology, as expressed in fundamental documents, and the information on organizational practices provided by the
interviewed organizational leaders and spokespersons. Having classified
the types of attitudes and behaviour of SMOs towards political institutions, I shall try to explain them by discussing some main hypotheses
developed in social movement studies, looking at the internal resources
of our organizations as well as at their environments.

Mapping attitudes towards institutions of multilevel governance

Social movement organizations were initially considered as societal
actors, with few contacts with politics. Since the development of a political process approach to protest, attention has focused on the interactions between social movements and the political sphere, as influencing
the forms, strategies, and outcomes of unconventional politics (see della
Porta and Diani 2006, chapter 8 for a review). Social movements have
not only protested for changes in policy, but also pushed for institutional changes towards larger grass-roots control. Under this pressure,
in many European countries administrative decentralization has taken
place since the 1970s, with the creation of new channels of access to
decision makers at the local level. New opportunities for 'conflictual co-
operation' developed within regulatory agencies set up to implement
goals also supported by movement activists (Giugni and Passy 1998,
p. 85). Collaboration took various forms, from consultation to incorporation in committees, to delegation of power and contracting out of
services (ibid., p. 86). Some regulatory bureaucracies established under
the pressure of movement mobilizations see activists as potential allies,

as movement activists are co-opted inside specific public bodies as staff members, or, in reverse, public agencies' administrative staff support movements.

The organizations we studied confirm, first, a strong concern with politics. This expressed political interest, at odds with interpretations of social movement organizations as only protesting in the street or even as 'anti-political' in nature, is often explicitly stated in fundamental organizational documents. The documents of our organizations frequently mention politics, although with varying meanings and emphasis; indeed, politics is perceived as part of the very self-definition of many of our organizations. The critical union Confederazione Unitaria di Base – CUB (2002) believes it indispensable 'to give a political breath to our initiatives', since 'the building of a basis union must start with the material conditions, but at the same time aim at the definition of values and general elements, in short an identity that opposes the social development founded upon neoliberalism'. ATTAC wants 'to contribute to innovate democratic political participation and favour the development of new organizational forms of the civil society, also through the activation of peaceful political instruments useful to conditioning, controlling and verifying from below the functioning of the local institutions' (ATTAC Italia 2003c). In the document synthesizing a discussion in its General Assembly, Rete Lilliput (2004) lists among the positive points its being 'a political subject', as well as, at the same time, the capacity to put pressure upon institutions, but also a 'disinterest in power... that makes us more free, independent and strong'.

However, politics is also perceived in somewhat different ways, as an expression of conflict (Giovani Comunisti, the youth organization of the Party for a Communist Refoundation), as conflict resolution (for Sinistra Giovanile, the youth association of the Democratici di Sinistra), or as a 'moment of growing' (Giovani Verdi, the youth association of the Italian Greens). A political commitment oriented to impact on the causes of war (singled out in the neoliberal economic policies and human rights violations by the powerful states) is promoted by the voluntary association 'Un ponte per...', although it perceives 'politics' mainly as the promotion of solidarity through sensitizing the public.

Within this political vision, we found many social movement organizations to be open to interactions with institutions of multilevel governance. As with politics, however, attitudes towards institutions vary. In the document analysis we coded references to different attitudes towards institutions ranging from open refusal to co-operation, distinguishing attitudes towards local, national, and international governmental

Table 4.1   Relationships with institutions and economic actors according to fundamental documents (% of yes)

No. of cases = 244

	Representative institutions	Local institutions	National institutions	IGOs	Economic actors
Collaboration	26.6	22.5	24.6	18.9	14.3
Democratic control	32.4	21.3	32.0	27.9	22.5
Refusal	11.5	4.5	9.0	7.4	14.8

organizations as well as economic actors. Although about half of our groups (concentrated in particular in some countries) did not mention relationships with institutions, our data indicate that, when they did, they were quite open to interaction with them: they were not simply emphasizing a negative message, but they also often accepted collaboration on specific problems. As we can see in Table 4.1, in relation to representative institutions in general, statements of open refusal of collaboration are rare (11.5%), while an attitude of either collaboration or democratic control is more frequent (about one-third each).

There are some differences in the attitudes towards the various territorial levels of governance. Collaboration with IGOs and economic actors seems less frequent than with national institutions, but still relevant. Additionally, the refusal of collaboration is mentioned more often for institutions at the national level than at the local or supranational ones. Statements about relations of collaboration are more frequent at the national than at the supranational level (where relations of control prevail). Differences in attitudes towards institutions at different territorial levels are limited, however, indicating that they tend to spread from one institution to the next. Although the refusal of interactions increases going from the local to the transnational and from the state to the market, the differences are smaller than one might have expected. In particular, the transnational level is recognized as an important institutional level for collaboration by about one-fifth of our groups (that is, two-fifths of those who mention relationships with institutions in their documents). Nevertheless, our organizations tend to be critical of institutions, perceiving their own role as the active engagement in citizens' control of institutional politics, through the implementation of channels of discursive accountability.

Statements in fundamental documents reflect the organizational ideology: as such, they provide clear-cut images of the differences within the GJM concerning attitudes towards institutions. However, as mentioned (see Chapter 1), we had to take into account the bias resulting from a certain degree of missing information, especially for small and grass-roots organizations. Additionally, documents tell us about the way in which groups argue, not directly about how they act. To extend the amount of information to more groups and add the level of (declared) practices, we can triangulate the statements in the documents with attitudes expressed by the interviewed representatives of GJMOs.

The results of our interviews on declared practices are highly compatible with those on organizational ideology (see Table 4.2). First of all, answers to the question 'how does your group relate to public institutions at different territorial levels?' confirm the openness of our organizations towards collaboration with institutions. Refusal of any collaboration is still very rare: from a very low 8.4 per cent for local institutions, to 11.8 per cent for the national and 13.5 per cent for the international level. The refusal rate is highest for IGOs, although still only a couple of percentage points higher than for national institutions and, in general terms, still very low. The groups that declare a lack of collaboration, either because of indifference towards relations with institutions or rejection by institutions, is larger but still limited to between one-fifth at the local and national levels and one-third at the supranational one. The rest of the sampled organizations tend to collaborate, especially with local (as many as 70 per cent) and national (67 per cent) institutions, but also with IGOs (more than half of our sample). Many groups declare collaborations with various territorial levels at the same time, showing an adaptation to multilevel governance. Here as well, however, our interviewees often qualify their collaboration with institutions as critical or selective, with

Table 4.2 Relationship with institutions according to interviews (%)

	Local institutions	National institutions	International institutions
Refusal of collaboration	8.4	11.8	13.5
Indifference/no contacts/ denial of collaboration by authorities	22.8	21.2	32.5
Critical/selective collaboration	29.7	34.5	24.5
Collaboration	39.1	32.5	29.5
Total	202 (100%)	203 (100%)	200 (100%)

less critical attitudes towards local governments and growing criticism towards the national and supranational levels.

Focusing on the Italian groups, a qualitative analysis of the organizational documents allows identification of the various specific ways in which GJMOs interact with institutions. Collaborations with local governments include local governments hosting meetings and signing petitions launched by social movement organizations (for example, for the abolition of the foreign debt of poor countries, see Sdebitarsi) or adhering to other social movement initiatives (such as the Internet portal Unimondo.org – Internet per i diritti umani e lo sviluppo sostenibile, oriented to spreading information on peace, civil rights, and sustainable development). The creation of dense networks of groups and local governments to elaborate political proposals, change politics, and stimulate politics is a constitutive element of the Tavola della Pace (2008), which aims at 'strengthening the sense of responsibility and the effectiveness of civil society, communities and local institutions'. Sympathetic local governments are targeted by Rete Lilliput in the campaign 'Tesorerie Disarmate', focused on discouraging banks from investing in arms by introducing 'good practices' in public administration. Specific campaigns also involve the local city councils in the approval of statements against international treaties (such as the GATTs), which are accused of disempowering local administrations and local democracy.

Collaboration with local governments is also promoted by groups offering various types of services to the public administration (from environmental education to social assistance for groups in need). Local governments might sponsor specific projects, as in the case of Un Ponte per... (2008), whose Web site declares its reliance upon the voluntary activity of its members and on local government contributions for specific projects. Even focusing just on the Italian organizations, examples abound. The constitution of Peacelink (1991), a voluntary association for the development of online communication on peace and human rights, promotes forms of collaboration with schools and public institutions in order to develop its cultural activities. Legambiente develops proposals on sustainable tourism or the public management of water, stressing the importance of the participation of citizens, the 'community', and local authorities. Arcigay collaborates with local institutions in projects and in co-ordinating tables oriented towards popular education against discrimination, as well as to 'find organizational headquarters and economic resources to activate help-desks, formation activity or new social instruments of interventions as, e.g., housing for young gays sent away by their family or lonely old ones' (Arcigay

2004). In a similar vein, the Italian Consortium of Solidarity stresses a dialogue with institutions based on specific projects (for example, in solidarity with intervention in former Yugoslavia), addressing the need for social practices of development from below through support to the local civil society. The Campagna Banche Armate asks for normative changes to allow for more transparency and 'active citizens control' on banks' financing of arms trade.

Especially notable is that social movement organizations (and campaigns) address different levels of governments to call for specific laws. The very formula of the 'campaign' is presented as 'actions of pressure and sensitization that aim at obtaining very concrete objectives, and last until that objective is reached' (Rete Lilliput 2003). Typically, a proposal for a law instituting a Tobin Tax had a strong mobilization and identification potential for ATTAC, which in fact addresses a broad set of specific requests (especially on fiscal policy) to both national and EU parliaments. Similarly, the Campaign for the abolition of the foreign debt of poor countries promoted laws in that direction – for example, in Italy, the law 209/2000 not only imposes debts remittance, but also encourages the Italian government to promote it at the international level. In the documents of the World March of Women, organized by 3000 organizations from 140 countries, a list of claims on specific policies ranges from the drastic reduction of military expenses to a social salary for women, also denouncing the absence of women in parliaments, governments, and high positions in the judiciary and central banks. The critical union CUB (2002) develops specific proposals against 'the privatization of public services, cuts to social expenditures, the dismantling of the public welfare and health systems...'. As the documents by the campaign Sdebitarsi indicate, social movement organizations also monitor the effects of such laws, often lamenting their lack of implementation.

Given the movements' noted concern with democracy, claims are also oriented to procedural issues, such as the 'confrontation with institutions in order to activate...participatory practices, inclusive and plural' (Venezia Social Forum 2001). The defence of freedom of information is stated in the constitution of the Internet cultural association Isole nella Rete, oriented to aid the self-organization of grass-roots activist groups. The documents of the 'critical unions' often contain references to democracy in the workplace, sometimes calling for specific legislation for union democracy and union rights as well as a 'universal public service' (COBAS). The Botteghe del Mondo raises specific claims for legal norms in support of alternative forms of trade, together with specific criticisms of cuts in local services. Rete Lilliput claims in its found-ing document (2008b) to 'oppose economic choices that jeopardize democracy', stressing that 'the forms of democracy and politics as we traditionally knew them, strictly tied to the national state, are largely inadequate'. More in general, participation in the movement against neoliberal globalization is defined as part of the unions' commitment to construct democracy together with social rights (FIOM).

The qualitative analysis of the organizational documents also points at some main elements of criticism and, sometimes, proposals for democratization of public institutions. First of all, our organizations are concerned with the accountability of IGOs. The international eco-nomic organizations (WTO, World Bank and FMI) are stigmatized as 'antidemocratic', and 'the search of a democratic alternative to neolib-eral globalization' stated as a main aim (for example, Torino Social Forum 2008). The critique of an involution of democratic politics is present even in the Catholic Pax Christi (2001), which denounces 'the serious involution of democracy that, from a participatory project of organization of social life according to the parameters of equality, free-dom, justice, international solidarity and peace, is transforming itself more and more in a mechanism of competitive management of power, dominated by a utilitaristic logic, and subject to the dominion of the market'.

The orientation toward strengthening the institutions of global gov-ernance, but at the same time democratizing them, is in fact especially visible in the attitudes towards the UN or the EU. In particular, the international campaign 'Reclaim our UN' (2005b) promotes a reform of that institution, based upon values of multilateralism, international co-operation, strengthening of international law, creation of democratic international institutions, subordination of the IFIs to the UN, extended competences for the International Court of Justice, establishment of an international judiciary police, development of world citizenship with 'responsible participation of every citizen within a grass-roots globaliza-tion', and increased access for NGOs to decision-making institutions. If this trust in the 'reformability' of the UN is not shared by all our groups, there is a widespread demand for transnational governance of economic processes and a return to politics against the dominance of the market.

Similarly, institutions of macro-regional governance – among them the EU – are also considered as necessary in order to reduce the damage of economic globalization. The EU is accused of protecting the interests of corporations, as the large presence of lobbyists for business groups in

Brussels would attest. In order to change their policies, Via Campesina proposes a multilevel intervention, with pressure upon national governments but also 'better' IGOs, such as the UN and some of its related organizations. The Seattle to Brussels Network (2008), after denouncing the undemocratic nature of EU decision making on trade ('EU trade policy-making... is opaque, non transparent and deeply undemocratic'), asks the EU to 'promote enhanced transparency and democratic participation and accountability in EU trade policy making', including consultations with parliaments and civil society groups (cf. also Zola and Marchetti 2006). Additionally, groups criticize the 'democratic deficit', linked to the lack of parliamentary control on the executive. Among others, ATTAC criticizes that the European Council, 'appointed by the governments of the Member States... can issue directives that constrain Member States. In charge of the "policy of competition", it is controlled in this field neither by the national parliaments nor by the European parliament, which creates a democratic deficit to the advantage of the powerful' (ATTAC Vaud 2004). The Italian National Council of ATTAC Italia defines as one of its five main aims the development of a 'democratic constitutive European process that starts from the peoples', rejecting the 'neoliberal process of a Europe of the powerful and the governments' (ATTAC Italia 2003a).

At the same time, calls for the defence of a European social model as an alternative to the American one are voiced, especially by trade unions (for example, on the Italian FIOM and CGIL, see Reiter 2006, p. 249). Typically, ATTAC promotes a social Europe, a Europe of civic and social rights for all residents, a Europe of the citizens, a Europe that promotes peace – as opposed to a Europe of the market, of trade, of the elites, of the governments, undemocratic, subject to the US. The instrument suggested is the development of a European public space. Criticizing the failure of the Convention for the Constitutional Treaty to involve (at least part of) the civil society, the Italian ATTAC declares that 'In the last two years a new public sphere was born in Europe; it has been promoted not by the consensus-catching sent by the commission to look for some dialogue with the civil society, but the oppositional movements. ... It would be a mistake however if, given the myopia of the European governments and to their frequent factual connivance with the imperial policies, one would look back, feeding the illusion that the national states are the terrain on which the movement can play its democratic instances' (ATTAC Italia 2002).[1]

Similarly, the Italian Consortium of Solidarity calls for the democratization and empowerment of a social and democratic EU, also through an open and participatory constitutional process. The International Consortium for Solidarity Italia (2004), calls for a 'Europe from below', emphasizing the 'centrality of democracy, rights and social cohesion within the process of European unification'. Rete Lilliput (2008c) lists the characteristics of 'the Europe we want', while stating that the existing one 'is not the Europe we want'.

The most moderate organizations are not the only groups to express interest in a European level;[2] even the more critical organizations call for 'another Europe'. Among them, EuroMayDay (2004) proclaims, 'We are eurogeneration insurgents: our idea of Europe is a radical, libertarian, transnationalist, antidystopian, open democratic space able to counter global bushism and oppressive, exploitative, powermad, planetwrecking, warmongering neoliberalism in Europe and elsewhere. Networkers and Flextimers of Europe unite! There's a world of real freedom to fight for'.

A deficit of accountability is also stressed with reference to national (and even local) government. National democracy is seen as undermined, not only by the growing influence of (non-democratic) IGOs on national decision making, but also by a lack of transparency and accountability to the public. For instance, Friends of the Earth stigmatizes the links between political parties and corporations, accusing the latter of funding and therefore controlling the former. Also with reference to local and national political arenas, the leading request is for the development of a 'real', read participatory, democracy.

Openness to interaction with institutions, but also dissatisfaction with previous experiences, emerge from an open question on the organizations' attitudes towards existing experiments with participatory public decision making. Based on the principle of participation of 'normal citizens' in public arenas for debate, these experiments have evolved in the last two decades, especially at the local level, in the forms of Citizens' Juries, Planungszellen, Consensus Conferences, Conferences de citoyens, and the like. Actors associated with social movements have intervened in the development of some of these processes, sometimes as promoters, sometimes as critical participants or external opponents. In particular, the participatory budget has been credited with creating a positive context for associational life, fostering more activism, better interconnectedness, and a city-wide orientation of associations (Baiocchi 2001; della Porta 2008b).

Here as well, we observed an interest among a large (although not majoritarian) part of our sample, but also some scepticism and criticism. While 42.3 per cent of the groups had not discussed this issue or had no clear stance on it, over one-third (38.5 per cent) declared that these participative experiments improve the quality of political decisions; the remaining about one-fifth (19.2 per cent) was sceptical. When asked to qualify their judgement on experiments of public decision making, almost one-fifth of the groups spoke of both advantages and risks, about half underlined the positive aspects, and almost one-third pointed at the negative side of these experiments, which emerges on both the input and the output sides of the decision-making process. Present in the responses is an interest in institutional politics, albeit coupled with strong mistrust in existing institutions.

First of all, those who support these experiments consider them as resonating with their own values: 'participation is one of the main elements of our strategy' (Rete Lilliput).[3] Participatory experiments are presented as 'one of our means of action: we seek more consultations of civil society. We promote a renewal of decision-making processes' (Alliance Sud); a way 'to stimulate civic responsibility' (Parti socialiste suisse – section genevoise); 'one of the principles we push for at a political level, we also monitor the quality of implementation of participation in practice' (European Network on Debt and Development – EURODAD). Many groups stress in fact their belief in participatory governance and in 'greater involvement of citizens and their groups in democracy, beyond voting' (Civicus).

Especially the more politically-oriented organizations appreciate the legitimating potential of this type of experiment, since 'participation is a fundamental element of democracy' (Italian union FIOM-CGIL); 'participatory instruments are fundamental even if they are often used to gain consensus' (Italian environmentalist association Legambiente) and 'allow for the full expression of citizenship' (Venezia Social Forum). In this sense, participatory experiments are considered even more important given the crisis of representative institutions. The experiments of institutional participation are welcomed as they, at the same time, 'signal a crisis of conventional politics and represent a good direction where to look in order to overcome this crisis' (Euromovement). The 'permanent engagement of citizens is fundamental' since 'the gap between social dynamics and their institutional representation widens when systemic complexity grows' (Italian union CGIL). Involving the people improves institutional accountability, since participatory democracy 'makes citizens more close to politics introducing an element of transparency in the decision-making (it becomes clear why a specific decision is taken)' (youth association of the Italian Green Party).

NGOs and voluntary associations involved 'in the field' stress more the positive effects of participatory decisions on the output side. Participation helps to make decisions fairer (Overseas NGOs for Development); it provides better information for decision makers (Comité Catholique contre la Faim et pour le Développement);[4] and it ensures the input of the grass-roots (Jubilee Debt Campaign), thus improving the quality of decisions (Organización de Cooperación y Solidaridad Internacional), as 'international cooperation should also actively involve the population on which it focuses' (Italian Consortium of Solidarity). Participatory decision making permits a 'better acknowledgement of the field reality, the proximity allows for a better understanding of the complex reality and a bridging of traditional political gaps' (Réalise), while its transparency 'allows catching ideas and problems of citizens' (Italian Greens), since 'If decisions are public and transparent their quality improves' (Tavola della Pace). Transparency is often related to citizens' control as fundamental for the functioning of democracy (for example, the French Agir ici and the British Catholic Agency for Overseas Development).

Also mentioned is the cognitive enrichment that results from participation from below. The representative of the Campagna Banche Armate, a network campaigning against the investment in arms, states that participatory experiments 'help creating a civil society that can pressure politicians towards the public good and produce a better political elite'. Local knowledge is stressed here, as 'decisions improve through proposals and ideas coming from concrete experiences of movements and the civil society' (Sdebitarsi). A few interviewees also point at the value of the discussion per se, as 'the contrast of ideas always ends up with a change, even small, of the initial positions' (Red con Voz); participatory processes facilitate the finding of solidaristic solutions (Ver.di, Vereinte Dienstleistungsgewerkschaft). Especially, but not only, for religious groups, participatory experiments imply the recognition of the dignity of each person. Thus, the representative of the Spanish Hermanidad Obrera de Acción Católica (HOAC) supports participatory public decision making 'because we assign a fundamental value to personal dignity, which has to be considered as the beginning and the end of all social, political and labour action'. A positive effect on individuals results from 'generating more responsibility among people who are involved and more sharing of the decisions' (Associazione Botteghe del Mondo).

Although supported in principle, experiments with participatory democracy are also criticized for their poor implementation (for example, Ligue Communiste Révolutionnaire). Several respondents qualify their attitudes towards participatory experiments by distinguishing among different institutional models. In fact, 'not all public decisional processes promoted by institutions produced a real improvement of the quality of political decisions' (Peacelink), and 'in some cases there is the possibility of institutional changes, in others not' (Ecologistas en Accion). Thus, experiments of participation are divided into 'true' and 'fake' ones. The representative of Attac Italia declares, 'We support these processes if they are real and not artificial ones'. 'Real' experiments are mainly 'bottom up' ones. The representative of the weekly Carta, one of the founders of the Rete Nuovo Municipio that promotes participatory experiments, states that they 'prefer when these initiatives are promoted directly by the citizens'. Similarly, the representative of the Abruzzo Social Forum recalled that 'We tried to engage in them but they become places for experts as a work of real promotion is missing. When they don't come from below, it is difficult that they are effective'.

In fact, the limits of these experiments in terms of 'real participation' are often mentioned. Critical organizations stress the failures in terms of citizens' involvement: 'We are very sceptical on participatory budget: in Porto Alegre only 1.5% of the population were involved (with little decisional power)' (Confederazione dei COBAS, Italian rank-and-file union; see also Koordinierungsstelle gewerkschaftliche Arbeitslosengruppen; London Rising Tide; Xarxa de Mobilitacio Global; Friends of the Earth).[5] Additionally, 'real' experiments are considered to be those in which decisions made in the participatory arenas count, that is, they are implemented (Espacio Alternativo). As with the representative of the British organization Global Justice Movement, many fear that 'the most conventional processes "hack at the branches" and don't "get at the roots" of challenging the laws governing property rights, corporate hegemony and the debt based interest bearing monetary system'. Even the Rete Noglobal, which co-ordinates groups in the area of the squatted youth centres, declares availability to participate but only 'when it is not a rhetorical artifact and when citizens can make decisions on significant resource'. The most critical opinions are linked to a perceived lack of concrete effects, making the participation 'often placebo politics' (ATTAC Germany) or a 'smokescreen' (Syndicat des Services Publics – Section genevoise), 'a simulacrum of democracy: the decisions which are then made do not take into account the opinions expressed by these bodies' (Confédération Paysanne). The empowerment of these bodies is thus linked to mobilization in the street (Colectivo de Solidaridad con la Rebelión Zapatista de Barcelona). What is more, a fear of co-optation accompanies involvement in these processes – stigmatized as 'PR for governments at the cost of the activists' (Bundeskoordination

Internationalismus'), or a trap of co-optation (World Economy, Ecology and Development), risking 'too strong a bond with established structures' (Weltfriedensdienst).

In conclusion, notwithstanding their critical positions, the GJMOs frequently *interact with the institutions of representative democracy*. Our organizations are in fact quite open towards public institutions – they do not emphasize a negative message, but often offer specific advice and co-operate on specific problems. At the same time, however, they tend to be critical of those institutions and to perceive their own role as actively engaging in citizens' control of institutional politics and implementing channels of discursive accountability.

Explaining attitudes towards institutions

Within the mentioned general openness to interactions with institutions, but also mistrust, both datasets indicated a range of attitudes towards collaboration with institutions within the same movement. If only a small percentage of organizations refuse interactions with institutions, there are however divided opinions about such collaboration, and about the need for control from below. Even experiments of participative democracy (including those sponsored by movement organizations) are supported by some of our groups, but looked at with scepticism by others. How do we explain these differences? Taking into account previous research, in what follows I look first at contextual variables, then focus on the structural and cultural internal characteristics that the literature on Social Movement Organizations (SMOs) has considered as relevant for strategic choices of this type.

Environmental characteristics

Organizations are clearly influenced by their environment. As Zald and McCarthy observed (1987, p. 45): 'Social movements are not created outside of the traditions and institutional bases of the larger society in which they are nested. Instead, the cadre and networks of adherents and activists grow out of, build upon, and use the repertoires of action, the institutional forms and physical facilities of the larger society.' Organizational structures can be imposed, authorized, induced, acquired, imprinted, incorporated or bypassed by their environment (Scott 1991, p. 170). Dependence on state agencies would increase pressure for isomorphism insofar as 'the greater the extent to which the organizations in a field transact with agencies of the state, the greater the extent of isomorphism in the field as a whole' (DiMaggio and Powell 1991b, p. 76).

The conditions governing access to public and private funding, tax exemption, or advantageous postage rates influence the organizational structure of groups who wish to benefit from these possibilities.[6] In fact, from within a neo-institutional approach, Debra C. Minkoff (2001, p. 287) has suggested that 'resources and institutional dependencies fundamentally shape movement development, as do competitive pressures that determine processes of organizational founding, survival and change...although compliance with such incentives is voluntary, a "tangle of incentives" provides advantages to certain organizational forms over others'.

A widespread hypothesis is that the more inclusive the political system, the more co-operative the social movement organizations. We cannot, however, generalize the argument that an open institutional system, offering resources to citizens' organizations, necessarily results in formal organizations positively integrated within the system. First of all, 'often, formal, hierarchical structures have been established to better fight a hostile state apparatus. ...Conversely, an open, decentralized political system may also facilitate similar trends towards decentralization and informality among movement organizations' (della Porta and Diani 2006, p. 153; see also Rucht 1996). Rather than assuming a rigid relationship between the form that activists give to their organizations and the characteristics of the institutional system in which they operate, it has been recognized that multiple organizational forms may be accommodated within the same system. This underlines the margins of choice available to social movement actors when trying to adapt creatively to their environment, rather than being determined by it – even if these margins are constrained by historically specific repertoires of organizational formats (Clemens 1996).

Our data do show country differences, but not always in the expected directions. Organizations mentioning in their fundamental documents refusal of relationships with institutions are more common in the Swiss case (although attitudes of collaboration and democratic control are also mentioned more often than in the other countries), and in the French and British samples (Table 4.3). Collaborative attitudes are more often present at the transnational level and in Switzerland, where control of institutions is also very often mentioned. Democratic control is less frequently mentioned in Spain and Italy. In all countries but Spain, democratic control tends to be the most widespread attitude towards international institutions, and collaboration towards local authorities (data not shown but available on request).

Table 4.3   Organizations' country and relationships with institutions according to fundamental documents

(No. of cases = 244)

Country	Relation with institutions and economic actors (%)		
	Any collaboration	*Any refusal*	*Any democratic control*
UK	44.7	18.4	52.6
France	34.4	18.8	43.8
Germany	25.8	16.1	25.8
Italy	22.0	4.9	16.1
Spain	21.6	5.4	10.8
Switzerland	48.6	20.0	65.7
Transnational	56.7	16.7	83.3
Cramer's V	0.292***	n.s.	0.517***

Note: Level of significance: *** significant at 0.001.

Cross-country differences also exist in the interviews regarding relations with institutions (see Table 4.4). Relationships of collaboration are frequent with international governmental organizations, but less so among Spanish and Swiss groups, mostly active at the local level. Refusal to collaborate grows to almost one-quarter for the Spanish and British samples. Unconditioned collaboration concerns as many as 39 per cent of the Swiss and 52 per cent of the transnational organizations, while critical/selective collaboration is particularly widespread among French, German, British and transnational groups. As for the relationship with national institutions, we noted a lower rate for the Spanish sample; selective collaboration more often mentioned by French, German,

Table 4.4   Attitudes of collaboration (unconditioned and selective) towards institutions at different levels per country according to interviews

(No. of cases = 210)

Collaboration with institutions	Country (% of Yes)							Total
	F	*G*	*I*	*SP*	*SW*	*UK*	*TN*	
International level	60.9	60.0	52.8	31.3	39.3	55.2	85.2	54.0
National level	83.3	64.0	75.0	35.3	60.7	75.9	81.5	67.0
Local level	87.0	60.0	89.2	54.5	75.0	51.7	63.0	68.8
Total (N)	23–4	25	36–7	32–4	28	29	27	200–3

Notes: Cramer's V is: 0.320*** (international); 0.341*** (national); 0.311*** (local).

and British interviewees; unconditioned collaboration with institutions most frequently used among Swiss and transnational groups. As for local institutions, refusal of collaboration is more frequently mentioned by German, Spanish, and British groups; selective collaboration is widespread among French, German, and Italian groups; while unconditional collaboration regards especially Switzerland and, again, Italy (where the lack of contacts with local authorities is almost absent).

Although, given our sampling strategy, we cannot measure our groups' representativeness, we can state that in all our countries we find the presence of varying attitudes towards authorities driving the search for explanations based on the internal characteristics of our groups.

Movement organizational structures

In social movement organizations resources vary in terms of *scale and type* (Rucht 1989, p. 73). Different SMOs have different 'organizational capacity', defined as 'the organization's financial and human resources as well as the administrative knowledge and capabilities to implement procedures and programs relevant to movement-related goals' (Zald et al. 2005, p. 265). The organizational conceptions of democracy have often been related to organizational resources. Availability of resources has been said to allow for the development of formalized models and, conversely, bureaucratization and centralization are expected to facilitate fundraising (Knoke 1989, p. 136). On the other hand, informal SMOs, based upon face-to-face interaction of people who know each other personally, are said to facilitate participatory democracy through reasoned debates followed by collective choices (Rosenthal and Schwartz 1989, pp. 45 ff.). In general, formalization and availability of resources have been considered to increase the likelihood that SMOs will collaborate with public institutions. Already, research on industrial relations have indicated a larger degree of co-optation of economic interest groups in public arenas at the national level, where these groups are richer in resources, better structured and more professionalized. Relations with labour movement organizations have tended to spill over towards new movements that, especially in neocorporatist countries, were incorporated into public decision-making arenas. This incorporation went hand in hand with trends towards organizational structuration, professionalization, and growing amounts of resources (Kriesi 1996). Our research confirms that, regarding interactions with institutions, some characteristics of the organizational structure have high explanatory power.

Table 4.5   Relationships with institutions and organizational structure according to fundamental documents

(No. of cases = 244; Cramer's V, or ETA for comparing means when explicitly noted)

Organizational structure	Relations with institutions and economic actors		
	Any collaboration	Any democratic control	Any refusal
Structural participation	0.162**	n.s.	−0.112°
Structural accountability	0.187***	n.s.	−0.224***
Formalization-mean	0.175*(ETA)	0.161* (ETA)	n.s. (ETA)
Territorial level (mean)	0.125* (ETA)	0.170** (ETA)	n.s. (ETA)
N. of individual members	0.285***	0.300**	n.s.

Notes: Level of significance: *** significant at 0.001 (2-tailed); ** significant at 0.01 (2-tailed); * significant at 0.05 (2-tailed); ° significant at 0.1; n.s. = non significant.

According to our analysis, the attitudes towards institutions emerging from fundamental documents are strongly (and significantly) correlated with particular organizational characteristics. In Table 4.5 we present the correlation coefficients between some indicators of organizational structure and (combined) mentions of collaboration, control, or refusal of interaction with any of the mentioned institutions. Indicators of organizational structuration, such as the presence of elements of structural participation and of structural accountability,[7] reduce the likelihood that refusal of relations with institutions is mentioned and increases the probability that collaboration with institutions at all levels is mentioned. At the same time and in a similar direction, the more formalized the groups and the more numerous their territorial levels of interaction, the more they tend towards relationships of collaboration and democratic control. Similarly, the availability of organizational resources in terms of large individual membership increases the likelihood that a relationship of collaborative control with institutions is mentioned.[8]

The data from interviews show similar relationships between characteristics of organizational structure and attitudes towards institutions, but with some specification for the different levels and forms of collaboration (see Table 4.6). First of all, indicators of organizational resources such as numbers of individual and collective members, as well

Table 4.6 Relations with institutions and organizational resources according to interviews

(No. of cases = 210; Kendall's Tau B)

	Relationship with IGOs	Relationship with national institutions	Relationship with local institutions
Number of individual members	0.305**	0.381**	0.225*
Number of collective members	0.237*	0.275*	n.s.
Budget	0.323**		0.230**
Presence of paid staff (dummy)	0.412**	0.369**	0.178*
Number of volunteers	0.249**	0.187**	0.243**
Organizational form	0.314***	0.317***	0.320***

Notes: Level of significance: *** significant at 0.001 (2-tailed); ** significant at 0.01 (2-tailed); * significant at 0.05 (2-tailed); ° significant at 0.1; n.s. = non significant.

as number of volunteers and size of budget, have strong and significant correlation coefficients with relationship with IGOs (especially), national and local institutions (less so). A similar, and similarly strong, correlation emerges between an indicator of professionalization such as the presence of paid staff (dummy) and the mentioned indicators of relationship with institutions. Here as well, correlation coefficients are particularly high when dealing with relationship with IGOs, but low(er) in dealing with relations with local governments, where party allies are more likely to be in power. Crossing relations with institutions and organizational forms, at all three levels of governance, refusal emerged more often among grass-roots SMOs; collaboration with restrictions among unions and modern networks; collaboration among NGOs and formal SMOs.

Relationships with institutions are also influenced by some characteristics of the organizational internal decision making. Our typology of internal democracy emerged as relevant in explaining relationships with institutions in both datasets. Focusing on the organizational ideology as expressed in fundamental documents, if we cross models of internal decision making with relationships with institutions, organizations belonging to the associational and deliberative representative models tend to more frequently mention collaboration (Cramer's V = 0.274***) and democratic control (Cramer's V = 0.224**), while refusal is more often mentioned by groups located in either the deliberative representative, deliberative participative, or assembleary models. Similar pictures emerged when looking separately at the attitudes towards local, national, and international institutions.

In the same direction, based on our interviews, collaboration with international institutions is more likely to occur for less participatory organizations (that is, when the main decision-making body is not the assembly); this is even more the case for collaboration with international and then national institutions. A consensual decision-making model in the main body also tends to discourage collaboration at these two levels (although not at the local level). This is true, more in general, for democratic model, which influences interactions at all three levels (but more so for the two highest levels: 0.345^{**}; 0.371^{**} and 0.162^{*} for IGOs, national, and local levels, respectively). The presence of an executive committee has the same type of facilitating effect on collaboration.

We may conclude that there is a strict relationship between choices made concerning internal organizational structure or, at least, structural characteristics of SMOs and their attitudes and behaviours towards institutions. This is all the more the case at the international level, where co-operation is much more likely the more structured, professionalized and resourceful an organization is. In particular, the more organizations adopt participatory and deliberative decision making, the more the choice of co-operating with institutions is discouraged.

Movement themes

If some approaches have linked choices of interactions with institutions to organizational resources, others have looked at cultural variables, suggesting that, within social movement organizations, judgements on organizational strategies are made not so much based on their efficiency or efficacy, but more on their symbolic appropriateness (for example, Melucci 1985; Klandermans 1989a and 1989b). In principle, choices about relations with institutions are not only strategically oriented, but carry with them important identity concerns. Attitude towards the state has traditionally divided the labour movement into revolutionary and reformist sides. More recently, some movements have been said to tend more towards instrumental orientation towards authorities (for example, the environmental movement), others instead to focus upon identity building (for example, the women's movement).

In our database on organizational documents, we coded democratic values on internal decision making as well as more in general. First, we crossed attitudes towards institutions as expressed in fundamental documents with organizational values on democracy. The expectation

Table 4.7 Relationships with institutions and (selected) organizational values according to fundamental documents

(No. of cases = 244; Cramer's V)

Organizational values	Relation with institutions and economic actors		
	Any collaboration	Any refusal	Any democratic control
Participatory democracy	n.s.	0.119°	n.s.
Inclusiveness	n.s.	0.201**	0.155*
Crit. Del. and non hier.	−0.229***	0.253***	n.s.
Autonomous org. or loc.	n.s.	0.148*	0.140*
Ind. or coll. autonomy	n.s.	0.177**	0.112°*
Participation (external)	0.161*	n.s.	0.130*
Equality	0.116°	0.136*	0.206
Inclusiveness (external)	0.147*	0.114°	0.319***
Dialogue/Communication	0.139*	n.s.	0.397***

Note: Level of significance: *** significant at 0.001; ** significant at 0.01; * significant at 0.05; ° significant at 0.1; n.s. = non significant.

here is that relationships with institutions can be facilitated by the presence of general democratic values that are more proximate to, or at least compatible with, those expressed by those institutions. Our data show in fact that attitudes towards institutions are influenced by general attitudes towards democracy. Looking at the association between attitudes towards institutions and the internal and general democratic values mentioned in organizational documents (Table 4.7), we can observe that references to participation correlate positively only with refusal of relationships with institutions, and references to inclusiveness with expressions of both refusal and democratic control. Critical references to delegation increase references to refusal and reduce those to collaboration. In addition, mentions of individual and collective autonomy and of autonomy of local chapters or member organizations seem to increase the tendency towards democratic control and refusal of collaboration. References to deliberative values increase for more collaborative and more control-oriented organizations. It seems, therefore, that explicit references to democratic values that are different from (if not opposed to) those implemented in representative institutions are associated with a lower tendency to collaborate and, especially, lead to stressing the role of civil society in making institutions accountable. Deliberative values are associated with a communicative attitude to existing institutions, but 'deliberative' organizations seem to stress especially their role as controllers. Looking at attitudes towards institutions at the various territorial levels, the same correlations emerge, although weaker for the local level (data not shown, but available on request).

Values seem linked to the organizational areas. Crossing movement area with relations with institutions, collaborative attitudes emerge as more widespread in the Old Left, new social movements, and solidarity/peace groups, while the New Left/anarchists but also the new global organizations are less oriented towards collaborative attitudes (Cramer's $V = 0.358^{***}$). In parallel, refusal of collaboration is more present in the last two areas (Cramer's $V = 0.278^{**}$), with democratic control equally spread across groups. Similar relations emerge from the interviews, with NSM and solidarity groups more oriented towards collaboration with both IGOs (Cramer's $V = 0.222^{**}$) and national institutions (Cramer's $V = 0.208^{*}$). While the New Left and anarchists more often express refusal, groups in the new global area more often present themselves as critical collaborators. These differences are less relevant (and not statistically significant) at the local level.

Although with statistical significance above 0.05, parties and NGOs/formal SMOs express a higher propensity towards collaboration (Cramer's $V = 0.217$, Sig. 0.094), while informal SMOs and modern networks (developed as organizational forms within the GJM) are more critical (Cramer's V with refusal of collaboration 0.211, Sig. 0.094). Attitudes of democratic control are more evenly spread across organizational forms.

Our data on organizational documents indicate that collaboration tends to increase with the age of the organization, with a Cramer's V coefficient of 0.230^{***} for the mentioning of collaboration (non-significant for refusal and democratic control). The correlations emerge as even stronger in the interviews' database, with coefficients of, respectively, -0.242^{**}, -0.266^{**}, and -0.181^{*} for co-operation with international, national, and local institutions. These data seem to indicate a sort of moderation with aging, or at least a more critical attitude by younger organizations.

Movements and institutions: Concluding remarks

The image of anti-political social movement organizations, jealous of their autonomy, is not supported by our research. First of all, our groups emerged as, in large part, open to interactions, although critical and selective, with institutions. In fact, they are politically committed, supporting 'another politics'. Even though our sampling strategy might have increased the number of more institutionally-linked organizations, we can nevertheless assess that a large part of the most relevant and visible organizations in the main areas of intervention of the GJM is in fact very interested in addressing policy makers in various ways. To a certain extent, the GJM itself represents a moment of repoliticization of the organizations of the civil society. Disillusioned by the meagre results coming from the sort of division of labour between political and social actors that had developed in the 1980s and 1990s, many NGOs, culturally-oriented groups, trade unions and voluntary associations started to bridge their frames and competences and to target the institutions of multilevel governance.

Not only do the large majority of our organizations interact with institutions, they address them at different territorial levels of governance. Groups structured at the local level tend also to declare interactions with the other territorial levels, as do national and transnational SMOs. Protest in the street, or even the focus on personal change, do not exclude attention to politics and public policy making. In fact, as it stands for a return of the state against the market, the GJM expresses an interest in the development of structures of governance at various territorial levels. In particular, the stigmatization of the democratic deficit in the functioning of international governmental organizations does not translate into a lack of interest towards this level of governance, but instead in strong demands for alternative policies and institutions. In this sense, our organizations are advocating not a return to nation-state sovereignty, but a 'global democracy' that can govern economic globalization (Marchetti 2008). Attention to the transnational level is in this sense very central: although the building of a 'democracy from below' at the international level is most challenging, it is perceived as an urgent need.

This is all the more true regarding the EU: most organizations strongly criticize the actual policies and politics of the EU, but at the same time stress the need for democratic European institutions and a social Europe. Civil society organizations have at times been considered as strong supporters of an identitarian vision of European integration, at times as among the strongest critics of the integration process. The campaign on the French referendum on the Constitutional Treaty spread the image of some social movement organizations as actively campaigning for a 'no' vote. Recent research has challenged the inclusion of those organizations and activists among the euro-sceptics, suggesting instead that they be defined as 'critical Europeanists' who are not against more competences for European institutions in principle, but are dissatisfied with its present politics and policies (della Porta and Caiani 2009). In this frame, the existing 'Europe of the market' is criticized as supporting neoliberal policies, but an alternative, 'social Europe' is called for (della Porta 2007a). With internal differences, our movement organizations do not seem, in fact, to favour a return to an exclusive power of the nation-state, but rather build up a process of 'Europeanisation from below' that includes the formation of European identities and organizational networks. Support and opposition tend to refer not only to (or not very much to) the integration process itself, but increasingly to its form and content. In fact, the intensification of the debate about Europe has brought about the symbolic linkage of the 'conflict over Europe' with other issues, layering various other cleavages over the original territorial ones.

This interest in politics and policies does not exclude mistrust of institutions and fear of co-optation. Co-operation with institutions is most often not excluded, but the role our organizations tend to assign themselves is mostly of democratic control. Collaboration is in fact qualified as critical and selective. Within this conception of democratic control, participation is stressed as a main value, but combined with a defence of the autonomy of the civil society from the state. Democratic decision making should be, first of all, transparent and accountable to the people. In order to be accountable, public institutions should open more and more channels of participation for the citizens. Mistrust towards public institutions is mostly not stated in principle, but as stemming from (direct or indirect) experiences.

However, our GJM organizations also emerged as internally diverse in their attitudes and behaviours towards institutions. In our research, we have looked at both external characteristics and internal environmental influences, focusing on their impact on attitudes towards institutions. We did not address them as rival theories, but looked at their respective impacts on our dependent variable, as operationalized in the organizational fundamental documents.

First, contextual characteristics emerged as significant, but association patterns did not easily confirm the hypothesis of more co-operative SMOs in more inclusive and consensual countries (in particular, in central–northern Europe) and more rebellious ones in more exclusive and conflictual ones (in particular, in southern Europe). In fact, more relevant was the degree of diversity within each country. Contextual impacts are especially filtered through a sort of imprinting in the founding period of our groups.

Instead, our analysis indicates a very high explanatory power for some structural organizational characteristics, allowing us to identify two main organizational constellations. The groups that are more open towards collaboration are usually richer in resources, better structured, more professionalized and have a larger membership. In contrast, the more critical ones are small, poor, voluntary, grass-roots groupings. This is all the more true when shifting from interactions with local to those with international institutions.

This does not mean, however, that the type of resources available automatically determines the attitudes towards institutions. Not only is the direction of causality not clear, but the attitudes towards institutions seem to be part of broader identities, involving also general values. From this point of view, the more the groups stress democratic values of participation and deliberation, the more they are critical towards existing institutions, which they perceive as not performing according to those values. Particularly organizations that emerged within the Global Justice Movement, as well as those who assumed a novel network structure, emerged as associated more with control than with refusal of interactions with institutions, which instead increases for the (more traditional) anti-capitalist values. Attitudes towards institutions are in fact influenced by the 'generation' a group belonged to. Younger organizations (those born with the GJM) emerged as especially critical in their collaboration.

Notes

1. Discussing the Constitutional Treaty, ATTAC France (2005) stresses 21 claims that European policies should address, among them the values of solidarity and gender equality (against those of competition and free trade), the defence of public services and public goods, a democratic control on trade policies and capital flows, and initiative rights for citizens. The Convention of European Attac for a 'Democratic Refoundation of Europe' (ATTAC Europe 2005) proposes, among other ideas, to increase the European budget in order to develop a social policy and increase structural funds for new member states, against social and fiscal dumping, concluding that 'the European Attacs care for European institutions that are authentically democratic', and 'Another Europe is possible. We shall build it together.'
2. In its constitution, the CGIL declares commitment to 'the construction of a European Union as a unitary federal subject, with a strong social dimension'. Sinistra Giovanile declares, in the name of a 'global generation', to 'believe in Europe', 'dream and project', while asking the EU for 'more commitment than in the recent past in becoming a promoting subject of a new multilateralism'; similarly, the Giovani Verdi declare support for a Europe of rights and peace.
3. Cordoba Solidaria takes part in participatory budgeting 'because the philosophy of the network is participation', and for the Swiss Parti du Travail, 'it goes along with our political philosophy'.

4. For example, the co-ordination on AIDS Act-up point at the essential role of the point of view of people living with the illness.
5. The pro-migrant rights Associazione 3 Febbraio criticizes the fact that these processes exclude some categories of immigrants. The Comitati di appoggio europei al MST brasiliano support those experiments but only in case of real popular participation.
6. See the concepts of 'funded' SMOs in McCarthy and Zald 1987a, pp. 358ff., or 'registered' SMOs in McCarthy et al. 1991, p. 68.
7. In measuring 'structural participation', we assigned a positive value to those organizations in which the assembly meets more than once a year, with the members of the executive, the president, or the spokesperson elected by the general assembly. 'Structural accountability' refers to the presence of a board of auditors and/or the approval of the budget by the assembly, the control of the executive by the assembly, the possibility for a certain percentage of members to convene an extraordinary assembly, and the mention of a quorum required for the decision-making body/bodies to deliberate.
8. The results on institutions at the various territorial levels (not shown, but available on request) are consistent with those shown in the combined index, although given the low number of mentions (especially on the case of refusal of interactions), the statistical significance of the correlation coefficients is reduced.

5
Why Are Social Movement Organizations Deliberative? Structural and Cultural Determinants of Internal Decision Making in the Global Justice Movement

Marco Giugni and Alessandro Nai

Introduction

Decision making in social movements, and democratic visions and practices more generally, vary strongly from one movement organization to another. This chapter looks at possible explanations of such differences in internal decision making observed among organizations of the Global Justice Movement. Indeed, the adoption of a given democratic model varies a great deal across the organizations included in the study (Table 5.1). Based on information derived from the organizations' online and offline documents, as well as a structured questionnaire submitted to them, the last column of this table shows that the associational model is the most common, followed by the two deliberative models and, lagging far behind, the assembleary model. Thus, half of the organizations put forward deliberation as their decision-making mode; about one-quarter of them follow the deliberative participative model.

The table also shows that the use of democratic models in general and, more specifically, the deliberative participative model vary across countries as well (see Chapter 2 in this volume for a more detailed presentation of the typology of democratic models). The associational model prevails in all countries except Spain, where the deliberative participative model is more frequently used. The latter model, in contrast, is much less widespread in France, Germany, and Switzerland than in the

Table 5.1   Democratic models by country (%)

	Britain	France	Germany	Italy	Spain	Switzerland	Total
Associational	45.0	42.9	55.2	36.6	24.5	54.8	41.3
Deliberative representative	25.0	34.3	20.7	31.7	26.5	25.8	27.6
Assembleary	0.0	8.6	6.9	4.9	8.2	3.2	5.3
Deliberative participative	30.0	14.3	17.2	26.8	40.8	16.1	25.8
Total	100%	100%	100%	100%	100%	100%	100%
N	40	35	29	41	49	31	225

Notes: Based on documents and questionnaire. Only valid cases are included (36 missing cases).

other countries, including Spain. While these differences are certainly due in part to our sampling criteria (see Introduction), they might reflect a greater sensibility towards participatory and deliberative democracy of the movement in Spain and partly also in Britain. Yet, it is difficult to interpret them as resulting from differences in national political opportunity structure, as no coherent pattern seems to emerge. In order to investigate this aspect, in our analyses we will include a more aggregated measure of country variation based on Lijphart's (1999) typology of democratic systems, in particular his distinction between majoritarian and consensual democracies.

The main purpose of this chapter, however, is not to explain cross-national variations in the adoption of a given democratic or decision-making model. Instead, we investigate some structural and cultural determinants for the adoption of a deliberative participative model by organizations active in the movement. We focus more specifically on the deliberative participative model, which is often stressed in the discourse of the Global Justice Movement. With its emphasis on the importance of consensus and broad participation in democratic processes (della Porta 2005b), this democratic model best represents the challenge to traditional forms of representative democracy (della Porta et al. 2006). Indeed, consensus and participation are two core values of the GJM.

We advance a number of hypotheses concerning the impact of three structural factors relating to the internal structuring of the organizations, and three cultural factors concerning the tradition of contention upon which their mobilization rests. In addition, we include a factor pertaining to the broader institutional setting of the country in which the organizations are located (type of democracy). We confront these hypotheses with the results of two kinds of analysis on a pooled sample of organizations from the six countries included in the study.[1] First, we run a logistic regression to see which of the organizational characteristics have an impact and to assess their relative weight. Second, we use qualitative comparative analysis (QCA) to explore multiple and conjunctural effects. Before we move to the results of the analyses, however, we need to elaborate upon our theoretical expectations and their operationalization.

Structural and cultural determinants of deliberative democracy: Some hypotheses

Our aim is not merely to describe the democratic models adopted in decision making within the Global Justice Movement, but above all to explain them. We focus on internal determinants, both structural and cultural, for the adoption of the deliberative participative model of democracy in our sample. Specifically, we examine the impact of the internal structuring of the organizations (degree of formalization, size, and territorial scope) and of the tradition of contention on which their political mobilization rests (belonging to the new social movement and Global Justice Movement area, identification with the GJM, and historical period in which the organizations were created). For each aspect, we advance a hypothesis about its impact on democratic models, specifically the deliberative participative model. However, we are in a more exploratory than a confirmatory mode. Therefore, these hypotheses are intended as a tool to guide the analysis rather than expectations to be tested against empirical evidence.

The first two aspects refer to the internal structuring of the organizations. These aspects have been given centre stage in the study of social movements by resource mobilization theory (see Edwards and McCarthy 2004 for a review). This theory has stressed the number of resources and the degree of internal structuring of social movements as crucial for movement emergence and mobilization (Jenkins 1983; McCarthy and Zald 1977). The organizations' internal structuring is also related to their development over time. For example, Kriesi (1996) proposes four dimensions for the analysis of organizational development: organizational growth and decline, internal structuring, external structuring, and goal orientations and action repertoires. Here, we focus on the second aspect, namely internal structuring. Specifically, we look at the impact of two indicators: degree of formalization and size.

The question is whether the organizations' internal structuring can plausibly be linked to the democratic model they follow in decision making, in particular to the deliberative participative model. We hypothesize that organizations with a lower degree of *formalization* (for example, in terms of paid staff, budget, and formal membership) will be more likely to follow the deliberative participative model (see Clemens and Minkoff 2004 for a review of work on the role of organization in social movement research). More formalized organizations, in contrast, will tend to delegate the most important decisions to a small group of leaders. This is partly because these organizations are more professionalized and therefore have a small, professional committee to take and implement decisions. Therefore, formalized organizations would favour representation over participation and majority voting over deliberation. In addition, we can expect a lower degree of formalization to be associated with a consensual rule of decision making rather than a majority rule, which better reflects the routines of a professional board and of formal organizations more generally (Meyer and Rowan 1977). Thus, if we combine the two dimensions, we expect organizations with a lower degree of internal structuring to adopt a deliberative participative model of democracy.

Similar reasoning can be applied to *organizational size* (see also Chapter 6 in this volume). Again, for pragmatic reasons, larger organizations can be expected to be more favourable to delegation of power in the decision-making body and less favourable to consensus as a decision-making method than smaller ones. Participation and deliberation are more difficult to attain in larger groups. Therefore, we expect smaller organizations to follow the deliberative participative democratic model.

Degree of formalization and size are internal characteristics of the organizations *strictu sensu*. A third aspect can also be considered as being part of the organizations' internal structuring: the *territorial scope* of the organizations (see also Chapter 4 in this volume). Here, we distinguish between organizations with an international/transnational scope and those with only a domestic scope (that is, local and/or national). Although it is more difficult to advance a clear-cut hypothesis for this aspect, one may argue that domestic organizations are more likely to adopt the deliberative participative model, as they can afford to be more open to participation and deliberation to the extent that they have a more limited reach. International/transnational organizations, in contrast, are more complex and therefore necessitate more effective decision-making procedures, which only a high degree of delegation and a majority rule can provide. Furthermore, the multilevel game implied by being active on both the domestic and the international/transnational levels makes consensus and broad participation more difficult to attain.

While the first three aspects are all structural conditions of the democratic models adopted by organizations, the remaining two can be seen as cultural conditions as they refer to their cultural roots. Students of social movements, especially in the European tradition, have stressed the role of social and cultural cleavages for the emergence and mobilization of social movements (for example, Kriesi et al. 1995). In particular, many have pointed to the different cultural underpinnings of the new social movements with respect to 'older' movements, above all the labour movement (see Buechler 1995 and Pichardo 1997 for reviews). Others have looked at the social basis of the new social movements, arguing that they reflect a division within the new middle class and that their mobilization potential is largely based on this line of conflict (for example, Kriesi 1989). In this perspective, the new social movements are ultimately rooted in the structural and cultural transformations that have characterized the European countries in the postwar period.

Here, we follow this line of reasoning to investigate the impact of the *movement area* to which the studied organizations belong on their propensity to follow a given democratic model (see also Chapter 1 in this volume). This gives us a measure of the organizations' broader position as resulting from their underlying cultural cleavage. In this regard, we can hypothesize that the organizations that reflect the cultural cleavage embodied by the new social movements should be more inclined to adopt a participative and deliberative mode of decision making. The new social movements have been characterized as promoting participation by civil society actors and 'softer' ways to take collective decisions (Polletta 2002). As a result, we may expect them to be more likely to accept the idea that decision making should be obtained through a lower degree of delegation and to more frequent use of consensus. Organizations not belonging to this tradition of contention, in contrast, should be more oriented towards delegation and towards majority rule in decision making. This should be particularly the case for traditional parties and unions, which tend to privilege representation rather than participation and are usually less prone to seeking consensus.

The *degree of identification with the Global Justice Movement* points in the same direction. The more an organization identifies with the movement, the more it can be said to share its values and claims. Therefore, we can expect organizations that display a strong degree of identification to be more likely to adopt a deliberative participative model of democracy, as they will be closer to participation and consensus as organizational values.

Furthermore, we look at the *year of foundation* of the organizations. This is meant to measure the impact of the historical period in which the organizations emerged. Although this aspect has been somewhat under-studied in the social movement literature, we think it is likely to influence the characteristics of the organizations studied and above all their visions of democracy (see Chapter 9 for a discussion of the relationship between time and democratic models). We distinguish between organizations created before 1989 and those founded after 1989. This year represents a watershed in the history of Europe and therefore also in the history of political contention. Organizations and movements that emerged after the fall of the Berlin wall clearly faced a totally different environment, less constrained by ideological cleavages and more open to work within cross-cutting cleavages. Most important for our present purpose, what we today call the Global Justice Movement can be said to have emerged around that time. We hypothesize that organizations created more recently (that is, after 1989) will be more inclined to adopt a deliberative participative model of democracy. These are the organizations that emerged within the protest wave carried by the GJM. Since this movement emphasizes the need for an open and inclusive democracy, we may expect the organizations that form the backbone of this movement to implement such a view of democracy in their internal functioning as well.

Finally, we control our results with a variable pertaining to the broader institutional setting of the country in which the organizations are located. Specifically, we want to see whether differences in the *type of democracy* characterizing the country can explain how some organizations are more likely to adopt more deliberative practices than others. To do so, we use Lijphart's (1999) well-known typology of democratic systems, which distinguishes between majoritarian and consensual democracies. Among the countries included in our study, France and especially Britain are examples of majoritarian democracies, while Germany and especially Switzerland are examples of consensual democracies. To these two 'pure' types, we can add mixed cases, intermediary situations in which the country has a high score on the executive–parties dimension and a low score on the federal–unitary dimension, or vice versa. In our data, this is the case for Italy and Spain. The rationale behind the use of this typology is that we may expect those organizations coming from consensual democracies to be more inclined to adopt a deliberative participative decision-making model given that the broader institutional setting is already attuned to inclusive, consensual, and horizontal forms of governance. Conversely, we expect organizations from majoritarian democracies to be less likely to follow this democratic model as they are located in more exclusive, unitarian, and vertical systems. Organizations in mixed democracies should stand somewhere in between.

In sum, we have advanced a number of hypotheses concerning the conditions that might lead an organization to adopt a deliberative participative model of democracy in internal decision making (that is, one that stresses the search for consensus and broader participation to arrive at a 'good' decision). Specifically, we expect such a democratic model to be adopted by recently created, smaller organizations with a low degree of formalization, a domestic territorial scope, a position close to the cultural cleavage embodied by the new social movements, and strong identification with the GJM. In addition, we expect organizations that are located in consensual democracies to be more likely to follow the deliberative participative model and, conversely, those located in majoritarian democracies to be less likely to do so.

A multivariate regression analysis allows us, in a first step, to confront these expectations with the empirical evidence at our disposal. Our analysis, however, does not simply aim to address these hypotheses separately or, as in a more traditional statistical approach, to look for the net effect of each of the five variables under control of all the others. We are also interested in exploring the configurations of conditions that lead organizations to opt for consensus and participation (rather than majority rule and delegation) in internal decision making. In doing so, we go beyond a linear and additive logic in explaining democratic models in the GJM and follow instead a method that allows us to identify possible combinations of factors leading to the choice of a given democratic model as well as different possible paths leading to such a choice. QCA is particularly suited to studying such multiple conjunctural causation (Ragin 1987).

Data and methods

The data were collected by means of a structured questionnaire submitted to a sample of organizations active in the Global Justice Movement in each of the six countries (see Chapter 1 for more details). Of the 225 organizations in our sample, only 168 were used in our empirical analyses.[2] In order to correctly apply the QCA, we need non-missing data on each variable. This is not the case for 57 organizations, which are therefore excluded from the analyses. Although the number of cases lost is relatively high (about one-quarter of the initial sample), this should not negatively affect our analyses. First of all, our initial sample of 225 organizations is not considered to be statistically representative. Even if the cases dropped are not randomly distributed among the variables (which is a problem for representative samples), this is not statistically relevant in our research. Second and most important, the missing cases are randomly distributed among the main variables. We can therefore assume that the removal of the missing cases does not affect the overall importance of particular kinds of organizations.

As discussed earlier, our model includes seven explanatory factors (six for the QCA). Most of them are simply operationalized directly through the data from the structured questionnaire. However, for some variables, there was too much missing information. In order to avoid excluding too many cases, missing information was replaced through data from other variables or with data retrieved in the documents produced by the organizations. Next, we present the operationalization of the variables included in the analysis, starting from the dependent variable.

Democratic models

To classify the selected organizations according to the typology of democratic models, we used both the information coming from the structured questionnaire and information derived from the organizations' internal documents, starting from the former and retrieving missing information from the latter. This allowed us to include as many cases as possible in the analysis. The definition of a given organization as assembleary, associational, deliberative representative, or deliberative participative (the type in which we are interested) is based on a complex operationalization involving a number of indicators allowing us to classify the organization on the two dimensions of the typology (delegation of power vs. participation in the decision-making body, and consensus vs. majority rule as a decision-making method).

Degree of formalization

To create the measure for the degree of formalization of the organization, we took into account three aspects: the size of the organization's staff (number of paid members), its budget, and the existence of a membership card. All three aspects were first computed as dummy variables with the following values: a paid staff of more than 30 people, a budget of more than 10 000 euros, and the existence of a membership card. The threshold concerning paid staff and budget was based on the median value on each aspect. We then created an additive index with the three indicators. The index thus obtained was finally recoded into a dummy variable (high/low degree of formalization).

Size

The size of the organization was computed through a variable measuring the number of individual members. If the number of members is higher than the median value (775 members), the organization is considered as large. When available, missing information on this variable was replaced by a variable measuring the number of people participating in the assembly (if higher than 100, then the size is considered as large) and two variables created based on the information retrieved from the documents produced by asking for information directly from the organizations: one measuring the number of individual members (large size if higher than the median value of the distribution) and another measuring the number of collective members (large size if higher than the median value). This was done for 123 cases.

Territorial scope

The territorial scope of the organization was operationalized through the highest level of its campaigns. The latter was measured through a direct question asking for the highest territorial level of the campaigns the organization usually conducts (local, national, or international/transnational). We distinguished between the domestic (local and/or national) and the international/transnational level. When available, missing information on this variable was replaced through a variable asking if the organization had some form of collaboration with international institutions (if yes, we consider the highest campaign level to be the international/transnational one).[3] This was done for 101 cases.

Movement area

To measure the belonging of the organization to a specific movement area, we used a variable that classifies the organizations on the basis of various sources (online and offline documents as well as the structured questionnaire). This variable distinguishes among six main areas: Old Left; New Left, anarchism, autonomy; new social movements; solidarity, peace, human rights; new global; and other issues (see Chapter 1). We created a dummy variable by merging the third, fourth, and fifth categories (new social movements; solidarity, peace, and human rights;

and new global), which we consider as belonging to the same broad area we may call 'new social global movements,' as opposed to all the other categories.[4]

Year of foundation

The year of foundation of the organization was operationalized in a simple fashion by using 1989 as a threshold. Organizations founded before 1989, which represents a watershed in the history of contention in Europe and in contemporary history more generally, are considered as 'old', while organizations created after 1989 are considered as 'new'.

Identification with the Global Justice Movement

The variable measuring the organization's degree of identification with the Global Justice Movement was operationalized through a question asking if the group considers itself as part of the overall movement. When available, missing information on this variable was replaced through a variable measuring whether the organization actively participated in events carried by the GJM (if yes, it is considered as identifying with the movement).[5] This was done for 83 cases.

Type of democracy

Variations in the institutional settings in which the organizations are located are operationalized through Lijphart's (1999) distinction between majoritarian and consensual democracies. In his perspective, countries may be classified according to a two-dimensional map built on two axes: the executive–parties and the federal–unitary axes. We used the scores he calculated in his analysis for each country on these two dimensions to place our countries in one type or the other. Thus, Britain and France are considered as majoritarian democracies, Germany and Switzerland as consensual ones, and Italy and Spain as mixed cases (see Lijphart 1999 for more details).

Given that our analyses are carried out on what is sometimes called a 'medium-sized sample' (formed, in our case, by 168 valid observations), we test our hypotheses through a triangulation of logistic regression and QCA. The logistic regression helps us to determine the relative importance of each explanatory factor on the democratic model adopted by the organizations. However, given the size of our sample, in general we do not expect highly significant results. QCA provides a more reliable tool when working with a limited number of cases (Ragin 1987). In addition, it has important logical and methodological advantages, especially for small to medium-sized samples such as ours (Harkreader and Imershein 1999). First, the method is based on an easily accessible logic, constructed on simple algebraic bases (the Boolean logic). The variables are entered in the model in the simplest possible form: the binary form.[6] Furthermore, QCA results are presented in a parsimonious yet comprehensive way, by distinguishing between necessary and sufficient conditions for the presence of a given outcome (Ragin 1987). This allows for direct and immediate understanding of the results. Second, QCA aims to integrate the complexity of the context into the core of the analysis. To do so, it integrates interaction effects among causal or contextual variables. As noted by Scharpf (1997), this method, by focusing on combinations of variables, not only stresses multi-causality, but also does not necessarily assume that variables are independent. Moreover, QCA has an equifinal or functional equivalent view, meaning that different configurations of the context can produce the same outcome (Scharpf 1997; Hall 2003; Mahoney and Goertz 2006).

The problem with QCA in our case is that our sample is not small enough. As reported in the literature on the subject, too small a sample increases the likelihood that no deterministic solution will be found (Hicks 1994). In such a configuration, the number of conflictive combinations is too high to allow a parsimonious solution. Second, a high number of independent variables increases exponentially the number of potential combinations of factors, again increasing the risk that no deterministic solution will be found (Scharpf 1997). We propose in this chapter an empirical solution allowing us to cope (at least in part) with these two problems that occur when the sample is not small enough. We present this solution in the discussion of the results below.

Regression analysis

Our main goal is to explore some of the structural and cultural factors that lead organizations active within the Global Justice Movement to adopt a deliberative participative model of democracy in internal decision making. Since we deal with a binary dependent variable (presence or absence of a deliberative participative model), in this first step we use logistic regression. In order to assess the explanatory power of each set of factors taken separately, we ran three separate models: one with only the three structural variables, another in which we added the three cultural variables, and a full model that includes the control by type of democracy (Table 5.2).

Table 5.2   Estimate of effects of selected independent variables on two contrasting decision models (odds ratios)

	Model 1	Model 2	Full model
Degree of formalization (low)	2.41	0.28	0.35
Size (small)	29.12***	39.59***	39.96***
Territorial scope (domestic)	1.34	1.33	1.30
Movement area (new social global)	–	4.46*	4.37*
Identification with the global justice movement (strong)	–	13.34+	10.89+
Year of foundation (after 1989)	–	4.18*	3.62*
Type of democracy (ref.: mixed)			
Majoritarian	–	–	0.39+
Consensual	–	–	0.45
Nagelkerke R^2	0.40	0.49	0.51
-2 Log likelihood	140.985	125.808	122.249
N	168	168	168

Notes: + $p \le .10$, * $p \le .05$, ** $p \le .01$, *** $p \le .001$.

If we compare the first two models, we can see that structural factors (model 1) have much more explanatory power than cultural factors do (model 2). Indeed, the explained variance for the former set of variables equals 40 per cent, while adding the latter only increases it by less than 10 per cent. The full model adds little to the explained variance but yields a significant effect concerning the institutional variable. Specifically, organizations located in majoritarian democracies are less likely to follow a deliberative participative model, as compared to those in mixed systems (category of reference). Certainly, the effect is significant only at the 10 per cent level and, moreover, the odds for the category of consensual democracies is also lower than 1, thus pointing to a negative relationship. Yet, this finding suggests that institutional setting influences the adoption of a deliberative participative model of democracy in the expected direction.

Among the three structural indicators we have included in our analysis, organizational size is by far the most important (model 1). In fact, it is the only one that displays a statistically significant effect. Furthermore, the odds of the occurrence of the deliberative participative model are extremely high: small organizations are nearly 40 times more likely to adopt this democratic model than are large ones, when controlling for the other factors (full model). Also, the effect is robust, as it remains significant across the three models. This finding is consistent with our hypothesis with regard to this factor. Larger organizations may be seen as posing a material obstacle to effectively deliberative and fully-inclusive decision making, insofar as the higher the number of members (which is an indicator of organizational size), the more difficult it is to include each one in a decisional process aiming to take into account the opinions of all. In contrast, degree of formalization and territorial scope have no effect. Thus, more loosely structured organizations and organizations focusing on the domestic level in their campaigns are not more likely to follow a more inclusive internal decision-making process.

Cultural factors play a smaller role, but their effect is still important, and all three of them are statistically significant (model 2). The strongest effect is shown by identification with the Global Justice Movement, as organizations that strongly identify with the movement are about ten times more likely to follow a deliberative participative model than are the others (full model). This effect, however, is significant only at the 10 per cent level. Belonging to the new social global movement area and creation after 1989 also show a statistically significant and strong effect. All three effects are robust and remain significant when controlling for type of democracy. Most important, they are all consistent with our hypotheses: confirming our expectations, organizations whose mobilization rests on the tradition of contention first carried by the new social movements and more recently by the GJM are more likely to adopt the deliberative participative model in their internal decision making.

In order to better understand the importance of the role of the statistically significant factors yielded by the regression analysis, we have transformed the results of the logistic models into predicted probabilities of occurrence (Figures 5.1, 5.2, and 5.3).[7] More precisely, we show the predicted probabilities of the deliberative participative model under the interactive effect of size with, respectively, movement area (Figure 5.1), identification with the GJM (Figure 5.2), and year of foundation (Figure 5.3). By doing so, we intend to set the structural factor found to be significant in the logistic regression in interaction with each of the three cultural factors for which we also observed a significant effect.

The pattern is very similar in all three cases. Starting with the effect of movement area and size (Figure 5.1), we can see that both small size and belonging to the new social movement and new social global movement area strongly increase the likelihood of using a deliberative participative democratic model, which is what we found in the logistic regression. The impact of organizational size, which is particularly strong, can be seen by comparing the two categories on the horizontal axis, while that of movement area can be observed by comparing the two segments of the vertical axis. However, the most important result here is the presence of a strong interactive effect insofar as the difference between organizations belonging to the new social movement and new social global movement area, on one hand, and those belonging to other movement areas, on the other, is particularly important for smaller organizations. Indeed, among larger organizations, there is almost no difference, while among smaller ones the predicted probabilities of the deliberative participative model range from around 20 per cent to more than 50 per cent. In other words, the likelihood of adopting this democratic model is much higher for small organizations that belong to the new social global movements, as compared to large organizations belonging to other movement areas.

A similar interactive effect can be observed in the case of identification with the Global Justice Movement (Figure 5.2). The predicted probabilities of the occurrence of the deliberative participative model are highest for small organizations with strong identification with the GJM and lowest for large organizations with only a weak identification with the movement. Again, size plays the bigger role, and the difference

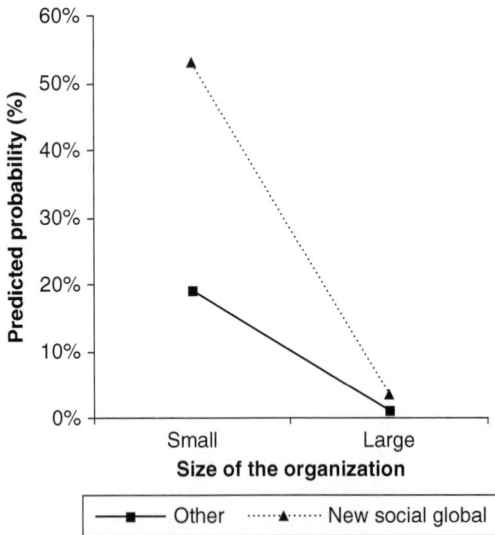

Figure 5.1 Predicted probability for a deliberative participative democratic model according to movement area and size

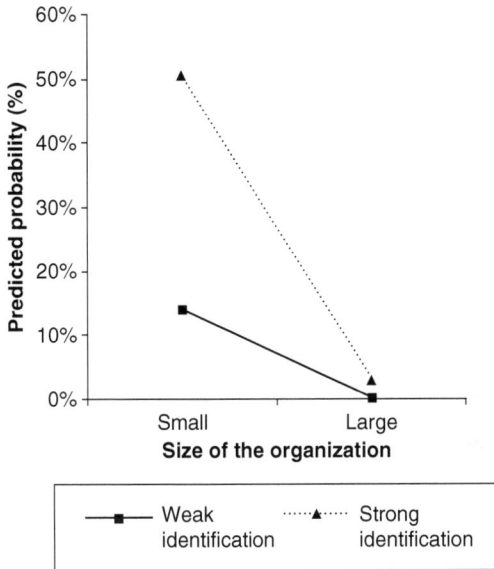

Figure 5.2 Predicted probability for a deliberative participative democratic model according to identification with the Global Justice Movement and size

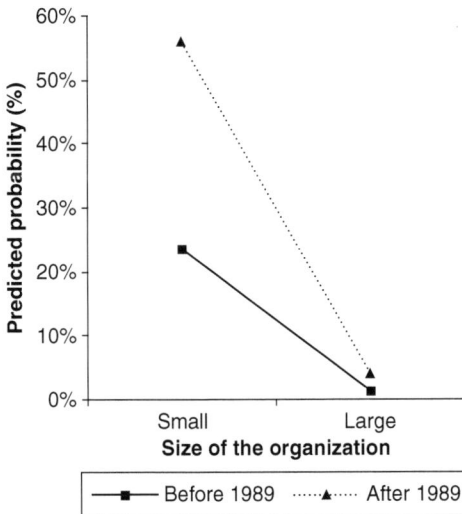

Figure 5.3 Predicted probability for a deliberative participative democratic model according to year of foundation and size

between organizations that identify with the movements and those that do not is virtually only present for those that are small.

Finally, the interaction between organizational size and year of foundation displays virtually the same pattern (Figure 5.3). Once again, size has a very strong effect, but only for smaller organizations, while the difference between recently created organizations and older ones is marginal for larger organizations. Thus, just as in the two previous situations, organizational size intertwines in a specific way with the historical period in which it was created to explain the adoption of the deliberative participative model, namely by increasing its likelihood among small organizations, but not so much among large ones.

Qualitative Comparative Analysis

The regression analysis gives us some hints as to the impact of the various explanatory factors on the adoption of a deliberative participative model of democracy. However, it is limited by the relatively low number of cases for this kind of analysis. In addition, it tells us nothing about the joint effects of the selected variables. Therefore, the findings obtained through logistic regression need to be complemented by means of alternative techniques. One way to do so is by applying QCA to our data. Built on a non-linear logic, QCA is particularly suited for small-N samples in which a set of explanatory factors is expected to jointly explain the presence or absence of a given outcome (in our case, a deliberative participative democratic model).

QCA is theoretically less stable and reliable when the number of observations is not small enough (the so-called medium-sized sample). In such a configuration, the likelihood that no deterministic solution will be found is much higher (Hicks 1994) owing to the increase in the number of conflictive paths (that is, identical configurations of independent factors that lead to different outcomes). In spite of the fact that our sample suffers precisely from this problem, we explore the role of structural and cultural determinants for the adoption of a deliberative participative model using QCA. However, in order to reduce the risk of non-determination due to the fact that our sample is not small enough, we need to adapt the classical crisp-sets QCA. We do so by introducing a pseudo-probabilistic approach that takes into account the probability for each conjunctural path to produce the outcome.

Following this approach, two scores are computed for each path composing the final causal equation: likelihood (L) and occurrence (O).

Likelihood measures the probability that the path leads effectively to the outcome predicted by the QCA and is calculated on the weighted ratio in conflictive combinations between the two different solutions the combination produces. For example, if a combination is composed by 9 cases leading to 1, and 1 case leading to 0, then the likelihood that the combination leads to 1 is 90 per cent. If a minimization occurred, likelihood is calculated through a simple weighting procedure based on the number of cases associated with each path that produced the minimization.[8] Occurrence simply measures the quantitative importance of each path. For example, if a path is built on ten cases in an $N = 40$ analysis, then we say that the path has a 25 per cent occurrence (O). Both scores, which are presented in a standardized form, provide better results when they are close to 1 (that is, 100 per cent). Similarly to what is done in standard probabilistic statistics, a threshold can then be set for the acceptation or refusal of a causal path. In this analysis, we decided that a path that does not lead to the predicted outcome in at least 50 per cent of the cases on which the path is formed ($L \leq 0.5$) and that is not based on at least 20 per cent of the cases entered in the model after resolution of the contradictions ($O \leq 0.2$) cannot be reliably accepted as relevant. These thresholds are consistent with what can be found in the literature (Ragin 2006) and are used to better understand the results provided by the QCA.

These two scores have several advantages. First, they provide a simple and intuitive way to assess the relative importance of each causal path that composes the QCA solution. This helps the researcher to better interpret the results and to single out the most important conditions for the outcome. Second, they allow us to increase the number of cases on which the QCA models are run. As we said earlier, a large number of cases increase the likelihood that no deterministic solution will be found owing to the increase in the number of conflictive combinations (Hicks 1994). Our solution avoids many of the problems posed by too large a number of conflictive cases, as the contradicting cases are directly integrated into the calculation of a likelihood score through a weighting procedure.[9] In brief, our solution allows the researcher to run QCA models with not-too-small samples by counterbalancing some of the major problems that typically emerge in such situations.[10]

We performed a first QCA in order to assess the conjunctural effect of the selected variables on the presence or absence of a deliberative participative model. The first QCA (not shown) did not yield any outcome, even after our procedure of resolution of contradictions. This is probably due to too low a ratio between the number of cases and the number of conditions. One solution to this problem is to exclude the variables of the lowest empirical and/or theoretical interest. Since we have included it in the logistic regression only as a control variable, although one based on specific theoretical expectations, we decided to exclude the variable pertaining to the institutional setting of the country in which the organizations are located. The results for QCA without this variable are much more satisfactory and can be summarized as follows:[11]

$$DELPART = SIZE^* YEAR^* IDGJM^* NSGM^* SCOPE_{<L=0.69;\ O=0.30>}$$
$$+$$
$$YEAR^* IDGJM^* NSGM^* scope_{<L=0.63;\ O=0.20>}$$
$$+$$
$$SIZE^* year^* nsgm^* scope^* formal_{<L=0.66;\ O=0.02>}$$
$$+$$
$$SIZE^* year^* scope^* FORMAL_{<L=0.35;\ O=0.03>}$$

The causal equation produced by the QCA is made up of four distinct causal paths (that is, combinations of conditions leading to the predicted outcome, in our case the presence of a deliberative participative democratic model), each composed of a unique combination of conditions. In order to assess the relative importance of each path, likelihood and occurrence scores are shown in brackets. If we take into account the thresholds proposed above ($L \leq 0.5$ and $O \leq 0.2$), which are quite restrictive, only the first two paths (indicated in italics) should be considered as sufficiently reliable given our data.

In the first path (SIZE*YEAR*IDGJM*NSGM*SCOPE), the presence of a deliberative participative model is the outcome of the joint presence of five conditions: small organizational size, recent foundation (after 1989), strong identification with the Global Justice Movement, belonging to the new social global movement area, and domestic (local and/or national) territorial scope (in terms of campaigns). This path is fully consistent with our expectations and shows very well the joint effect of structural and cultural factors for the adoption of the deliberative participative model. The only explanatory factor, among those we are investigating, that does not appear as a condition for this democratic model is degree of formalization, which was also not significant in the logistic regression. It is important to stress that only the simultaneous presence of these conditions leads to the outcome. Taken individually, they do not represent conditions for this democratic model to exist. This first causal path has quite a high likelihood of producing the desired outcome (L = 0.69) and is built on a sufficient number of cases (O = 0.30).

The second path (YEAR*IDGJM*NSGM*scope) is made up of the joint presence of four conditions: recent foundation, strong identification with the Global Justice Movement, belonging to the new social global movement area, and an international/transnational territorial scope. While the first three conditions are once again consistent with our expectations, the fourth is not. Here, we find that having activities that reach beyond the national level combines with the other three factors to lead to the adoption of the deliberative participative model, which contradicts what we found in the first path. The fact that size does not matter here may give us a clue to explaining this apparent contradiction: small organizations probably tend to focus more on the domestic level, so when (small) size is not part of the causal path, having an international/transnational territorial scope enters the explanation.

Yet, the important point here is that, if we compare the factors appearing in the first two paths, we can see that the result of the QCA points to three necessary conditions for an organization to adopt a deliberative participative model of democracy:[12] creation after 1989, identifying with the GJM, and belonging to what we called the new social global movements. The joint presence of these three conditions (YEAR*IDGJM*NSGM) is needed for a deliberative participative model to be adopted. In other words, this means that this democratic model is not adopted without the joint presence of these three factors, although it does not exclude the possibility for other factors to combine with them.

All three conditions are consistent with our hypotheses. We expected organizations created more recently to be more inclined to adopt a deliberative participative model of democracy, as they emerged within the protest wave carried by the Global Justice Movement. Since this movement emphasizes the need for an open and inclusive democracy, we expected the organizations that form its backbone to implement such a view of democracy in their internal functioning as well. This is confirmed by the results of the QCA. Similarly, we expected that the more an organization identifies with the GJM, the more it can be said to share its values and claims. A strong identification with the movement was therefore expected to increase the chances that a deliberative participative model of democracy is followed, as the organization will be closer to consensus and participation as organizational values. Again, the results of the QCA support this hypothesis. Finally, organizations belonging to the new social global movement area, which emphasize consensus and broad participation, were expected to be more inclined to adopt the deliberative participative democratic model. Here, too, the results of the QCA confirm our prediction.

All three factors comprising the necessary condition (YEAR*IDGJM* NSGM) belong to what we have defined as the cultural determinants of democratic models. This is consistent with the results we found earlier in the regression analysis. Indeed, the logistic regression models showed that all three cultural determinants have a statistically significant effect, going in the expected direction, on the presence of a deliberative partic- ipative model. These factors therefore seem crucial for this democratic model to be adopted by organizations of the Global Justice Movement. Furthermore, the necessary condition (YEAR*IDGJM*NSGM) combines in the first causal path with the presence of small organizational size. This is again in line with the results found in the regression analysis, where organizational size was found to be the strongest predictor for the deliberative participative model of democracy. In contrast, the QCA suggests that that territorial scope of the organizations also matters in one way or the other. This factor was found not to be statistically sig- nificant in the logistic regression. Finally, the QCA confirms the lack of impact of degree of formalization, and therefore that our prediction with regard to this aspect was incorrect. Just as in the logistic regres- sion, this factor does not appear in the QCA as a condition leading to the deliberative participative model (meaning that a minimization has occurred), at least if we consider only the first two causal paths.

However, the QCA results look different if we do not take into account the two relevance scores (Likelihood and Occurrence) and we there- fore interpret all four causal paths as yielded by the analysis. In fact, the third and fourth paths are far more complicated to understand, as they provide counterintuitive results. For example, if we look at the third path, the deliberative participative model seems to be, as expected, the outcome of the presence of small organizational size, but jointly with earlier year of foundation, belonging to another movement area, international/transnational territorial scope, and high degree of for- malization. All of the latter four conditions seem to work against our hypotheses and are not consistent with the results of the regression anal- ysis. Similarly, the fourth path points to the impact of two factors in line with our predictions (small organizational size and low degree of for- malization), but again in combination with two unexpected conditions: an earlier year of foundation and an international/transnational terri- torial scope. Furthermore, if we do not take into account the relevance scores, no necessary condition emerges from the results of the QCA. As we said, however, we think that failing to consider them would put our conclusions on shaky ground. In particular, occurrence is in both cases extremely low. This means that the outcome is based on only 2 per cent (third path) and 3 per cent (fourth path) of the cases. In addition, likelihood for the fourth path is quite low. Under these conditions, it is obviously difficult to draw firm conclusions.

Conclusion

Deliberative democracy has become fashionable in recent years. Yet, while normative discussions of this concept abound in the political theory literature (e.g. Habermas 1996b; Dryzek 2001; Benhabib 1996), there is a lack of knowledge about how deliberation works in concrete settings (see Steiner et al. 2004 for an exception). In particular, we still know little about the reasons pushing social movement organizations to stress consensus and participation in internal decision making. This is all the more important insofar as the Global Justice Movement and the new social movements before it have put much emphasis on these aspects.

In this chapter we have focused on a number of structural and cultural factors that may explain why organizations active within the Global Justice Movement in several European countries adopt a deliberative participative model of democracy, which stresses the search for consensus and broad participation in internal decision making. We conducted two types of analysis that follow different underlying logics, also with the idea of triangulating them: regression analysis, based on a linear logic and looking at the net effect of each variable, on one hand; and QCA, in order to examine multiple and conjunctural causation, on the other. The findings show that both the internal structuring of the organizations (structural factors) and the tradition of contention upon which their mobilization rests (cultural factors) should be taken into account to explain the adoption of this democratic model. On one side, the logistic regression suggests that organizational size matters most. Specifically, small organizations are more likely to adopt a deliberative participative democratic model. It also shows that organizations belonging to what we called the new social global movement area (that is, close to the new social movements and the Global Justice Movement), that have a strong identification with the GJM, and that were created after 1989 are more likely to follow the deliberative participative model. All of this is in line with our hypotheses. On the other side, again confirming our expectations, the QCA points above all to the importance of the cultural factors. In particular, we have found the joint presence of the three cultural factors to be a necessary condition for the adoption of the deliberative participative model.

The results of the QCA are consistent with those yielded by the regression analysis: the three cultural factors are all important determinants of the choice of a given model of democracy in internal decision making. However, while the regression analysis also suggests that one of the structural factors, namely organizational size, has the strongest impact in quantitative terms, the QCA adds to the explanation by showing that the cultural factors combine qualitatively to lead the organizations to opt for the deliberative participative democratic model.

To conclude, we should stress a finding that was not at the core of our study, but that deserves to be mentioned. We are referring to the fact that organizations located in majoritarian democracies, according to Lijphart's (1999) typology, are less likely to adopt the deliberative participative democratic model in internal decision making. Certainly, this effect does not stand the contrast with the other type of democracy singled out by Lijphart, as organizations located in consensual democracies are less likely to follow this democratic model. Yet this finding suggests that there might be some kind of institutional isomorphism between social movement organizations and their broader institutional setting.

Notes

1. We exclude from our analysis the transnational organizations. Since we look, among other factors, at the impact of the international/transnational scope as well as the type of democracy of the country in which the organizations are located, including purely transnational ones would bias the analysis.
2. By combining data from the structured questionnaire and from the documents produced by the organizations (and sometimes from information presented on the organizations' Web sites), we obtained a sample of 225 (non-transnational) organizations that included information about their democratic model of decision. Of these, only 168 are included in the analysis owing to missing information.
3. This is not only theoretically, but also empirically justified: among organizations that qualified their highest level of campaigns as international, the majority also declared having partial or full collaboration with international institutions.
4. Following previous work (e.g. Kriesi et al. 1995), we think that solidarity, peace, and human rights organizations belong to the new social movements, although they might have certain specificities such as, for example, religious roots, the involvement in project development, and a strong international orientation.
5. Again, this is not only theoretically, but also empirically justified: among organizations that consider themselves part of the GJM, nearly all declared having participated in events carried by the movement.
6. The dichotomization of the variables is not a sine qua non condition. For example, 'fuzzy-set' QCA uses more fine-grained measures (Ragin 2000).

Similarly, Cronqvist (2003) has proposed an approach using categorical variables. Here, however, we prefer to stick with the original version of QCA in order to keep our analysis as simple as possible.

7. Predicted probabilities refer to the likelihood, expressed in percentages, for an observed unit (here, an organization) to display the characteristics to be explained (here, to adopt the deliberative participative model) under the effect of one or more explanatory variables. They are calculated through the following equation (Menard 2002):

$$P(Y = 1) = [e^{(\alpha + \beta 1 X 1 + \beta 2 X 2 + \ldots + \beta k X k)}] / [1 + e^{(\alpha + \beta 1 X 1 + \beta 2 X 2 + \ldots + \beta k X k)}],$$

where Y is the outcome to be predicted, X_1 to X_k are the independent factors, α is the intercept of the model, and β_1 to β_k are the unstandardized regression coefficients.

8. Minimization refers to the process by which QCA aims to identify regularities among a medium number of cases. The researcher starts with a maximum level of complexity, then Boolean algebra allows for a systematic minimization of this complexity to varying degrees (depending on the inclusion or exclusion of 'logical case'), so that one or several configurations of conditions are identified as leading to a given outcome.

9. Simply put, when a conflictive situation exists while explaining an outcome, it is resolved: (1) by eliminating all cases leading to the opposite outcome, and (2) by integrating a measure of the relevance of the combination of conditions that takes into account the ratio between kept and eliminated combinations (likelihood).

10. It should be noted that the likelihood score and the occurrence ratio are roughly equivalent to the notions of consistency and coverage in QCA (see Ragin 2006).

11. In QCA, upper case usually indicates the presence of a condition and lower case its absence. In our case, we use upper case for conditions that meet our hypotheses and lower case for conditions that go counter to the hypotheses. Thus, 'SIZE' indicates a small organization and 'size' a large one; 'YEAR' indicates an organization created after 1989 and 'year' one created before 1989; 'IDGJM' indicates an organization that considers itself as part of the Global Justice Movement and 'idgjm' one that does not; 'NSGM' indicates an organization belonging to the new social global movement area and 'nsgm' one that belongs to another movement area; 'FORMAL' indicates a poorly formalized organization and 'formal' a highly formalized one; 'SCOPE' indicates an organization whose campaigns are prevalently domestic (local and/or national) and 'scope' one that has at least some campaign activity on the international level. The logical operator 'and' (*) means that two or more conditions need to be present jointly for the outcome to occur (conjunctural causation, in the QCA jargon). The logical operator 'or' (+) means that there is more than one path leading to the outcome (multiple causation, in the QCA jargon).

12. Perhaps better: one necessary condition, which is the joint presence of three conditions.

6
Organizational Size and Democratic Practices: Can Large Be Beautiful?

Clare Saunders[1]

Introduction

One of the Global Justice Movement's central concerns is the lack of democracy of international financial institutions (IFIs) such as the G8, the International Monetary Fund, and the World Bank (della Porta and Reiter 2006). These organizations make decisions through no more than a handful of elite politicians, who are often heavily biased towards the interests of Western corporations and are notorious for their lack of democracy. With particular reference to the G8, but equally true of other IFIs, George Monbiot (2003, p. 52), for example, states:

> While the rulers of the world cloister themselves behind the fences of Seattle or Genoa, or ascend into the inaccessible eyries of Doha of Kananaksi ... they leave the rest of the world shut out of their delib-erations ... They, the tiniest and most unrepresentative of the world's minorities, assert a popular mandate they do not possess, then accuse us of illegitimacy. Their rule, unauthorised and untested, is sovereign.

Because this type of critique of IFIs is a cornerstone of the GJM's frame, it becomes a special challenge for Global Justice Movement Organiza-tions (GJMOs) to ensure that they themselves do not lack democratic qualities in their own decision making. It is hypocritical of GJMOs to sustain a critique of rule by a minority that ignores the deliberation of the majority if they do not practise what they preach. Thus, to be immune from charges of hypocrisy, GJMOs themselves should avoid being ruled by a small, unrepresentative minority and should involve rank-and-file movement members in decision making. To do this prop-erly requires using 'beautiful' decision making that is open, inclusive,

transparent, and accountable. Such decision making allows creative freedom to flourish and is rewarding for its participants. It is the converse of
'ugly' decision making, which suppresses participation and creative freedom by prioritizing organizational efficiency, and, by so doing, becomes
closed, exclusive, non-transparent, and non-accountable, resulting in
frustration for participants.

Yet, beautiful decision making is difficult to implement, especially for
large organizations which, as often cited, tend to become increasingly
oligarchic as they develop their resource base. It is certainly the case that
many GJMOs have become formal and complex in their organizational
structures as they have increased in popularity and size, while they
struggle to address multifaceted issues of local, national, and transnational scope. But is it true, as the literature on this topic tends to
predict, that smaller GJMOs, which are less well resourced and have
smaller memberships, seem to find it easier to defy the 'iron law of
oligarchy' (Michels 1959 [1915]) and to implement 'beautiful decision
making' than their larger and better resourced counterparts? In other
words, are smaller GJMOs better than larger ones at practising what they
preach with regard to democracy? Are they better able to work horizontally using prefigurative politics to create an ideal democratic setting, or
do they too have some democratic weaknesses? Do large organizations
always have oligarchic structures, or are they able to find ways to involve
their rank-and-file in decision making? Or have GJMOs, of whatever size
or degree of formality, managed to successfully avoid the oligarchy they
so despise at the level of international policy making?

We could hypothesize that small organizations are more likely to
be able to avoid oligarchy than larger ones. However, as we shall see,
this simple hypothesis overlooks the tendency for small groups, in
the absence of rules – such as rotation of facilitation, circular seating
arrangements, transparency, and the use of hand signals – to have 'informal oligarchs'. It also ignores the proclivity for GJMOs, whatever their
size, to experiment with innovative forms of participation that make
them less susceptible to oligarchy than some other types of SMOs.

This chapter begins by reviewing the literature on organization and
oligarchy in social movements, using Schumacher's (1973) postulation
that 'small is beautiful' as a framework. It then looks at the results of a
survey of the decision-making practices of 210 GJMOs of various sizes to
see whether it is true that larger GJMOs are more oligarchic than smaller
ones. Next, it looks at the extent to which both large and small organizations really are 'beautiful' by considering the presence or absence
of rules serving to prevent the development of informal oligarchy, such

as rotation, transparency, working groups, seating arrangements, and/or hand signals. Before concluding, it will look in more depth at two contrasting transnational GJMOs: ATTAC – which, at least in France, fits the stereotype of 'large and ugly' – and Indymedia, for which a better characterization is 'large but beautiful'. The discussion of ATTAC will contrast its decision making with ideal small group politics and demonstrate that its activists, in accordance with academic critiques of oligarchic decision-making structures, view its non-participatory nature as 'ugly'. As a contrast, the discussion of Indymedia will illustrate how a large network has managed to avoid oligarchy by approximating the beauty of ideal small group decision making.

Is small beautiful?

> In any organisation, large or small, there must be a certain clarity and orderliness; if things fall into disorder nothing can be accomplished...Therefore any organisation has to strive continuously for the orderliness of the order and the disorderliness of creative freedom. (Schumacher 1973, p. 227)

Although he was writing about economic organizations, Schumacher clearly recognized in his seminal economic text, *Small is Beautiful* (1973), that the size of an organization matters. In particular, he noted the need to balance 'structurelessness', which reduces order, with 'oligarchy', which stifles creative freedom and participation. The former – structurelessness – is supposedly more common in smaller organizations, and the latter – oligarchy – is more apparent in larger organizations. Nonetheless, for Schumacher, small organizations are preferable because they allow creative freedom to flourish and prevent organizations from becoming 'moribund and a desert of frustration' (1973, p. 227). According to Schumacher, small organizations are especially preferable when the nature of the organizational activity is 'active and intimate' (1973, p. 60), as, indeed, much social movement activity is.

The balance between clarity and orderliness on the one hand, and disorderliness and creative freedom on the other, is especially important in social movements. As resource mobilization theorists have endeavoured to show (for example, McCarthy and Zald 1977), some kind of organizational 'structure' is necessary in order to bring people together to fight for a common cause. Yet, as others have warned (most notably Michels 1959), too much organization can result in alienation of the majority by an exclusive decision-making cadre. In a small organization, the majority are unlikely to be alienated from their cadre because the few group members involved will be easily able to meet and conduct intense discussions. In an organization with many members, such intense involvement from all members is not always possible because of the amount of time and the organizational dilemmas it would involve. The challenge for social movement organizations, then, is to balance organizational size and effective decision making. We might expect decision making in small organizations to be inclusive and creative, but rather disorderly. In larger movement organizations we would, instead, expect more order, but more frustration and less creative freedom.

The idea that 'small is beautiful', or that 'large is ugly', can be related to Michels' (1915) 'iron law of oligarchy', upon which there is a 'continuing scholarly fixation' (Minkoff and McCarthy 2005, p. 298). This 'iron law' stresses the inevitability of large-scale organization resulting in oligarchy: 'It is organisation which gives birth to the dominion of the elected over the electors, of the mandatories over the mandators, of the delegates over the delegators. Who says organisation, says oligarchy' (Michels 1959 [1915], p. 401). Smaller, or informal organizations can, supposedly, more easily avoid this tendency because they are much better able to encourage the participation of all members.

But is it really inevitable that large organizations follow the 'iron law'? Although many scholars think so, the GJM provides an interesting challenge to the 'iron law' – and a novel case upon which to test it – because of its widely recognized support for open and inclusive decision making and its unwillingness to fall prey to the same criticisms it levels upon its main adversaries, the International Financial Institutions (IFIs). Della Porta (2005b), for example, demonstrated that deliberation and consensus are not only desirable, but also possible, in social forums – the debating arenas of the GJM – which bring together and invite participation from thousands of participants. Perhaps GJMOs are novel cases to which the iron law does not apply; we shall see. But first, let us return to those scholars whose ideas support Michels' thesis.

Jordan and Maloney (1997) are among the scholars whose findings support the idea of an 'iron law'. They argue that modern campaigning organizations, such as Friends of the Earth and Amnesty in Britain, tend to have a large and passive membership, which does not participate in decision making and can make its own voice heard only through exit.[2] Run by elites, such 'protest businesses' lack internal democracy (Jordan and Maloney 1997, p. 190). This, they argue, is unsatisfactory:

> Campaign organisations have become bureaucratised and hierarchically controlled. The elite or policy entrepreneur controls the policy agenda while the volunteers do the 'depoliticised' mundane work of sending in the funds, selling raffle tickets, or buying goods from catalogues – and there is as much of a danger in glamorising this as in describing it as being meaningfully involved in the political process. (Ibid., p. 188)

There are three things worth pointing out in relation to Jordan and Maloney's work. The first is that, in agreement with Michels, they see the lack of participation in decision making as undesirable, or 'ugly'. This is because it restricts the role of volunteers to demeaning tasks, while excluding them from the 'real' work of the protest businesses in which they are 'involved'. Second, their findings are remarkably similar to McCarthy and Zald's (1973) seminal observations on the professionalization of movement organizations – a process that, for them, involves organizations employing full-time staff, reducing dependence on volunteers, and consequently eroding and eventually removing adherents' control over the organization. Third, and probably most important, just like McCarthy and Zald (1973), they do not have an independent variable for explaining *why* campaign organizations have become bureaucratized, and, by implication, oligarchic. Is it because of their age, their size, their quest to achieve efficiency, or something else? Other scholars have mostly tested the 'iron law' by using age and size as their dependent variables.

Rucht (1999), for example, used age as the independent variable for determining oligarchy in environmental organizations in Germany, finding that the iron law was much easier to 'bend' than other scholars had implied. Environmental organizations, he claimed, go through phases and even attempt to purposefully work against oligarchization, or as Michels said, to 'paralyse' it. This was an aim shared by the 'New Left', which has been much lauded by Breines (1980). Yet Rucht focused on age, ignoring the importance of organizational size. It seems rather strange to overlook organizational size, probably one of the most important factors in determining decision-making structures. Although there is a relationship between organizational age and size, we should be aware that the two do not always develop in tandem. Old organizations that have sought to remain informal and non-professional may remain small and consequently more participatory than their counterparts that are formal, professional, and large (Staggenborg 1988, p. 597).

With regards to size, it is obvious that when a political party (or, by implication, any type of social movement organization) has tens of thousands of members, 'it is impossible to carry on the affairs of this gigantic body without a system of representation' and that 'such a gigantic number of persons belonging to a unitary organization cannot do any practical work upon a system of direct discussion' (Michels 1959, p. 65). Thus, organizational size should be regarded as a key independent variable in determining oligarchic tendencies: it seems to lead to representative forms of democracy, which are often controlled by a few *without* direct participation from the majority.

The hypothesis that large organizations have a tendency to become oligarchic has not escaped scholarly attention. Tan (1998), in his study of political parties across Europe, found that larger political parties had more complex decision-making structures and tended to be less participatory than their smaller counterparts. However, he also found that *some* complex organizations, even if a minority, actually *were* participatory, their complexity resulting from their attempts to involve their grass-roots networks. Similarly, Hands (1971, p. 169) notes that 'most parties and unions have fairly elaborate governmental structures designed to allow, or to ensure, rank and file control over the leadership'.

Thus, we can see that previous research suggests that SMOs and political parties have a tendency, but not an inevitability, to become less participatory as they become larger. But does this necessarily imply that informal small organizations, which lack bureaucracy and are more participatory, are exemplars of democracy-in-action? Previous research suggests that the answer seems to be 'no' – small is not always synonymous with 'beautiful'. Just as it is possible to have both 'formal' and 'informal' organizations, it is also possible to have formal and informal oligarchs. 'Formal oligarchs' might be legitimately in charge of bureaucratic structures, whereas 'informal oligarchs' are likely to illegitimately dominate collectivist structures (Leach 2005, p. 318). This argument is in tune with Jo Freeman's classic article on the 'tyranny of the structurelessness', in which she notes that a lack of formal rules can lead to what Leach (2005) calls 'informal oligarchs'. Informal oligarchs are those social movement activists who are the most gregarious, or who are in the strongest friendship groups, and who therefore assume illegitimate group leadership by default. According to Freeman, small and informal decision-making procedures are only 'beautiful' when there is delegation, responsible power, distribution, rotation and allocation, diffusion of information, and equal access to power (Freeman 1970).

But how does this play out in relation to GJMOs, which we should expect, as a result of their critique of IFIs, and regardless of size, to take a more proactive role in avoiding oligarchy than other types of social movement organizations do?

Measuring oligarchy and organizational size

In this chapter we are concerned with the *extent* of participation in the main decision-making bodies of GJMOs. It is a crucial first step for us to operationalize the term 'oligarchy' in the context of this chapter because of the often-sloppy use of the term in the literature. Schmidt (1973, p. 10), for example, states that, 'Since Plato and Aristotle, most writers who discuss oligarchy fail to define the concept, apparently because they assume the word is understood in light of its Greek etymology (the rule of a few).'

So far, our discussion of oligarchy has implied, yet not explicitly declared, that it primarily involves a decision-making cadre, which excludes the majority. In short, we define oligarchy here as 'ruling power that belongs to a low proportion of SMO membership'. Thus, we have, for the purposes of this chapter, calculated a quantitative measure of oligarchy, the *oligarchy score*, which divides the number of people in the main organizational decision-making body – whether it be a president (one person), an executive committee (five people), a thematic group (ten people) or an assembly (number as specified in the questionnaire) – by the total number of members. Highly oligarchic organizations have low oligarchy scores because they are dominated by a small cadre in the manner Michels (1959) would predict. In contrast, a high score is indicative of a low degree of oligarchy because a large proportion of members participate in decision making. For example, an organization that has 10 000 members but has its decisions made by the president is highly oligarchic because decision making is concentrated in the hands of a very small minority. Consequently it has a low *oligarchy score* (1 divided by $10\,000 = 0.0001$). In contrast, an organization with 500 members which makes its key decisions by an assembly with 1000 participants (including 500 non-members) is non-oligarchic, yielding a high *oligarchy score* (1000 divided by $200 = 2.0$).[3]

Deliberation alone does not make participation meaningful if it is confined to a small cadre – such practice still alienates the majority from organizational practices and can be viewed as oligarchic. Therefore we do not test how the extent of deliberation is affected by organizational size because we already know that many large organizations, such as democratic representative organizations, do use it. In any case, if the manner in which deliberative representative organizations use deliberation still excludes the majority of participants, they can still be regarded as oligarchic because they are closed to broader participation. Therefore, instead, we shall look to see whether it is true that those GJMOs that involve a low proportion of their members in decision making tend to be large, and that those that involve a high proportion of members tend to be small.

We use annual operating budgets, the number of members (individual, and, if appropriate, collective), and the numbers of paid staff and volunteers to define 'large' and 'small' organizations. We consider organizations to be 'large' if they meet at least one of the following criteria: have an operating budget greater than 500 000 Euros, have more than 100 volunteers, have over 50 staff, have in excess of 10 000 individual members, and have, if the organization concerned is a network, over 100 collective members. These measures of 'largeness' were chosen because they represent approximately the largest one-quarter of the organizations within our sample – less than 60 organizations meet the criteria in each category. We consider organizations to be 'small' if they have at least one of the following: less than 15 volunteers, no paid staff, an annual budget less than 1000 Euros, and between one and 100 individual members (excluding organizations with collective members only).[4] The cut-off values for 'smallness' were chosen because they represent an approximate threshold after which, because of size restrictions, ideal small-group decision making becomes difficult to implement.

It should be remembered when interpreting the data based on these measures that the criteria for 'large' and 'small' organizations are not mutually exclusive categories – for example, at the worst extreme, 45.1 per cent of the organizations that are 'large' according to their budget are classified as 'small' on the basis of their number of volunteers. For this reason, it is important to consider the measures of organizational size largely in isolation from one another and as approximate indicators of size. Nonetheless, it should also be noted that most measures of largeness are more exclusive than the measure of budgets. For example, of those organizations with a 'large' number of individual members, none have 'small' numbers of staff, just under one-quarter have a 'small' budget, and only 6.1 per cent have a 'small' number of volunteers.[5]

The data is derived from Work Package 4 of the Demos Project based on structured interviews with organizational elites from 209 global justice movement organizations across western Europe. The interviews sought details of actual organizational decision-making practices (see Chapter 1 for more details).

Are large organizations more oligarchic than small ones?

Let us now look more closely at how the *oligarchy score* relates to our measures of organizational size.[6] Does oligarchy seem to increase in tandem with size, and if so, which measures of size are most discriminating?

Tables 6.1 and 6.2 indicate that, generally speaking, larger organizations have greater oligarchic tendencies. Oligarchy seems to steadily increase as organizations grow in terms of their staff, annual budgets, and numbers of volunteers and members. The most oligarchic GJMOs,

Table 6.1   Oligarchic tendencies of large organizations (% for columns)

Degree of oligarchy	Measures of organizational size				
	>100 volunteers (n=56)	>50 members of staff (n=29)	>€500000 budget (n=51)	>10000 individual members (n=33)	>100 collective members (n=28)
High <0.1	89.3	86.2	76.5	93.9	89.3
Medium 0.11–0.5	5.4	6.9	13.7	6.1	3.6
Low 0.51–5	5.4	6.9	9.8	0.0	7.1
Cramer's *V*	0.256***	0.142	0.085	0.231***	0.466***

Note: *** p ≤ .001.

Table 6.2   Oligarchic tendencies of small organizations (% for columns)

Degree of oligarchy	Measures of organizational size			
	<15 volunteers (n=88)	No members of staff (n=66)	<€1000 budget (n=71)	<100 individual members (n=32)
High <0.1	65.9	62.1	64.8	25.0
Medium 0.11–0.5	17.0	21.2	15.5	34.4
Low 0.51–5	17.0	16.7	19.7	40.6
Cramer's *V*	0.094	0.118	0.132	0.391***

Note: *** p ≤ .001.

with an *oligarchy score* of less than 0.1, are largest on all accounts. The most discriminating variables are the number of volunteers and the number of individual and collective members. The difference that the size of individual membership makes to the degree of oligarchy is particularly striking – whereas 93.9 per cent of the organizations with over 10 000 members are highly oligarchic (Table 6.1), only one quarter of those with less than 100 members are (Table 6.2).

However, we cannot, by any stretch of the imagination, conclude that small organizations are resistant to oligarchy. Table 6.2 indicates that, by most measures of size – with the exception of the number of individual members – a majority of small as well as large organizations have a high degree of oligarchy. Additionally, the tendency for small organizations to lack rules designed to avoid the domination of 'informal oligarchs' (Leach 2005) is slightly disconcerting. Table 6.3 shows the proportion of small organizations that claimed to use certain types of rules that might reduce informal oligarchy in their assemblies/open meetings, cross-tabulated by measures of 'smallness'. Overall, less than one-tenth of our 'small' organizations uses at least one of these rules. Circular seating arrangements and use of hand signals are the most commonly, even if infrequently, used. Yet, rotation of moderation or facilitation – one of the strategies recommended by Freeman (1970) to prevent 'the tyranny of the structurelessness' – was only mentioned by four small organizations. Nonetheless, 'large' organizations seem to use specific oligarchy-prevention rules in their meetings even more sparingly. Only one organization within our sample with more than 100 volunteers

Table 6.3 Rules for small organizations (% for columns)

Rules to prevent oligarchy	Measures of organizational size			
	<15 volunteers (n=88)	No members of staff (n=66)	<€1000 budget (n=71)	<100 individual members (n=32)
Rotation of facilitation	4.5	3.9	1.8	2.0
Transparency/ accountability	4.5	7.8	3.5	0.0
Working groups	3.0	2.0	1.8	2.0
Circular seating arrangement	9.1	2.0	1.8	2.0
Use of hand signals	9.1	7.8	5.3	2.0

claimed that it uses rotation, explicitly seeks transparency, or uses hand signals, and none of those with budgets over 500 000 Euros claimed to use any of the five rules shown in Table 6.3.

Not only do some of the small groups in our sample defy the theory of 'small is beautiful', but some of the larger ones also defy the parallel one that 'big is ugly'. Contrary to the expectations of Michels (1959) and Jordan and Maloney (1997), we can see that *some* GJMOs with large budgets and with a considerable number of staff have been able to resist oligarchy, even though they are not as common as their more oligarchic counterparts. Even traditionally organized trade unions, for example, are influenced by the 'tide of democracy from below' that has risen with the GJM. The Italian Confederazine General Italiana del Lavoro (CGIL) and the Federazione Impiegati e Operai Metallurgici, for instance, have at least experimented with deliberation and facilitation, and CGIL additionally declares that it seeks to protect the rights of minorities, to reduce excess bureaucracy and assure participation (Reiter 2006). Nonetheless, many socialist organizations have remained hierarchically structured, and consequently tend to be fairly oligarchic. For them, though, this is not related to their age or size, but to their ideology, especially their attempt to give birth to a top-down revolutionary socialist movement (see Teune and Yang 2006). Other GJMOs, still, have had lively debates about their internal decision making or have purposefully avoided hierarchy. Those avoiding hierarchy have done so by mimicking, whether intentionally or not, the beauty of small, non-oligarchic organizations.

Can large be 'beautiful'?

'Beautiful' decision making involves broad participation in the real politics of the organization concerned. To allow this to happen, decision making needs to approximate ideal small group decision making. As discussed in the introduction, it needs to be open, inclusive, and plural, but also accountable and transparent to members and supporters. Furthermore, to recapitulate Freeman (1970), it also requires that leadership roles be rotated, that participants have equal access to information, and that they share their skills to prevent power relationships from forming. The discussion that follows will illustrate that it is precisely because these characteristics of good internal democracy are missing in ATTAC that its members express discontent. On the other hand, the discussion of Indymedia that follows demonstrates how it is possible for a large organization to approximate beautiful decision making.

True, as these cases illustrate, broad participation in the real politics of an organization can come at the expense of efficiency. But compromised efficiency is probably preferable to the 'desert of frustration' (Schumacher 1973, p. 227) that results when participation is restricted. In ATTAC, in France in particular, the 'desert of frustration' resulting from restriction of grass-roots participation has stemmed from the struggle for power within the organization. In Indymedia, by contrast, there has been some concern regarding the loss of efficiency that accompanies broad-ranging participation. In contrast to ATTAC, though, Indymedia's dilemma over its internal democracy stems not from a power struggle, but from the now entrenched norms of open publishing. These two cases have also been selected because although they are both 'large' organizations, they have highly contrasting *oligarchy scores* (for example, 0.06 for ATTAC France, making it highly oligarchic, compared to 1 for Indymedia UK, which is very open to and participatory for its members).

ATTAC

Although ATTAC is an organization born with the rise of GJM, it has struggled to meet the democratic aspirations that its grass-roots membership demands. ATTAC is also a good case study because it allows us to compare national branches of different sizes to see how their decision-making structures vary, without worrying that any differences we find are due to vastly contrasting ideologies. If, on the other hand, we were comparing the decision making of socialist and autonomous organizations, we would expect to see differences in decision-making styles that are more attributable to ideology than to size, or, indeed, to anything else. ATTAC is also an important case study because it demonstrates how a democratic crisis can develop as a direct result of organizational growth: its oligarchic decision making was not deemed problematic when membership was small, as there were far fewer people suffering the disempowerment of exclusion.

After comparing the *oligarchy scores* of different ATTAC organizations, we will discuss the democratic dilemmas that ATTAC has faced in France, Germany, and Italy (beginning with the founding organization, ATTAC-France) and explore, in particular, what it is that makes ATTAC's decision-making 'ugly' – both theoretically and for its activists.

All three of the ATTAC organizations for which we have data have a low *oligarchy score* (0.06 for Germany, 0.1 for France, and 0.13 for Italy); yet they use different models of decision making, some more deliberative than others. The largest, ATTAC France, with 25 000 individual members and 50 collective members, uses an associational model of decision making (few involved, with voting heavily used). The other two, considerably smaller with around 15 000 individual members, use a deliberative representative model (few involved with consensus/deliberation heavily used) of organization. Does this mean that we can claim the triumph of the iron law of oligarchy in explaining the differences between the larger and smaller ATTAC groups? If ATTAC Germany and ATTAC Italy were to expand by another 10 000 members, would they too become associational?

This does not seem to be the case. Size seems to have no discernable impact on the decision-making styles adopted by different ATTAC organizations. One of the problems of assuming that size leads to associational behaviour in this case is that ATTAC France was never anything other than associational, even when it was a small, nascent organization. As it has grown, its *oligarchy score* has reduced, suggesting increased oligarchy, and the discontent of its grass-roots has become apparent. In addition, ATTAC Germany and Italy learned of the unpopularity of associational decision making from their progenitor, developing slightly more deliberative decision-making styles as a result of their reflections upon ATTAC France's experience, rather than because of their size. Nevertheless, all three ATTACs have low *oligarchy scores*, which, as we shall see, have proven unpopular with their rank-and-file activists.

ATTAC was born in France in 1998, the brainchild of Bernard Cassen, and founded by a number of leaders of aid, trade and development organizations. Its initial imperative was to ensure a tax on international financial institutions to create a development fund and prevent stock market speculation. It has since broadened out to campaign more generally against unfair trade regulations, the World Trade Organization, tax havens, and other international development issues.

For the first two years of its existence, ATTAC France continued to work according to its founding constitution, which was ill equipped to cope with the large network of local groups that rapidly developed. The problem, from the local groups' perspective, was that they were not invited to participate in decision making, which seemed to be dominated by the leadership. Thus, several key characteristics of 'beautiful' decision making – being open, inclusive, and plural – were missing. As a result, local groups began to 'continually denounce the absence of democracy' (Combes and Ekovich 2006, p. 123). As a result of local groups' dissatisfaction with the 'democratic' practices of the national organization, a Board of Directors–Local Committees (CA–CL) was established to research ways to alter the constitution to give local groups more substantive opportunities for input. Local group members could thus be admitted to the Board of ATTAC; but this was only a partial success because they were still not allowed to vote.

Dissent increased when minority initiatives for more participation for locals and for participatory budgeting failed, and, in 2004, the rift between the local and national organization nearly reached a crisis point. The critical moment seemed to be when the leadership was heavily suspected of secretly arranging the constitution of 100 per cent No Global Candidates for the European elections, with vigorous opposition among national and local board members alike. Thus, it became apparent that decision making in ATTAC France lacked the 'beautiful' qualities of accountability and transparency, further fuelling discontent.

Although the initiative was abandoned, it, and the preceding events, left a legacy of two opposing factions: one consisting of current leaders unwilling to relinquish power to locals, and another of the founding members (leaders of associations and unions) who wanted locals to have more influence and the power to join as co-presidents. At the 2005 general assembly, 70 per cent of participants claimed that they wanted better representation for grass-roots members, and 59 per cent were in favour of co-presidency. Despite this, the apparently oligarchic leadership remains intact (Reiter 2006; Combes and Ekovich 2006). Contrary to idealized small group 'beautiful' politics, a small unaccountable leadership continues to dominate, the leaders stubbornly cling on to their leadership roles, and inclusivity is lacking. The result of this internal power struggle, as Schumacher (1973) would predict, is a 'desert of frustration' amid its activists.

It is not just in France where local ATTAC activists have decried and become frustrated by the lack of democracy of their mother organization. In Germany, local group members can only attend assembly meetings as delegates, and participation is highly formalized. In Italy, ATTAC sought to be democratic and open from its conception. However, it soon had to compromise on deliberation in the interests of efficiency, adopting the slogan 'federative but not fragmented, participative but not inefficient' (Reiter 2006). Although ATTAC Italia seeks to make decisions mostly by consensus, it is prepared to vote if required. It is also far more centralized than some Italian activists desire, and it has been criticized for being too vertical. These criticisms are not without substance – the national council has relevant power, it discusses and decides which issues are of interest to the network, and it sets the agenda for the assembly and decides on themes for consultation. This is very different from 'beautiful' small group decision making. Yet, in Italy and Germany, the leadership is considerably more accommodating to participants than are the centralized leaders of ATTAC France, who are unwilling to relinquish their power.

There are three other important points to raise with respect to ATTAC. First, it is illustrative of how Schumacher's (1973) call for the need to strike a balance between orderliness and creative freedom is recognized in practice. This is expressed most clearly in ATTAC Italia's almost synonymous slogan: 'federative but not fragmented, participative but not inefficient'. The challenge seems especially acute in the case of ATTAC France, which seems to prefer organizational efficiency over participation of the grass-roots. The second point relates to the reasons for the democratic crisis in ATTAC France, which became manifest for two reasons: the internal power struggle between (committees of) locals and the centralized leadership, and the rapid expansion of an organization ill prepared for a model of participatory democracy. Third, the case of ATTAC (particularly in France) highlights the gap between its own praxis and its critique of IFIs. ATTAC France, for example, claims that:

> We are out of reach of the direct citizen control. Furthermore, at the time of neo-liberal globalization, the decision-making power is concentrated in the hands of international political institutions (G7, European Commission, IMF, World Bank, WTO) which are widely out of reach of democratic control. (http://france.attac.org)

However, it could equally be charged that ATTAC France's decision-making power is concentrated in Bernard Cassen's hands, which are also widely out of the reach of democratic control. Thus, ATTAC France might consider taking steps to remedy the situation before it can be accused of failing to practise what it preaches. Such a discrepancy between discourse and praxis has the potential to destroy the progress made in building up a successful movement organization. At the time of the 2005 general assembly, 17 per cent of activists had already left (Combes and Ekovich 2006), many of them presumably disillusioned with its lack of participatory democracy.

Indymedia

In contrast to ATTAC, Indymedia has been able to remain relatively efficient, yet at the same time participatory, even with many members. Perhaps the best example of an organization that bucks the tendency for sizeable organizations to implement formal and exclusive structures for decision making, Indymedia is a network of free communication that seeks to deliver 'passionate tellings of truth' through stories uploaded from independent journalists and activists across the globe. It is facilitated through Internet discussion lists and an open access Web site that can allow access to any Internet user.

Our survey of the democratic practices of GJMOs included three Indymedia collectives: Indymedia Italia, EH (Euskal Herria, Basque Country), and UK (within the UK, but the acronym stands for United Kollectives), all classified as deliberative participative. This is despite Indymedia Italia being substantially larger in membership (with 400 members) than Indymedia EH (which has only ten). All three organizations have *oligarchy scores* of 1, which means that all members get a say in the decisions regardless of organizational size. This case clearly defies the 'iron law': size does not, in this case, seem to lead to oligarchic tendencies. But how has Indymedia managed to escape the clutches of the iron law?

Indymedia groups such as Indymedia EH meet face-to-face to conduct deliberative discussions. Others, however, like Indymedia Italia, make decisions through their email list, which contains up to 400 members, by conducting what Reiter (2006, p. 260) referred to as a 'telematic assembly', in addition to physical meetings. In the UK, Indymedia has formalized some of its decision making because of its concerns about the lack of editorial quality, structurelessness, and the networks' early development into a 'free for all' (Spicer and Perkmann 2008, p. 18). Yet, even in the UK, it remains firmly committed to the principles of horizontality and transparency, and it prioritizes the production of news items over bureaucracy (Spicer and Perkmann 2008, p. 13). Like in all Indymedias, there has been an attempt to purposively avoid the model of hierarchical decision making caricatured in the praxis of many groups of the Left (Alt.Media.Res Collective 2007).

At a global level, Indymedia has been experimenting with a 'spokes council' model, with at-a-distance facilitation made possible by the use of electronic tools for communication. Conducting inclusive and consensus based decision making in the global Indymedia network of approximately 5000 individuals, 150 groups, and 50 countries on six continents (Pickard 2006, p. 317) is no small feat. Yet, it has not been without some, albeit slight, divergence from Indymedia's founding concept of 'principles of unity', which express what Pickard (2006a, p. 316) calls 'radical democratic principles' of 'inclusivity, plurality, diversity, openness, transparency and accountability'.[7] Principle six from this informal constitutional document is the most relevant to this chapter. It states that:

> All IMCs [Indymedia Collectives] recognize the importance of process to social change and are committed to the development of non-hierarchical and anti-authoritarian relationships, from interpersonal relationships to group dynamics. Therefore, [all IMCs] shall organize themselves collectively and be committed to the principles of consensus decision-making and the development of a direct, participatory democratic process that is transparent to its membership.

However, as Pickard (2006b, p. 26) points out, the notion of consensus may be defined differently by different groups, with some even seriously considering majority voting. Furthermore, it is difficult to reconcile cultural and international differences and debates about strategy. Overall, though, it seems that even in periods of disagreement, the norms of consensus and participation remain guiding principles, despite many tensions. Pickard (2006a), for example, discusses how the global Indymedia network managed to survive a difficult debate about whether it should accept Ford Foundation funding for an international conference in 2002.[8] Indeed, the global network has been at pains to maintain these principles in cases in which organizational efficiency and rationality may have been preferable, again making clear the need to balance efficiency and creativity. 'Yet...', as Pickard (2006a, p. 316) points out, 'despite such formidable obstacles, the IMC network somehow continues to function and thrive'.

Indymedia's open, inclusive, and consensus-based decision-making style can, in no small part, be attributed to being *au fait* with electronic forms of decision making that make direct democracy possible even in larger groups (on parties, see Budge 1996). Open email lists and Internet relay chat rooms make open and horizontal decisions possible in a manner that face-to-face meetings could not easily achieve alone, partly because of the limits of physical space. Despite its unprecedented success at radical democracy, it is certainly the case that, in any Indymedia, those with the most time or expertise may become de facto leaders. But certain organizational practices, similar to those recommended by Freeman (1970) to prevent informal oligarchy in informal groups, have developed to keep the power in check. In Seattle Indymedia, for example, these practices include the introduction of 'vibes watchers', who can raise awareness of latent power structures, or of non-vocalized discontent; rotating schedules for spokes positions and facilitation; and 'empowering certain groups and individuals to operate in ad hoc fashion beyond consensus, and relying on rational self selection' (Pickard 2006a).

So, although it has sometimes been difficult for Indymedia to prioritize 'beautiful' decision making over efficiency, it has been successful most of the time. Therefore, Indymedia is almost a textbook archetype of 'large but beautiful' decision making, with its open and participative ethos, its skill-sharing agenda, its rotation of leadership roles, and the existence of rules to prevent the 'tyranny of the structurelessness'. This is all made possible by its commitment to radical democratic principles, which have become entrenched norms throughout the organization, and its innovative use of the Internet.

Conclusion: Is large or small beautiful?

Looking at our entire sample of 208 GJMOs, it generally seems to be true that larger organizations – whether measured by budget, numbers of voluntary or paid staff, or number of members – tend to be more oligarchic and less 'beautiful' than their smaller counterparts. It is simply untrue that all large organizations become oligarchic. Certainly, there are compromises to be made in balancing organizational efficiency and participation; but some large organizations do surprisingly well at including their members. The most notable success story is that of Indymedia, which, in various locations, independent of size and organizational dilemmas, seems to hold true to its deliberative and consensus-based decision-making model. Several things make this possible: commitment to the 'principles of unity'; the Internet; and a set of rules that help to avoid oligarchy. Thus, large is not always ugly, especially in the presence of working groups and/or a spokes council model and with innovative use of the Internet.

In recent years, some large organizations such as Friends of the Earth in England, Wales, and Northern Ireland have become more participatory conterminously with the rise of the GJM, as they aim to keep apace with modern political innovations such as those expressed in the Aarhus Convention (a United Nations Economic Commission for Europe treaty that seeks to improve engagement in decision making through provision of information, widening the scope of public participation, and providing access to justice), and with new SMOs demanding more grass-roots involvement. Increasingly, SMOs are acting upon demands for more involvement from grass-roots members, often with the assistance of the Internet to facilitate broader participation. GJMOs are also pushed towards wider participation by their need to keep abreast with trends in the broader movement: as more GJMs turn towards participative (and deliberative) decision making, it becomes a more attractive decision-making model, which diffuses through the movement (Saunders and Andretta 2009).

Just as it is untrue that all large organizations inevitably become oligarchic, so is it also untrue that all small organizations approximate the perfect picture of democracy in action. They may well have principles and practices of consensus and deliberation, but very few seem to have specific rules to ensure that their organizations do not become vulnerable to implicit and unintentional oligarchies or power structures. Yet, that does not mean to say that small cannot approximate beauty. As Freeman (1970) suggested, attempting to share skills to increase equality, increased inclusivity and diffusion of information are all helpful. However, the formation of friendship groups and informal oligarchy is hard to avoid – some participants will always be more involved and/or committed than others, and natural friendship groups are inevitable and not necessarily 'ugly'. To reduce tendencies towards 'ugly' decision making, best practice would be for participants in small groups to at least be aware of inevitable implicit power structures and to attempt to militate against them by fostering inclusivity and equality as much as possible.

However, GJMOs must not forget that perfect democracy is illusory – it simply cannot be achieved. For small groups, friendships and informal power structures are virtually unavoidable. For large groups, the Internet is a useful tool for avoiding oligarchy; but it should not be forgotten that access to the new technologies remains uneven due to the 'digital divide' – which in practice means that white, wealthy, young males remain the social group most likely to use the Internet (Norris 2001), hardly fostering inclusivity among ethnicities, genders, and classes. The compromise solution for both is to aspire to as much 'real' participation as possible, allowing for creative freedom from all those who desire involvement. For large groups, the most meaningful way to allow such freedom to flourish is to create smaller working groups and/or to implement a spokes council system. However, even in such a system, the more experienced or the most confident can become informal oligarchs, suggesting, again, the need for skill-sharing and/or confidence building for all movement participants.

However, prioritizing creative freedom can make organizations less efficient. In the background of most activist debates about internal organizational decision making is the dilemma over whether to compromise *creative freedom* or *orderliness*, or, to put it another way, *participation* or *efficiency*. Some organizations have a clear preference for creative freedom and participation over orderliness, as in Indymedia, where consensus and participatory decision-making strategies seem to prevail even in the face of conflict. Other organizations prefer orderliness over participation, particularly emphasized by the case of ATTAC France. Others still seek a balance between the two, as does ATTAC Italia, which seeks to be 'federative but not fragmented, participative but not inefficient' (Reiter 2006).

Although size may determine oligarchic tendencies to an extent, there are other important factors too. The ideological approach of the organization seems to matter, as does its preferred approach to organizational matters. Formal left-wing organizations can only hope to create the type of revolution they are seeking through hierarchically controlled organizations with a largely passive rank-and-file that follows a clearly defined chain of command. If an organization seeks to make quick and efficient decisions, the consensus model will clearly be ill favoured. Yet it should not be forgotten that, as the case study of ATTAC illustrates, organizational efficiency can come at the expense of discontent from members, supporters, and local group activists.

Probably the most important lesson that GJMOs might learn from this is the importance of practising what they preach with regards to democracy. ATTAC (especially in France) seeks radical changes in the manner in which decisions are made by undemocratic IFIs, while at the same time it does not, or cannot, practise its ideal in the microcosm of its own organization. If ATTAC wants democracy at the global level to be 'beautiful', it should perhaps try to prefigure that manner of organization in its own decision making. Although decision making in Indymedia is by no means perfect, it provides a model to which most large GJMs could aspire, and from which ATTAC, seemingly, could learn much.

Notes

1. Many thanks to Donatella della Porta for her extremely helpful comments on earlier drafts of this chapter. In this, as in the other chapters, by Global Justice Movement we refer to the broad movement, not the British organization with this name.
2. Jordan and Maloney are actually wrong about Friends of the Earth, which is much more participatory – through its local groups' network – than they assume (Saunders 2007).
3. Where the president was the main decision-making body, the equation was $O = 1/m$, where O stands for 'oligarchy score', m stands for the number of members of the organization, and 1 refers to the one person (the president) making the decisions. Where the executive committee (or similar) was the

main decision-making body, the equation was $O = 5/m$, where 5 refers to the estimated number of members of the executive committee (often a chair, a vice-chair, a secretary, a treasurer and a co-opted member). Where a thematic group was the main decision-making body, the equation was $O = 10/m$, where 10 refers to the estimated number of people in a thematic group. Where the assembly/open meeting was the main decision-making body, the equation was $O = a/m$, where a refers to the number of participants in the assembly as given by respondents. A score higher than one indicates that there are more participants in the main decision-making body than there are members of the organization – this occurs, for example, in organizations in which the assembly is the main decision-making body, and in which non-members can participate.

4. These figures are based on interviews with organizational representatives in the year 2005. Where respondents gave ranges (for example, 'somewhere between 10 000 and 15 000 members'), the mean score was calculated (in this example 12 500 members) and used for analysis.

5. The best measures of 'largeness' are staff numbers and individual members – at least half of the organizations in these categories are 'large' by the other measures too. The best measures of 'smallness' are staff numbers and budget; over three-fifths of organizations with 'small' numbers of staff are 'small' by the three other measures of smallness, and more than half of the organizations with a small budget are small according to the other measures.

6. NB: Discriminant analysis and regression failed to predict a model or significant effects based on variables measuring organizational size. This was presumably because of a number of outliers in the data that the author was reluctant to erase as this would have downplayed the diversity of organizational sizes within the sample.

7. For more information and debate on the 'principles of unity', see Pickard (2006b).

8. Indymedia Argentina initially blocked the proposal, and it was finally cancelled.

7
Forms of Action of Global Justice Movement Groups: Do Conceptions and Practices of Democracy Matter?[1]

Dieter Rucht and Simon Teune

To make their critique of neoliberal politics heard, the Global Justice Movement Organizations (GJMOs) have used a wide array of forms of action, ranging from prayers and petitions, to marches and blockades, to the destruction of property. This complex grammar of activity mirrors the often proclaimed diversity of the movements advocating a just and peaceful globalization. Yet it is very unlikely that the forms of action actually used spread randomly across the GJMOs. Rather, the selection of different kinds of activities from the available stock of means is influenced by structural and ideational factors. Thus far, repertoires of action have mainly been studied with regard to choices of individuals and in protest event analysis. Studies exploring repertoires of movement organizations – our central reference point – have tended to focus on small samples (for example, Carmin and Balser 2002; Crossley 2002; Meyer 2004; for exceptions, Minkoff 1999, Edwards and Foley 2003). We add to this literature with an analysis of the link between GJMOs (and their environments) and their action repertoires.

In this chapter, we will first clarify our main categories, offering typologies of forms of (protest) action and theoretical arguments about the conditions and variables that impact upon the choice of kinds of actions. Second, we will present our database and the way in which we operationalized the forms of action chosen by GJMOs. Third, we provide a descriptive account of the empirical distribution of forms of action, our dependent variable, and how these forms are co-related. The fourth and main section is devoted to the analysis of factors, both internal and external to GJMOs, that correlate with their action repertoires. Finally, we summarize and interpret our main findings.

Conceptual and theoretical reflections

Forms of action can be understood very broadly, including all kinds of internal activities that movement groups undertake (for example, researching facts, discussing problems, introducing new members, and networking with allies). Our focus, however, is on outwardly-directed actions that are meant to publicly promote the group's cause. Because we are studying social movement groups, many of these activities fall under the rubric of collective protest or collective contention.

Forms of action can be conceptualized at different levels of aggregation (Rucht 1990), ranging from very specific activities (for example, tabling, street theatre, and hunger strikes) to somewhat broader categories (for example, confrontational acts, violent acts) to generic types or general strategies (for example, public education or protest). We – that is, the multinational group of researchers[2] who conceptualized the research and collected the data on which this chapter draws – did not create a fine-grained list of actions that might include dozens of categories. Still, we remain on a relatively specific level in distinguishing some basic and frequently used activities such as demonstration, strike and occupation of a building.

These activities are elements of what Tilly (1986a, p. 2) has called a repertoire of contention, 'a set of means [a group] has for making claims of different kinds on different individuals or groups'. He suggested the concept of action repertoire as a grammar of interaction between a challenger group and its target groups in a given historical context. This repertoire can be analysed in terms of breadth – that is, the range of alternative means available in a given situation – and structure, exploring the interrelation of different forms of action as compatible, distant, and so on (Ennis 1987). Tilly assumes that groups do not dispose of the full range of the theoretically available repertoire but only of that 'limited set of routines that are learned, shared, and acted out through a relatively deliberative process of choice. Repertoires are learned cultural creations, but they do not descend from abstract philosophy or take shape as result of political propaganda; they emerge from struggle' (1995, p. 26). Accordingly, the actions chosen by a single group or a broader set of groups also tell us something about how these groups perceive a conflict and their targets. Among the potentially available means, an organization chooses a limited subset that it can handle as an adequate and conducive tactic to reach, or at least to come closer to, its goals.

Different forms of action rest on different requirements and carry different messages. Consider just a few examples. The strike is a classical means of – usually legal – protest typically organized by a particular social group (workers, employees) to make claims (higher salary, better working conditions, and so on) vis-à-vis an employer. With the exception of a genuine political strike, state authorities are not, or not directly, addressed. This contrasts with an act of civil disobedience – for example, the blocking of a gate to a military camp to protest the deployment of nuclear weapons. In this case, the form of protest is not inherently bound to a specific social group. Also, it does not target a private enterprise but rather state authorities. Moreover, it usually involves the breaking of rules. Hence, it is an illegal and therefore non-institutionalized protest activity. In the case of either a strike or a blockade, the protest can be very demanding for the participants and may imply the risk of sanctions, for example, losing a job or being sentenced by a judge. Personal investment and risk is virtually absent when it comes, for example, to signing a petition urging a local administration to create a children's playground. Moreover, this activity does not require the physical co-presence of all protestors, nor does it have a disruptive character.

In various attempts to categorize and systematize different forms of contentious actions, social scientists have used scales with varying forms of graduation. Tarrow (1989, p. 69), for instance, presents a tripartite categorization separating 'conventional' from 'confrontational/symbolic' and 'violent' forms of collective action based on a more refined list of forms of action. In their classification of political participation of individuals, Marsh (1977, p. 41) and, with some modifications, Dalton (1988, p. 64) have located forms of 'unconventional political behaviour' on a categorical scale with the poles of 'conventional politics: voting, lobbying, formal interest groups, etc.' on the one hand, and 'sabotage, guerrilla warfare, hijacking, assassination, bombing, revolution, kidnapping, war' on the other. According to Dalton, between these extremes, four groups of 'unorthodox' activities can be located: (1) petitions, slogans, lawful demonstrations; (2) boycotts; (3) unofficial strikes, rent strikes; and (4) unlawful demonstrations, occupations, damage, violence. The forms attributed to items 2 to 4 are defined as direct action, those attributed to 3 and 4 as illegal action, and those in category 4 as violent.[3] It is assumed that a threshold must be crossed to move from a more conventional to a more unconventional kind of behaviour.

Survey research has shown that for contemporary democracies in a situation of normalcy (hence, in the absence of deep crises or even civil war), the more radical an activity, the less people participate (Dalton 1988, p. 65; Jennings et al. 1990). This, presumably, has not only to do with the greater risk of sanctions in cases of radical action but also with the moral values of most citizens. To them, breaking laws is unacceptable or only acceptable in very special cases. And only a tiny proportion of the public approves the use of violence by political actors to reach their goals.

A categorization somewhat similar to that of Marsh and Dalton can also be applied to political groups such as GJMOs. When considering the total of GJMOs, they occupy the wide range from 'conventional' politics to moderate forms of 'unorthodox' to certain forms of 'violent behaviour' (for example, violent clashes with police, arson attacks), though with the exclusion of the most destructive forms of guerrilla warfare, bombing, and so on.[4] Yet, as the literature on the GJMs suggests, the organizational field of these movements is ideologically and otherwise very diverse (della Porta 2007c; Sommier et al. 2008b), so that most groups are far from combining all these forms of action. In specific situations as well as regarding more general strategic preferences, these groups have an affinity to some forms of action but not to others: they are likely to stick to a certain 'style' or sub-field of action (Crossley 2002, p. 51). This is because the choice of an action repertoire is not a mere instrumental requirement made in reaction to a given situation. It is predetermined by a habitus[5] that makes the use of one kind of action appear almost natural while alternative forms are perceived as unreasonable and inappropriate, and therefore not even taken into consideration.

This argument is the point of departure for our first hypothesis. It is commonly thought that some groups, particularly the segment comprising the more formal NGOs, have a pragmatic tendency and are ready to interact and even to co-operate with both state administrations and private corporations (Rucht 2006). By contrast, radical groups refuse such co-operation and tend towards the use of disruptive means, though not necessarily excluding all forms of moderate action. In Germany, for example, we have shown the existence of two clusters with quite different positions which, however, are bridged by a relatively strong intermediate cluster that is ambivalent towards both the moderate and the radical branch (Rucht et al. 2007). Because this intermediate cluster is weak or almost absent in some other countries (for example, France), we expect the GJMOs, with regard to their preferred forms of action, to fall into two (moderate or disruptive) or three (moderate, confrontational, disruptive) broad categories (hypothesis 1).

Regarding the question of which factors shape or even determine the action repertoire, the available state of knowledge is quite uneven. On the micro-level, that is, the participation of individuals, both theoretical assumptions and empirical findings are based on extensive research. For example, it has been shown that highly educated people have a greater interest in politics, and are more engaged in both 'conventional' and 'unconventional' political participation. Also, it has been found that well educated and young people have a higher propensity to take part in unconventional (and more radical) actions than less educated and/or older people. As a rule, however, the questions asked in this kind of survey research decontextualize political participation so that we usually do not know for which political aims, in which organizational framework, and in which specific conflict the respondents participated. On the level of social movement organizations, the knowledge about repertoire choices is rather fragmentary (Clemens and Minkoff 2004). We assume that factors directly bound to the organization (for example, ideology, political aims, organizational type, structure, and resources) as well as contextual factors (for example, political regime, orientation of the government, availability of allies) come into play.

This leads us to further hypotheses. We assume that so called anti-systemic groups (Arrighi et al. 1989), in our case anti-capitalist groups, favour confrontational forms of action, whereas the opposite holds for groups with a moderate (reformist) ideology (hypothesis 2). We also assume that groups tending towards a 'strong', participatory, or grass-roots democracy – both within their own ranks and on the societal level at large – are more inclined towards the use of confrontational action than groups favouring representative democracy (hypothesis 3). Moreover, the former groups have a greater tendency towards more formal and professional structures (hypothesis 4). Finally, the context of social movement organizations is of paramount importance to understanding repertoire choices. While variations within a geographical region are best explained by SMO structures and values, variation between regions can be traced back to national trajectories in political culture and political opportunities (Meyer 2004). We suppose that organizations in countries with a strong left–right cleavage and/or countries ruled by a decidedly conservative government have a greater propensity to confrontational forms of action than groups in other countries (hypotheses 5 and 6).[6]

Dataset and operationalization

The analysis presented in this chapter rests primarily on interviews with GJMO representatives in six countries and on the transnational level (N = 210).[7] In telephone or face-to-face interviews, representatives or activists were asked about their organization (size, structure, and values), its engagement in the protests, and its relationship with state institutions. The GJMOs' tactical choices were the subject of one question phrased: 'Has your group engaged in any of the following forms of action within the last five years?' The related list comprised eight kinds of action[8] and included the option to write in other forms of action. For the analysis, we added to the responses on this question the results for the item on lobbying that was introduced in the interview as a strategic choice.[9] Although lobbying was specified as a 'main strategy' to reach the organization's goals, we assume that the common practice of meeting political and administrative representatives can also be treated as a tactical choice similar to organizing a demonstration or blocking a road (see Taylor and Dyke 2004, p. 263). No question about violent forms of action was asked in the interview, as we assumed that GJMOs rarely resort to violence and, even if so, their representatives would be hesitant to admit their group's participation in the destruction of property or the use of violence against people.

To determine the independent variables, we can rely on answers from the interviews and, to a minor extent, on data from an analysis of the GJMOs' written documents. On this basis, we are able to reconstruct internal structures and values on the one hand and information about the groups' relation to their environments on the other.

To interpret the results of the analysis, we must be clear about the composition of the sample. The selection criteria for the sample – to choose GJMOs that are 'most relevant' with regard to a certain sector in the national context (for details of the sampling strategy, see the introductory chapter) – favour large and formalized organizations that are visible on the national level. For countries whose GJMs inherit a strong horizontal network structure from the new social movements (such as Switzerland, Spain, and Germany) rather than being dominated by parties and trade unions (as in France and Italy), an analysis of contentious repertoires would have brought different results if the sample had been tailored individually for every national branch of the GJMs. However, this strategy would have reduced the ability to compare movement sectors across countries.

Descriptive findings on action repertoires: Not dichotomy but plurality

A first glance at the data shows that GJMOs use multiple forms of action. When asked which kinds of action their group had used repeatedly, the interviewees named up to nine action forms (that is, all options offered by the interviewer). Three-quarters of the respondents named more than two tactics. The distribution of the most common forms of action in the sample has already been presented in the introductory chapter of this volume (see Table 1.7). As shown, demonstration (almost 80 per cent) and petition (around 76 per cent) are used by a very large proportion of all organizations, while confrontational tactics such as blockade and occupation have been applied by roughly one-quarter of them.

This first and rough finding needs to be further investigated. In order to test our first hypothesis, we ran a hierarchical cluster analysis interrelating the action forms on the basis of interviewees' responses. The analysis confirms the distinction between two sets of actions. The validity of the theoretical distinction between confrontational and nonconfrontational forms of action is supported insofar as strike, blockade, boycott, occupation, and civil disobedience emerge as one distinct cluster, while petition (which includes the collection of signatures), demonstration, lobbying, and artistic or cultural performance comprise another (see Figure 7.1).[10]

In the first cluster, blockade and the occupation of buildings, the two action forms with the highest costs (in terms of potential confrontation with the police and juridical sanctions), emerge as most proximately linked. Civil disobedience, a term that allows more room for interpretation but usually implies the violation of laws or other formal rules, is close to the pair of blockade and occupation. Strike, as a highly regulated form of protest, and boycott add to the cluster. Notwithstanding their lower intensity, civil disobedience and strike are still confrontational in the sense that they are designed to harm the adversary, either economically or symbolically.

The second class of action forms links demonstration and petition most closely. As seen in Table 7.1, both tactics are most common. Artistic or cultural performances as a creative, public display of dissent are associated next. Lobbying, a tactic not addressed to the public and usually invisible to outsiders, has the largest distance from other forms of action, but still is part of the second cluster.

As stated above, the distinction between confrontational and nonconfrontational (or moderate) forms of action is quite common in the

Rescaled distance cluster combine

Label	Num	0	5	10	15	20	25

```
Label              Num    0         5        10        15        20        25
                          +---------+---------+---------+---------+---------+
Blockade            5      ─┐
Occupation          6      ─┘ ┐
Civ. disobedience   7      ───┤ ┐
Strike              3      ─────┤                                            ┐
Boycott             4      ─────┘                                            │
Petition            1      ───┐                                              │
Demonstration       2      ───┤ ┐                                            │
Performance         8      ─────┤                                            ┘
Lobbying            9      ─────┘
```

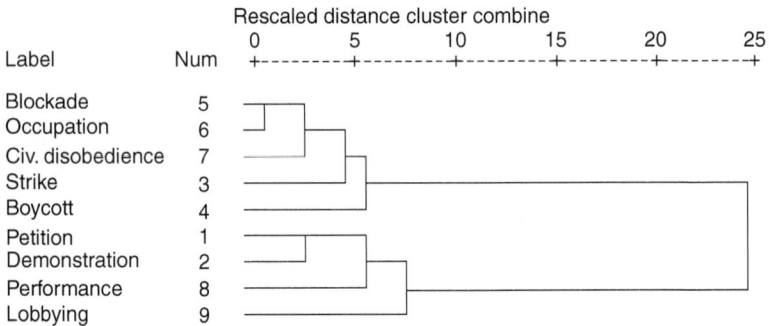

Figure 7.1 Dendrogram depicting results from the hierarchical cluster analysis, N = 210 (GJMOs)

analysis of social movements' tactics.[11] However, scholars have been inclined to understand this distinction as a dichotomy. This is mainly due to its use in the study of protest events on an aggregate level. When action repertoires are analysed on a macro level, protests, on the basis of newspaper reports, are usually attributed to a categorical scale in which the dichotomous distinction between non-violent/violent, moderate/radical, conventional/unconventional is used to undertake comparisons and to analyse trends.[12]

A look at the meso level, however, reveals that for GJMOs, moderate and confrontational forms of action are not mutually exclusive. Non-confrontational action, that is, the use of at least one form attributed to this category, is common among virtually all interviewed groups. In addition to these, many groups also used confrontational tactics to make their case. Of 202 organizations, 130 (64.4 per cent) deployed at least one confrontational form of action in addition to their moderate repertoire. This finding contradicts our first hypothesis. GJMOs do not fall into groups using moderate forms of action and other groups using radical means. Instead, confrontational action forms are appended to the moderate repertoire. The case of the German Bund für Umwelt und Naturschutz Deutschland (BUND) illustrates the parallel use of different action forms: in the 1990s, this environmental NGO participated in the UN conferences on environment and development, a milestone in global governance. At the same time, the group took part in protest activities outside the conference venues to criticize the official summits.

For the remainder of this chapter, we assume the parallel use of moderate and confrontational forms of action and distinguish between those groups that use non-confrontational forms exclusively and those that add confrontational means to their repertoire of action. The analysis of

Table 7.1 Forms of action used by moderate and confrontational GJMOs (%; N = 203)

Action forms	Proportion of groups using only *moderate* actions (N = 73)	Proportion of groups using also *confrontational* actions (N = 130)
Moderate forms		
Petition	72.6	81.5
Demonstration	57.5	96.2
Performance	49.3	69.2
Lobbying	63.0	52.3
Confrontational forms		
Strike	–	39.2
Boycott	–	50.8
Blockade	–	44.6
Occupation	–	39.2
Civil disobedience	–	66.2

repertoire choices will be made on the basis of this simple bisection of the sample.

Probably because groups engaged in confrontational action tend to be highly motivated and generally exhibit a high level of activity, the proportion of groups that make use of the moderate repertoire is generally higher among those groups that also use confrontational action (see Table 7.1). The only exception to this pattern is the use of lobbying, which is more common in groups with an exclusive use of moderate actions (63.0 versus 52.3 per cent).

The activities that interviewees added to the pre-existing list give an impression of the actual breadth of the groups' protest repertoires. For example, GJMO representatives named speeches at stockholders' meetings, alternative walking tours, protest camps, calls for ethical consumption, and street theatre. Adding to these, many of the activities mentioned in the interviews reveal the importance of knowledge-based forms of action. GJMO representatives specified events such as conferences and speeches as well as leafleting, film screenings, and the production of publications as major forms of action.

The influence of democratic values and structures

Are the internal practices and preferences for particular organizational models (our first set of independent variables) related to the use of moderate or confrontational actions (our dependent variable), as exemplified by grass-roots groups practising civil disobedience (see, for example, Epstein 1991)? The correlations between these sets of variables show that organizational values and forms indeed make a difference. GJMOs embracing horizontality and 'first-person-politics' are more likely to engage in confrontational actions than those that are hierarchically structured and practise the principle of delegation. This connection becomes obvious when the four-fold table based on the degree of delegation and the consensus versus the majority principle (see Chapter 1, Table 1.8) is crossed with the dependent variable. The two fields that imply a low level of delegation (the 'assembleary' and the 'participative deliberative' model) correlate strongly with the use of confrontational forms of action (see Table 7.2). Four of the five groups preferring the assembleary model also use confrontational actions, and only one group applies moderate actions only.

More specifically, the inclusiveness of the main decision-making body is related to the kind of action used. GJMOs that decide primarily in assemblies are more prone to confrontational tactics such as blockade, boycott, or civil disobedience than organizations in which decisions are made in other settings. This relation found on a structural level is confirmed for the preferences for specific organizational models and related procedures: those GJMOs endorsing the idea of 'non-hierarchical decision making' are less likely to restrict themselves to the moderate repertoire of action than the other groups. While degree of delegation of power seems to be quite a good predictor for action repertoire, the other axis in the four-fold table does not emerge as a relevant factor. The difference between those groups that make decisions by majority rule and those adopting the consensus principle is not mirrored in the use of moderate and confrontational forms of action, respectively. If we look at the use of the consensus versus majority principle in general, or at the decision-making method of the assembly in particular, differences between these categories are not significant.

Coming back to hypothesis 3, our analysis confirms that democratic principles within the groups have an influence on the preferred action repertoire. Those GJMOs that embrace horizontal decision making and that are – supposedly – critical of the representative system at large tend to use confrontational forms of action to make their case.

The influence of the groups' themes and structural characteristics

In addition to values, which contribute to particular forms of decision making and organizational structure, factors directly related to cultural and structural properties of the organization can also be expected to

Table 7.2 Organizational forms and forms of action (%)

	GJMOs using exclusively moderate actions	GJMOs using also confrontational actions	N
Organizational model (0. 183°)[a]			
Assembleary	20.0	80.0	5
Participative deliberative	23.5	76.5	51
Associational	38.6	61.4	70
Deliberative representative	44.9	55.1	69
Delegation of power (0. 193°)			
Low delegation	23.2	76.8	56
Medium low delegation	42.6	57.4	47
Medium high delegation	46.4	53.6	56
High delegation	35.0	65.0	40
Main decision-making body (0. 292**)			
President/leader/ secretary	68.4	31.6	19
Executive committee or similar body	35.4	64.6	82
Assembly/open meeting	22.2	77.8	54
Non-hierarchical decision making aspired (n.s.)			
Yes	27.0	73.0	74
No	39.5	60.5	81
Consensus vs. majority principle (n.s.)			
Non-consensus based	35.3	64.7	119
consensus based	27.8	72.2	36

Note: [a]The numbers given in brackets are correlation coefficients (Cramer's V, 2-tailed). °$p < 0.1$, *$p < 0.05$, **$p < 0.01$, ***$p < 0.001$.

influence the choice of action repertoires. For example, while organiza-tions based on mass numbers of formal members are generally reluctant to use confrontational actions, many small and informal groups, not least because they usually lack nominal representatives that could be held accountable, may also be more inclined to apply confrontational actions – as can be seen with regard to the so-called autonomous groups from the radical Left.

To name a second assumption: organizations that are dependent on external subsidies, in particular those from state administrations, may tend to be more moderate in their action repertoires than financially independent groups. This connection has been observed, for example, for a number of organizations working on environmental or immigrant issues at the level of EU politics. The European Environmental Bureau, an EU-wide umbrella organization of national environmental groups, receives a large proportion of its running costs from the EU. Not by chance, it is definitely more moderate in both its claims and its activities than, say, Friends of the Earth Europe, which receives only little EU funding, and Greenpeace European Unit, which categorically refuses to accept money from state and industry. Finally, to name a third finding, Dalton (1994) showed a strong correlation between the ideological tendency of environmental groups and their preferred actions.

When organizations in our study are attributed to broader social movement segments according to the context in which they originated, their ideological leanings, and their affiliations to large networks, we find that groups belonging to the New Left/anarchist/autonomous sector are most inclined to confrontational actions (see Table 7.3). Next are those we coded as new social movements, followed by Old Left groups. While one might expect that groups focusing on peace and human rights would not strongly tend towards disruptive actions, it came as a surprise that the groups attributed to the 'new global' category – that is, the youngest cohort of groups that most directly relate to the core themes of the GJMs – are least inclined to use confrontational actions. This stands in stark contrast to images of those groups in most mass media. In addition, groups based on collective members are less prone to confrontational actions than those based on individual members. We assume that this latter result can be explained by the greater reluctance of organizations as a whole (compared to individuals) to take risks, particularly when organizations have a nominal leadership that can be made accountable for illegal acts. In addition, because of organizational logics and internal dynamics, it seems plausible that in the context of a GJMO it is easier for individual members than for collective members to support confrontational actions.

When looking only at the groups that are flatly anti-capitalist in their self-descriptions, we get an unsurprising and clear result. Anti-capitalist GJMOs are significantly more inclined to the use of confrontational actions than all other groups.

Table 7.3 Characteristics of GJMOs and forms of action (%)

	GJMOs using exclusively moderate forms	GJMOs using also confrontational forms	N
Movement area (0.276**)[a]			
New Left/anarchism/ autonomy	5.3	94.7	19
New social movement themes	24.0	76.0	25
Old Left	29.6	70.4	27
Solidarity/peace/ human rights	44.4	55.6	63
New global	45.5	54.5	66
Type of membership (0.234**)			
No individual membership	53.8	46.2	26
Individual membership	26.1	73.9	111
Anti-capitalist group (0.164°)			
Yes	19.4	80.6	36
No	37.8	62.2	119
Type of organization (0.291**)			
Unions	9.5	90.5	21
Grass-roots SMOs	15.4	84.6	13
Parties, youth organizations and foundations	19.0	81.0	21
'Modern' networks	42.4	57.6	59
NGOs/formal SMOs	45.0	55.0	80
Co-operatives	57.1	42.9	7

Note: [a]The numbers given in brackets are correlation coefficients (Cramer's V, 2-tailed). °$p < 0.1$, *$p < 0.05$, **$p < 0.01$, ***$p < 0.001$.

Considering the type of organization, we find trade unions having the greatest propensity to engage in disruptive actions, followed by grass-roots social movement organizations, political parties and youth organizations. Least inclined towards disruptive actions are NGOs and formal social movement organizations, and co-operatives. The lead of trade unions does not necessarily indicate their high inclination towards disruptiveness in general. Rather, it stems from the use of strikes as the natural weapon of unions which, according to the cluster analysis presented above, was part of the confrontational cluster.

Other group characteristics, in particular group age (categorized in different ways), self-attribution to the GJMs, number of volunteers, size of budget, existence of fee-paying members, and existence of formal statutes, do not show a significant correlation with form of action.

The role of two further organizational characteristics – degree of formalization and professionalization – is worth exploring, especially because following the writings of Robert Michels (1962 [1911]) on the 'iron law of oligarchy', both organizational tendencies are often seen as resulting in ideological and tactical moderation, eventually causing the group to become 'toothless' (see also Piven and Cloward 1979). When five available indicators for formalization are combined, a relationship with form of action can be found (see Table 7.4). However, this finding is based on only two of the five indicators, namely the existence of a formally adopted programme and a formal membership (regardless of individuals or groups). These two characteristics clearly correlate with the use of confrontational actions. Even when trade unions (for which a programme and formal membership are the rule) are omitted from the analysis, the result holds. This finding contradicts Michels' assumption.[13] The only explanation we have is that radical groups may also adopt a formal resolution or a kind of programme and rely on formal membership, for example in most Trotskyist organizations.

With regard to professionalization, however, the results are fully in line with Michels' and many others' assumptions. More professionalized groups exhibit a greater tendency towards the moderate spectrum of actions. Significant correlations could be found when considering the number of paid members/staff and the existence of funds from outside (as opposed to funding by members).

Taken together, the findings on formalization and professionalization leave us with an inconclusive pattern when it comes to common assumptions about the link between organizational properties and forms of action. Michels' assumptions on the impact of professionalization on the action repertoire are confirmed, while for formalization the result is inconclusive.

The impact of the groups' environment

The activity of social movement organizations cannot be sufficiently explained by organizational properties. GJMOs, when expressing dissent and promoting political and social change, interact with a complex political environment, including target groups, opponents, and

Table 7.4 Measures of formalization (%)

	GJMOs using exclusively moderate actions	GJMOs using also confrontational actions	N
Normalized index of formalization (0.278*)[a]			
Low level	17.6	82.4	17
Moderate level	37.5	62.5	56
High level	11.4	88.6	35
Presence of formally adopted programme[b] (0.170*)			
Yes	24.2	75.8	66
No	40.4	59.6	89
Presence of formal membership[b] (0.253**)			
Yes	13.0	87.0	46
No	35.5	64.5	62
Number of paid members (0.214*)			
None	22.0	78.0	59
Up to 15	44.9	55.1	89
Between 15 and 100	32.1	67.9	28
More than 100	45.5	54.5	22
Financial sources (0.184*)			
Only from members	27.4	72.6	95
Receiving funds	45.1	54.9	102

Notes: [a]The numbers given in brackets are correlation coefficients (Cramer's V, 2-tailed). $°p < 0.1$, $*p < 0.05$, $**p < 0.01$, $***p < 0.001$. Normalized Index of Formalization = (Presence of Constitution + Presence of Document of Fundamental Values + Presence of Formally Adopted Programme + Formal Membership + Presence of Fee Paying Membership)/5. Low (< 0.34), Moderate (< 0.67). High (> 0.67). When unions are excluded from the analysis: Cramer's $V = 0.277$, $p = 0.029$.
[b]Only these components of the index are significant (this finding holds true when unions are excluded from the analysis).

third parties (Gamson 2004; Rucht 2004b). This is partly reflected in approaches stressing the relevance of both 'objective' and perceived political opportunities (for example, Tarrow 1998, chap. 5).

To begin with, the groups' structural and ideational characteristics referred to above are already influenced by external factors. For instance, groups that emphasize grass-roots democracy are likely to do so in contrast and as an alternative to representative institutions, which are perceived as offering very limited participation. In a similar vein, groups adhering to grass-roots democracy may have a critical view even on some of their allies who rely on more formal and hierarchical structures.

Likewise, GJMOs' struggles to adequately frame issues, to make marginalized groups visible, and to bring about or impede political decisions are based on prior experiences and imply ongoing interactions with reference groups such as governments, other political organizations, and an audience such as bystanders or the public at large. The way in which GJMOs address these reference groups, and thus the specific forms of action they choose, are shaped by their conceptions of democracy and social change. These concepts evolve and are transformed in an interactive process. The left-radical black bloc, for instance, which is present in many large protests of the GJMs, expresses detachment from and opposition to the state and its representatives. Even in its physical appearance, the black bloc symbolizes resistance to governmental attempts to embrace and pacify protest. State institutions react to the black bloc with the deployment of riot police, thus producing experiences of exclusion which, in turn, reaffirm the symbolic distance of the bloc vis-à-vis the state.

As expected, our data confirm that confrontational forms of action are more likely to be found in GJMOs that lack a close relationship with state institutions and do not aspire to such contacts (see Table 7.5). Organizations that mention the refusal of relationships with representative institutions as a positive value are more inclined to resort to confrontational actions. Obviously, for these groups there exist no positive relations with authorities that could be jeopardized by confrontations. More importantly, these groups perceive their confrontational repertoire as a means to affirm their challenger position in the field of conflict.

While confrontational action is correlated with the claim to refuse collaboration with state institutions regardless of geographic level, this relationship is significant only on the national and transnational levels. On the local level, however, there seems to be some ambivalence in interacting with administrations. This can be illustrated by the example of the Berlin Social Forum, which leans towards confrontational actions. Although the group would not consider collaboration with administrations a positive value, they had to engage in negotiations with the district mayor to safeguard the survival of a squatted social centre.

Such an experience of being forced into negotiations to reach short-term goals is common for a number of other groups with a predominantly confrontational action repertoire. Once GJMOs ask for state funds or intend to collaborate with state institutions – an aim that obviously not all groups share – they are likely to abstain from confrontational actions. The obvious reason for this self-restriction is the ambition to be acknowledged as moderate player and a reliable partner

187

Table 7.5 GJMOs' environments and forms of action (%)

	GJMOs using exclusively moderate forms	GJMOs using also confrontational forms	N
Refusal of relationship with representative institutions as positive value (0.176°)[a]			
No	36.2	63.8	141
Yes	7.1	92.9	14
Relation with transnational public institutions (0.284**)			
Refusal	8.3	91.7	24
Indifference	40.0	60.0	40
Collaboration	45.8	54.2	72
Relation with national public institutions (0.206°)			
Refusal	14.3	85.7	21
Indifference	30.4	69.6	23
Collaboration	41.3	58.7	92
Relation with local public institutions (n.s.)			
Refusal	20.0	80.0	15
Indifference	50.0	50.0	18
Collaboration	39.2	60.8	97
GJMO receives governmental funds (0.179**)			
No	30.3	69.7	119
Yes	48.0	52.0	75

Table 7.5 (Continued)

	GJMOs using exclusively moderate forms	GJMOs using also confrontational forms	N
GJMO receives non-governmental funds (0.248***)			
No	28.6	71.4	126
Yes	53.7	46.3	67
GJMOs' home country (0.330***)			
France	11.1	88.9	27
Spain	23.5	76.5	34
Italy	27.8	72.2	36
Switzerland	38.5	61.5	26
United Kingdom	46.4	53.6	28
Germany	48.0	52.0	25
Transnational	63.0	37.0	27
Dominant government in home country during the last five years (0.225**)			
Conservative	20.6	79.4	63
Ambivalent	30.0	70.0	60
Social democratic	46.3	53.7	54

Note: [a]The numbers given in brackets are correlation coefficients (Cramer's V, 2-tailed). °p < 0.1, *p < 0.05, **p < 0.01, ***p < 0.001.

who deserves support. The situation is different for groups from the radical Left spectrum. These groups would not ask for funds, nor would the state be willing to grant them. However, a publicly highly appreciated organization like Greenpeace, which cannot be called left-radical, also refuses to accept state funds in order to maintain its autonomy. After all, Greenpeace started its career with, and continues to engage in, acts of civil disobedience.

One indicator for relationship with the state is dependence on state funding. GJMOs that are supported by the government have a strong tendency towards the use of moderate actions (for similar findings in other contexts, see Rucht et al. 1997). The same applies to groups that receive funds from non-governmental sources beyond their own ranks.[14] The influence of nongovernmental funds can be illustrated by the Bundeskoordination Internationalismus (BUKO), a German network of leftist groups promoting solidarity with the global south. For several years, the network and its annual congress were financially supported by the Protestant Evangelischer Entwicklungsdienst (EED). When participants in a BUKO-congress positively referred to shoplifting as a political form of action, the EED cancelled its contribution in 2005. While in this case the BUKO accepted a severe financial loss to avoid condemning the tactics of political shoplifting, it is obvious that for other groups the threat of losing funds influences their choice of actions. It is not surprising that groups from the radical Left blame moderate NGOs for compromising their aims and repertoires of action for the sake of securing external funding.

Self-restriction in terms of action repertoire does not occur only with regard to the state as a target. Boycott, the action primarily directed against corporations, can also be a double-edged sword to be handled with caution. Some organizations do not consider boycotts a powerful tactic because they have little confidence in the awareness of most consumers. They fear that a call for boycott followed by only few people is more harmful to its initiators than to the targeted company because they will lose reputation and potential influence on companies and decision makers. The Italian Campagna Banche Armate, for instance, which opposes the involvement of banking houses in the production and trafficking of arms, chooses not to call for boycotts. Instead, it maximizes support through distributing information and organizing mailing actions.

Apart from concrete interactions with their environments, we must keep in mind that GJMOs develop in broad political and cultural contexts. In fact, the notion of action repertoires was originally developed to explain the scope and forms of contention in a national context (Kitschelt 1986; della Porta and Rucht 1995; Kriesi et al. 1995). Scholars argued that national communities had developed a shared understanding of what forms of action are 'normal' and appropriate to express dissent. This domestic protest culture does not, or does not significantly, fade away in times of transnational mobilization (Tarrow 2005). Rather, national contexts are amended and permeated by non-domestic and international influences.

Our data show that national background is indeed closely connected with the prevalence of a moderate or confrontational action repertoire (see Table 7.5). Roman countries, which generally tend to have a more salient left–right cleavage, are characterized by a more confrontational protest culture. By contrast, Switzerland, Germany, and the UK seem to have developed relatively effective mechanisms to reduce conflict, for example, through an openness of state institutions to addressing problems that are articulated 'from below'. In these countries, this is indicated by a lower inclination of GJMOs to resort to confrontational actions.

In France, for instance, the nation in our sample where confrontational actions of GJMOs are most common, civil disobedience is widespread even in formal organizations such as the communist trade union Confédération générale du travail (CGT) and the green party. Actions such as the destruction of genetically-modified crops or the support of immigrants on the verge of deportation are not restricted to a radical minority but widely accepted. Elected representatives of the Left take part in acts of civil disobedience, presenting their mayoral insignias or waving the French flag (Combes and Sommier 2006, p. 91).

Apart from national protest cultures, another feature at the national level seems to play a role. In hypothesis 6, we assumed that the political tendency of the national government had an influence on choice of repertoire. Indeed, the deployment of confrontational forms of action can be found in countries with a conservative government during the five years before the interviews were conducted.[15]

Summary and conclusion

What are the forms of action that Global Justice Movement Organizations (GJMOs) choose, and which factors influence these choices? We have tried to answer this two-fold question based on a dataset derived from interviews with 210 organizations in six European countries and on the transnational level. The respondents were given a list of action forms that they could supplement. Also taking into account a second question on the organization's preferred strategy, we ultimately identified nine different forms of action.

In the aggregate, the groups cover the full range from very moderate to very disruptive actions,[16] although they engaged significantly more in moderate than in disruptive actions. A cluster analysis, which can show whether specific forms of action group together, reveals a clear-cut pattern. The set of nine basic forms of action applied by the organizations falls neatly into two distinct categories. On the one hand, the moderate actions (petition, demonstration, cultural performance, lobbying) represent a cluster in which petition and demonstration are the most closely connected. On the other hand, the more confrontational or disruptive actions (blockade, occupation, civil disobedience, strike) represent a second cluster, with the closest link between blockade and occupation.

However, the groups do not fall completely into two subcategories by employing either moderate or confrontational actions. While approximately one-third of the groups used exclusively moderate forms of action, a much greater proportion, in addition to moderate actions, also used at least one form of confrontational action. Only one group relied on confrontational forms only. These results largely contradict our hypothesis 1, in which we linked political leaning and a distinct action repertoire. This finding corresponds with much earlier results from the Political Action Study, based on surveys with individuals who also tended to combine 'conventional' and 'unconventional' forms of political participation (Barnes, Kaase et al. 1979).

Overall, it came as no surprise that GJMOs, in line with their ideological, thematic, cultural, and structural diversity, also vary considerably in their forms of action. As we have assumed from the outset, the specific actions chosen by groups are not only related to each other, but are also influenced by factors both internal and external to the groups.

Several organizational values and characteristics are conducive to the choice of confrontational strategies: endorsement of horizontal structures, avoidance of delegation, prefer decision making in assemblies, and/or are based on individual membership, as well as belonging to the New Left/anarchist/autonomous sector and having a clear anti-capitalist stance. These results support our hypotheses 2 and 3. Contrary to common expectations, groups having a formally adopted programme and formal membership are more inclined than other groups to resort to confrontational action. This runs counter to one part of hypothesis 4. On the other hand, in line with Michels' oligarchy thesis and another part of hypothesis 4, more professionalized groups tend towards the use of a moderate action repertoire.

With regard to external factors – that is, the context in which the groups act – we found, as one might assume, that groups that refuse to establish links with representative (state) institutions in general and with national and international public institutions are more inclined to use confrontational actions, while the picture is inconclusive with regard to local institutions. The data also confirm the assumption that groups receiving funds from governments or from non-governmental institutions are less prone to confrontational action. Moreover, groups from Spain, Italy, and France (that is, countries with a salient left–right cleavage) and groups from countries that were predominantly ruled by conservative governments (Italy and France) in those years relevant for the interviews are more inclined towards confrontational actions than groups from Switzerland, Germany, and Britain. This confirms our hypothesis 6. Interestingly, the genuinely transnational groups in the sample have the strongest tendency towards moderate actions.

To conclude, two major and robust findings should be highlighted again. First, although a considerable proportion of GJMOs remain within the confines of the moderate action repertoire, a greater proportion relies on both moderate and confrontational action, and only one group used exclusively tactics from the confrontational repertoire. Second, ideological leanings, moral values, and structural characteristics of the groups as well as characteristics of their context have a strong impact on which kinds of actions are chosen. Rational choice theories stressing instrumental reasons for the selection of actions do not provide a sufficient explanation. Democratic values and internal practices of decision making do affect the action repertoire. Groups preferring a participatory model of democracy, making decisions in assemblies, and avoiding delegation are more prone towards confrontational and disruptive tactics. This is probably no news for insiders, but still deserved to be proved by systematic empirical research.

Notes

1. We are grateful to Donatella della Porta for her comments on an earlier version of this chapter, and to Wolfgang Stuppert for statistical calculations and the creation of most tables and figures.
2. The research was undertaken in the framework of the DEMOS project (see Introduction to this volume). We are grateful to all our colleagues who took part in the conceptualization, data collection, and data input of this part of the project, which essentially focused on the study of GJMOs.
3. The fact that Dalton subsumes unlawful demonstrations and occupation to violent action points to a far-reaching notion of violence that is not shared

by the authors of this chapter. Both forms of action can be absolutely non-violent.

4. This is indicated, for example, by the fact that the organizers of World Social Forums choose not to have representatives of guerrilla groups or militant separatist organizations at their meetings.

5. Crossley (2002, p. 51) holds that the concept of habitus 'seeks to capture the manner in which an agent's or group's actions and choices are shaped by their respective histories. By the same token it captures the manner in which their choices and actions can have durable effects upon their manner of being-in-the world, so as to affect further, future choices.'

6. Thus far, little research has been undertaken to empirically test these assumptions. Regarding hypothesis 6, Koopmans and Rucht (1995) did not find a consistent pattern when comparing the proportion of radical protests in Germany, France, Britain and the Netherlands.

7. Interviews were conducted with representatives of 210 organizations. For most analyses, we excluded three of them from the sample because these had not provided answers on forms of action, our dependent variable.

8. The list includes: petition, demonstration, strike, boycott of certain products, blockade, occupation of buildings, civil disobedience, and artistic/cultural performance.

9. Wording: 'Which are the main strategies your group uses in order to reach its aims?'

10. The fact that we did not discriminate legal from illegal forms of actions in the interviews is likely to have an influence on this result. Based on a distinction between legal and illegal demonstrations and strikes, the classification would be more fine-grained.

11. Soule et al. (1999), for instance, distinguish between insider and outsider tactics that are more or less congruent with the distinction between confrontational and non-confrontational action forms.

12. Note that some researchers use more differentiated categories. Kriesi et al. (1995, p. 44), for example, used the items direct democracy, petitions, festivals, demonstrative, confrontational, light violence, heavy violence. They referred to the four latter items as 'unconventional'. Neidhardt and Rucht (2001) use 21 items that can be attributed to the broader categories of appeals, procedural, demonstrative, confrontational, and violent types of actions.

13. Note that Rucht et al. (1997, p. 105) found in their study on left-alternative groups in West Berlin that, in the aggregate, growing institutionalization of groups is not paralleled by deradicalization.

14. By contrast, there is no significant relation between fees and dues from members as a financial source and the action repertoire that a group chooses.

15. For the period from 2001 to 2006, we coded the dominant government as social democratic for Germany and the United Kingdom, conservative for Italy and France, and ambivalent for Spain (with a change of government in Spring 2004) and Switzerland (with a concordance democracy).

16. As the political leaning of the governments goes hand in hand with specific national protest cultures, this finding has to be interpreted with caution.

8
Unconventional Politics Online: Internet and the Global Justice Movement[1]

Lorenzo Mosca and Donatella della Porta

The Internet and social movements: An introduction

As with other communication technologies, the Internet influences the behaviour of individuals and organizations, intervening on the mode of interaction at the individual and collective levels. Even more than with other means of communication – such as press, telegraph, radio, television, telephone, fax, and so on – it seems that social scientists expect such important changes from the electronic revolution as to require specific concepts. *E-participation*, *e-governance*, and *e-voting* are all specifications of a more general transformation brought about by the new technologies, to the point of promoting an *e-democracy*, defined by increased opportunities for citizens to participate in politics, thanks to the Internet (Rose 2005). As with other technologies, the debate on their advantages and disadvantages has long polarized observers between sceptics and enthusiasts. From this point of view, the debate and research on the Internet has been intertwined with that on the various qualities of democracy with which this volume is concerned.

Regarding *participation*, in contrast to television and other expensive means of communication, the Internet has been presented as a technology that could augment not only the number of information consumers, but also the quantity of information producers. Increasing the information available to citizens would also facilitate the participation of the more powerless, thus reducing inequalities (Myers 2001). However, research on the digital divide has challenged this view, underlining that, as with other technologies, the Internet facilitates those who are better endowed with individual and collective resources (Margolis and Resnick 2000; Norris 2001; Rose 2005). As for the *deliberative* quality of democracy, it has been argued that the Internet could enrich it by improving the quality of communication as well as contributing to the creation of an alternative public sphere (Klinenberg 2005). From this point of view, the Internet has certainly increased not only the quantity of information available, but also the plurality of its sources. Its use is also correlated with more intense social relations (for a review, della Porta and Mosca 2005). Here as well, however, more sceptical views have emerged on the capacity of new technologies to promote communication across ideological and social barriers (Sunstein 2001). As for the quality of communication, on- and offline arenas do not seem to differ much from each other (Schlosberg et al. 2005).

Focusing on political actors and institutions, the first studies stressed the low interactivity on the part of Web sites of political parties (Cuhna et al. 2003; Gibson et al. 2003) and institutions (Coleman et al. 1999). In this sense, the way in which the Internet is used by political parties and politicians alike does not seem to differ very much from their use of other media technologies, as potentialities are constrained not only (or not so much) by material resources but by deep-rooted cultural habits (van Os et al. 2007; Zittel 2003, p. 3).

Given their larger flexibility, social movement organizations (SMOs) and, more in general, loose networks and unconventional forms of politics have emerged as more open to experimentation and permeable to technological changes, with a more innovative and dynamic use of the Internet.[2] In particular, the new technologies seem to have provided those actors with an inexpensive and fast means for communication beyond borders, fostering mobilization and favouring more flexible and looser organizational structures (Smith 1997; Bennett 2003). Even in the field of social movement studies, however, other authors have presented a more pessimistic view on the Internet's democratic potential in terms of a limited offering of interactive channels, but also the low use of these applications when offered (Rucht 2004a, p. 80). Indeed, if the Internet presents new opportunities to resource-poor actors, it also creates new challenges for their collective action as, apparently, not only conventional political actors but also unconventional ones have difficulty exploiting its full democratic potential (Mosca 2007).

In our empirical research, we have addressed the general question of the use of the Internet by social movements by introducing specific questions in a survey of participants in the 4th European Social Forum in Athens (della Porta 2009) and in our questionnaire to organizations involved in the Global Justice Movement (GJM) in our selected countries, as well as by systematically analysing some general qualities of the Web sites of 261 organizations belonging to the GJM (see Chapter 1).

In what follows, we shall first present some data on Internet use by GJM activists and organizations. Subsequently, we shall focus on relevant qualities of Web sites, assessing the empirical performance of our population of sites on indicators related to provision of information, identity building, transparency, mobilization, and reduction of users' inequalities in accessing and using this medium (digital divide). Next, we will single out potential explanations for the varying attention given to various potential qualities of the Web sites: after looking at the internal correlation among the various qualities we identified, we shall assess the influence of contextual and organizational characteristics on Web sites' qualities.

Unconventional politics online: How activists use the Internet and how they perceive its impact

As with other means of communication, the Internet can be used for various purposes. Research on social movements has stressed in particular some of these purposes. First of all, the Internet has been said to improve the potential to *mobilize* people, through the diffusion of alternative information and through protest. Helped by the Internet, epistemic communities and advocacy networks (Keck and Sikkink 1998) spread information on global issues, highlighting the negative consequences of economic globalization, possible alternatives to neoliberalism, and various struggles in different parts of the world (on the paradigmatic case of the Zapatistas, see Olesen 2005). These groups supported the creation of the GJM, providing alternative knowledge on specific issues, access, and visibility on the Web, and linking organizations acting on diverse parts of the globe. Cheap communication has been particularly relevant for the mounting of transnational campaigns (Reitan 2007). There is growing evidence that 'protests are increasingly conceived, planned, implemented and evaluated with the help of the Internet' (O'Brien 1999). Computer-Mediated Communication allowed for the use of *e-petitions*, which have also been used to denounce specific human rights violations, pressure national governments against the death penalty, and target European institutions (Mosca and Santucci 2008); the *net-strike*, in which a large number of people connect simultaneously to the same domain at a prearranged time, 'jamming' a site considered a symbolic target and making it impossible for other users to reach it (Jordan 2002); and *mailbombing*, consisting of sending emails to a Web site or server until it overloads and jams.

Second, it has been observed that the Internet plays an important role in the *management* of social movement organizations. Organizational structures can in fact be shaped differently by Computer-Mediated Communication, making more decentralized organizational structures viable (Smith 1997, p. 58). The Internet 'fits with the basic features of the kind of social movements emerging in the Information Age (...) To build an historical analogy, the constitution of the labor movement in the industrial era cannot be separated from the industrial factory as its organizational setting (...) the internet is not simply a technology: it is a communication media, and it is the material infrastructure of a given organizational form: the network' (Castells 2001, pp. 135–6). As Naomi Klein (2002, p. 16) observed, the use of the Internet is 'shaping the movement on its own web-like image', with hubs at the centre of activities, and the spokes 'that link to other centers, which are autonomous but interconnected'. In fact, thanks to the Internet, transnational campaigns have become more long lasting, less centrally controlled, more difficult to turn on and off, and more flexible in terms of networks and goals (Bennett 2003).

Third, the Internet has been praised for creating a public space open to *deliberation*, allowing for the creation of new collective identities. Social movement scholars have underlined the Internet's capacity to generate new identities. As indicated by our previous research on the use of SMOs' Web sites during the mobilization against the G8 in Genoa in 2001 (della Porta and Mosca 2005), the Internet provides opportunities for reflexivity. Online forums and mailing lists promote debates on specific choices (such as forms of actions, alliances, slogans, and so on) before a protest takes place and, later, a collective reflection on a demonstration's success and failure among 'distant' activists. True, the Internet's contribution to the collective identities of social movements is mainly in reinforcing existing ones (Diani 2001): it 'can be helpful in organizing and educating within social movements, but in terms of expressing identities, it is a useful but limited tool' (Wall 2007, p. 274). However, even 'real communities can and do take root in internet-based space' (Gurak and Logie 2003, p. 43). Virtual communities can in fact develop an identifying function, creating social networks with internal solidarity and common beliefs, acting online and offline (Freschi 2002).

The DEMOS survey of participants in the Athens ESF (May 2006) confirms that the Internet represents a fundamental means of communication among activists of the Global Justice Movement (see also della

Table 8.1 Use of the Internet by GJM activists (%)

Frequency	Internet use			
	Online petitions/ campaigns	Net-strikes and/or other radical online actions	Exchange of information with own group	Political opinions online
At least once a week	14.9	3.8	48.7	21.2
At least once a month	26.0	6.6	16.2	21.9
Less frequently	44.3	20.2	15.1	32.7
Never	14.8	69.4	20.0	24.3
Total	100.0	100.0	100.0	100.0
(N)	(1054)	(1025)	(1035)	(1038)

Source: DEMOS survey of participants in the Athens ESF (2005).

Porta and Mosca 2005, p. 171, on the first ESF in Florence in 2002). In particular, a very high percentage of respondents (between 75 and 85 per cent) uses the Web to perform moderate forms of online protest (less than one-third employ more radical ones such as net-strikes); to exchange information with their own group; to express political opinions online (see Table 8.1). With very high frequency (by almost half of respondents at least once a week), the Internet is used as an instrument to exchange information with one's own group, and very often it is also used for petitioning and campaigning. Less frequent, even though present, are occasions to express political opinions online.

While gender and education have no relation with the frequency and type of use,[3] Internet use is related with the level of activism of the interviewees, as the more mobilized population also uses the Internet more (Table 8.2). The various uses of the Internet all increase with identification with the movement, multiple organizational memberships, participation in GJM protest events, and the use of multiple forms of political participation. As already noted elsewhere (della Porta and Mosca 2005), offline and online protests are strongly related and tend to reinforce each other. The more activists identify with the GJM, the more they use the Internet to take part in moderate forms of action online and to express their political opinions, both in their own group and outside of it. The importance of being part of one or more groups is also demonstrated by the fact that the higher the number of groups in which activists are involved, the more they use the Internet as an instrument for political protest and expression of political opinions.

Table 8.2 Relation between offline and online activity (Kendall's Tau-B)

Offline activities	Internet use			
	Online petitions/ campaigns	Net-strikes and/or other radical online actions	Exchange of information with own group	Political opinions online
Identification with the GJM	0.137**	n.s.	0.199**	0.149**
Multiple membership	0.201**	0.081**	0.288**	0.222**
Participation in GJM protest events	0.193**	0.098**	0.296**	0.183**
Multiple forms of action	0.192**	0.100**	0.235**	0.234**
Total	100.0	100.0	100.0	100.0
(N)	(1033–45)	(1019–29)	(1005–16)	(1014–26)

Note: ** = significant at 0.01 level (2-tailed); * = significant at 0.05 level (2-tailed); n.s. = not significant.

Similar trends can be noted if we consider the level of mobilization (as measured by participation in GJM protest events and multiple repertoires of action). The lower scores of correlation coefficients concerning Internet use for net-strikes and activists performing other radical forms of online protest confirm the peculiar characteristics of these activists, who tend to belong to particular types of loose organizations (that is, alternative media and social centres) and to have a repertoire of action more oriented towards radical forms of protest than do the rest of the sample.

These results at the individual level are highly compatible with the assessment made by the speakers for GJMOs that we interviewed during a part of our research (see Chapter 1), asking questions on the effect of the Internet in general, and of their organizations' Web site in particular, on their communication with various actors and constituencies (Table 8.3). The overall judgement concerning the impact of the Internet on communication with *public administrators* is mostly negative, although more than 40 per cent of the groups registered a positive impact. The judgement on the impact on relationship with the *mass media* is significantly different: only one-fifth of the interviewees give a negative evaluation, while for more than 70 per cent the Internet

Table 8.3   Evaluation of the role of the Internet (%)

Internet's impact	Target		
	Public administrators	Mass media	Members and sympathizers
Negative	52.9	21.6	3.3
Both negative and positive	3.2	7.0	15.4
Positive	43.9	71.3	81.3
Total	100.0	100.0	100.0
(N)	(157)	(171)	(182)

Note: Cramer's V is: n.s. (public administrators); n.s. (media); 0.246^{**} (members).

according to interviews with GJMOs improved communication with the mass media. Finally, optimism prevails particularly when respondents are asked about the contribution of the Internet to communication with *members and sympathizers*. In this case, negative evaluations are very few and were recorded only in southern European countries, where about one-quarter of the groups showed a mixed position.

The widespread ideas about the Internet's impact on different publics are synthesized by a spokesperson of a local social forum, who states:

> it doesn't seem to me that the Internet favoured more interactions with *public decision-makers*. On the contrary, they often ignore the actions made via the Internet that are frequently ineffective. This was the case of a netstrike that we directed against the Web site of the National Institute of Nuclear Physics within the framework of our campaign against the big infrastructures planned by the Berlusconi's government. We also organized a mail-bombing at the European level using the email addresses of MPs during the discussion on directives concerning issues such as genetically modified food, water, and Bolkestein directive but it was not effective. This is because public decision-makers are not competent on these online actions. As for the relation with the *media*, I think that the Internet is fundamental because press releases, photos, and documents are published on our Web site and they are used by journalists as a source for their articles... However, I believe that the Web site served us mostly to attract people that are informed and already interested but it didn't prove to be very effective for the communication with the whole *public opinion* because TV and face-to-face interactions are more important for that.

Hence, it is especially useful for specific sectors of public opinion that are already informed but not for the masses of people.

Although less trusted, Computer-Mediated Communication with public administrators and politicians are not totally discounted by our activists. As one spokesperson for the ecopacifist group Rete Lilliput notes, 'The Internet has a pivotal and strategic role for us; it is part of our strategy of communication and pressure. ... We are using it in a very interesting way to organize online pressure campaigns on national deputies and also on representatives at the local level. We have used the mail-bombing on political representatives and it has given interesting results.'

It is worth noting that during our research, the issue of Internet communication was raised spontaneously and framed as crucial by most of the interviewees beyond our specific questions. Particularly with regard to the effect of the Internet in the internal life of the organizations, some interviewees highlight that new technologies can facilitate the spreading and sharing of power. In particular, Internet tools such as mailing lists become 'permanent assemblies'. Open publishing and open management systems are employed by some groups in order to widen participation in organizational life and to democratize the organization, avoiding the concentration of power in the hands of few technology-skilled individuals. Some interviewees stigmatize, in fact, the risks of new inequalities as technical expertise gives power to a limited amount of people. Fear of excluding some activists led in some cases to limiting the use of new technology and favouring face-to-face communication – or, in other cases, to setting up groups of people specifically dealing with Internet issues, in an effort to spread knowledge on Internet use among its participants.

In addition, in some cases interactive tools are not used by GJMOs because they feel that they would require great effort. This concerns especially more traditional organizations such as trade unions. In the words of the Webmaster of the Italian left metalworkers union Fiom: 'we don't give users the possibility to express themselves directly and to publish their judgment on platforms and agreements even if this is what they ask us for more. ... the opening of a forum would mean a different management of the web site because it would imply to devote one person to the forum but we don't have such possibility'.

Some of our interviewees refer to a generational divide within and between 'old' and traditional organizations/members and 'new' and innovative groups/activists in conceiving and understanding the Internet, with older generations not conceiving the new media as something radically different from traditional ones. Going beyond an instrumental vision of the Internet, some activists stress the peculiar capacity of the Internet to promote participation and deliberation. According to a member of the executive of the Italian Young Communists:

> web tools represent an amazing innovation in doing politics. The internet is really a political space. It's not just an instrument. It's a place where, notwithstanding the great push towards privatization and control, millions of people cooperate to build critics and to attack the private idea that Microsoft and Windows propose of the Net. It is also a political space in that it represents a place of confrontation and discussion without precedents.

The use of Internet cannot, however, be conceived in isolation from communication by other means. Many interviewees underline that face-to-face relationships are very important for the construction of virtual nets, which do not emerge spontaneously. In addition, the Internet is often considered as something adding to existing relations, rather than as an alternative to them. As the spokesperson for Rete Lilliput states, 'the internet is very important for us but it is just an instrument and it cannot be a substitute for other forms of interaction that we consider fundamental. ...We have chosen to have a series of physical meetings like seminars and assemblies because we think that some events cannot be mediated or replaced by the internet.' Other interviewees strongly emphasize the need for visual and physical contacts. As a local social forum spokesperson states: 'We also need to practice militancy, to draw posters and write leaflets, and to have physical contacts with the people otherwise we won't change the world!'

Summarizing, the Internet is seen as a means for widening participation in organizational life, but it also raises concerns of the risk of exclusion for people without access to it, and the related power inequalities. It facilitates interactions with journalists and allows deepening relationships with members. However, it mainly serves to complement face-to-face relations, as none of our interviewees thinks that the Internet could replace face-to-face communication: it simply multiplies the possibilities and frequencies of communication among territorially dispersed individuals.

Web sites' qualities

If our SMOs and their activists are indeed interested (even more than other actors) in the Internet as an instrument that might reduce the cost of communication and make it more inclusive, we considered the actual implementation of these possibilities as a matter for an empirical investigation that, following some previous research, we have focused on the organizational Web sites. Additionally, we assumed that the attention to the different 'qualities' of Web site design can vary. In what follows, we will analyse various strategic choices in the construction of one relevant instrument of Internet technology, the Web site, presenting the sites' performances on some main analytical dimensions.

A first relevant contribution of the Internet, especially in terms of allowing for better deliberation, is the *provision of information*. A Web site can fulfil an important function in that it organizes a set of meanings, selects a part of reality, and proposes an interpretation of it. SMOs belonging to the GJM stress, more than most social movements in the past, the importance of building a specialized knowledge base (della Porta et al. 2006). Most of the Web sites we analysed present a significant amount of information. They frequently offer opportunities for political education via articles, papers, and dossiers (90 per cent of the cases), even providing bibliographical references (40 per cent). More than half of the sites (53 per cent) publish conference and seminar materials that allow interested users to deepen their knowledge on specific topics; a news section is present in almost four-fifths (78 per cent) of our sites. In order to put our data in a wider comparative perspective, we can recall that the Web sites of Eastern European NGOs offered a news section in a much lower 48 per cent of the cases and information about conferences in only 16 per cent (Vedres et al. 2005, p. 154).

An important aspect that affects the quality of information is also the *usability* of a Web site – that is, the potential for users to find relevant information easily. The presence of search engines and site maps should help the user to rapidly find what he/she is searching for. It seems that SMOs perceive this necessity: almost 60 per cent provide a search engine and almost 30 per cent a site map. Only about one-quarter of the Web sites, however, offer translations of basic information on the group, and about one-fifth translate the section identifying them. This seems a comparatively low proportion, if we consider the highly transnational nature of the movement's frames and action (additionally, about one-third of Eastern European NGOs translate at least part of their Web sites; see Vedres et al. 2005, p. 154). Although one could argue that borderless communication develops more through mailing lists than on Web sites, it seems that, in a globalizing world, national civil society organizations still find it difficult to speak to each other across borders: language differences still represent problematic barriers to transnational communication.[4]

A second important opportunity offered by the Internet is its capacity to contribute to deliberation by facilitating the *building of new identities through the Internet*. Web sites serve as opportunities for self-presentation to the general public, while specific tools like forums and mailing lists favour ongoing communication and discussion among activists. The activists that we have interviewed often underline the importance of Web sites as a means for constructing a memory of the activity of the organization, and for disseminating information. Web sites are in fact considered as 'electronic business cards' that reflect and represent the identity and past history of the organization. One type of information generally published on the Web sites of GJM organizations does concern the identity and the history of the group itself. Overall, around two-thirds of those we analysed provide an archive of press releases (also an important source of information for journalists of traditional media) and an archive of annual reports or a chronology of the history of the organization. Additionally, about two-fifths of the surveyed organizations have online archives of old leaflets (informing users about the history of the organization: its actions, campaigns, mobilizations, and so on) as well as documents on past assemblies that are considered fundamental steps in their collective history. More than 50 per cent of the analysed Web sites have a newsletter that in the large majority of cases is accessible by all users, while less than 25 per cent publish online the internal work agenda of the group. The organizations that are more interested in enhancing internal communication with their members can provide a members-only section on their Web sites; this is the case in one-quarter of the analysed Web sites.

This takes us to another characteristic, also relevant for the formation of a collective identity through online debates. The presence on a Web site of specific applications like forums, mailing lists, blogs, or chat lines indicates the organization's commitment to multilateral interactivity through the creation of open spaces for discussion among diverse people. Applications for multilateral interactivity are variously spread on the analysed Web sites.[5] About one-third of the Web sites provide an asynchronous space for discussion (forum and/or mailing list). This is not a comparatively low proportion – similar indicators show that about one-fifth of the Eastern European NGOs provide instruments for participation via bulletin boards, chat rooms, and the like (see Vedres et al. 2005, p. 154). However, it also indicates that a majority of our groups do not consider Web sites as instruments for open debate. Additionally, the newest forms of information management such as open publishing (all users can publish news, calls, proposals, and so on, without a filter) are used in only 10 per cent of the cases; the same percentage of Web sites offers the possibility to respond to the organization's specific request for comments, or for surveys and questionnaires to collect users' opinions on various topics.

The high information storage capacity of the Web sites also provides opportunities for improving *transparency and accountability*, another relevant feature of democracy. A large majority of our sampled SMOs uses Web sites to improve transparency about their internal life. As many as 80 per cent offer information on the physical existence and reachability of the organization (a similar percentage was noted for Eastern European NGOs; see Vedres et al. 2005, p. 154), which in 70 per cent of the cases are directly published on the homepage or just one click away from it. Even more (85 per cent) publish online the statute (or an equivalent document) of their organizations, and almost two-thirds contain information on the organizational structure of the group. Less frequent is information on the Web site itself: in only one-quarter of the sites do we find information about the last updating, and only 16 per cent give some kind of indication on users' access to the site (although those statistics are often unclear and very imprecise, as well as lacking a temporal reference). Probably also because of often low budgets, only 25 per cent of the Web sites provide information on their organization's finances.

The presence of contact information for people actively involved, both with leading and with other identified roles, indicates the organization's willingness to open to public scrutiny by creating direct channels of communication with Web site users. In this sense, the presence of contact information represents a step beyond unidirectional instruments of communication (like a newsletter). Almost 90 per cent of the Web sites provide a general email address for the organization, 30 per cent of them on their homepages. A similar percentage (85 and 87 per cent, respectively) was found in the case of Eastern European NGOs (Vedres et al. 2005, p. 154) and in the analysis of European parliaments online (Trechsel et al. 2003, p. 23). However, the provision of email addresses of other people involved in the organization is not very widespread on the analysed Web sites: the Webmaster's address is provided in only 40 per cent; for other people/departments within the organization in 31 per cent; and for the person responsible for international relations in 14 per cent. Among the groups that identify the presence of a leader, less than half give information on that person, and about a quarter provide leader contact information to the general users. The responsiveness of the general information service and of the Webmaster is also indicated by the responses to an email we sent (using the email addresses published on the Web site) to request information about the site's management.[6] Overall, the response rate varied from 31 per cent for the request sent to the general email address, to 45 per cent for the one sent to the Webmaster.[7]

As mentioned, activists are especially sensitive to the potential for *mobilization through the Web*, and thus improved opportunities for political participation. The Web sites of our sampled SMOs perform mobilization functions to very different degrees. Most widespread is the use of the Internet for *offline protest*. More than 60 per cent of the organizations publish their action calendars online, a significant proportion when compared with 42 per cent in the case of Eastern European NGOs (Vedres et al. 2005, p. 154). About one-third also publishes online the action calendar of other organizations belonging to the GJM; the same proportion provides concrete information (through handbooks or links to useful resources) on offline forms of action. The organization of physical meetings for offline forms of action is covered by almost one-fifth of the analysed Web sites (between 16 and 22 per cent organize workshops and help desks to socialize people to offline forms of action); information on offline forms of action is present in about one-third of them (36 per cent).

As many as two-thirds of our Web sites advertise the participation of their organization in a protest campaign. The Internet also provides instruments for *online protest*, such as e-petitions, net-strikes and mail-bombings. Many hackers – with their attention to the Internet and online protest – belong to the GJM, struggling against copyright and for the right to privacy (Jordan 2002). In our Web sites, however, online forms of action are promoted less often than offline tactics: almost 30 per cent of the analysed Web sites use the online petition; almost 18 per cent propose to their users a form of online mobilization like the e-postcard; and 15 per cent publish concrete information about online forms of action. The percentage is even lower if we consider the presence of calls to net-strikes and/or mail-bombings; other forms of online mobilizations are much more widespread, although still limited to a minority of sites.

A final quality of Web sites could be in contributing to participation by *intervening on the digital divide*. The extent to which the Internet allows for mobilizing different groups of the population, especially the least 'technologically educated', is an open question often discussed in the literature on the Internet (Norris 2001) and by activists alike. Our own data from a survey of activists participating in the first European Social Forum in Florence confirm to a certain degree the existence of a digital divide within social movements, although they also point at the role of movement organizations in socializing their members to the Internet (della Porta and Mosca 2005). The organizations we selected for our analysis, however, do not seem very concerned with this issue. In fact, less than 10 per cent provide laboratories, help desks and other electronic applications to socialize their users to the Internet; 5 per cent offer free email to their users; and just 8 per cent host Web pages or Web sites. A text-only version of the Web site, allowing those with slow connections or older hardware to access its contents, is available in only about 5 per cent of the sites. Only very seldom did we find reference to the accessibility issue on the homepage of an analysed Web site. The issue of the digital divide, then, is addressed mainly by a limited number of SMOs specifically engaged with this problem, while others clearly do not consider it a priority.

Contextual characteristics, organizational features, and web sites' qualities: Some explanations

How can we explain the varying emphases of the various Web sites on the diverse dimensions of communication? Technological explanations have frequently been used to account for the effects of technological innovation. Similarly, technological skills have been cited in explaining the qualities of Web sites, for example when the sites of political organizations demonstrate significant improvement due to contracting out their design and management to professional Webmasters. However, recent research has identified various models that adapt technology to organizational styles and strategies (Vedres et al. 2005), as well as to contextual dimensions. Criticizing the technological interpretation of the Internet as able – thanks to its inherent networked logic – to favour decentralization of power and empowerment of citizens, most scholars now agree in underlining the role of the agency in shaping the online environment (Oates and Gibson 2006, p. 3). Relations between technology and its users are therefore considered as bi-directional: technology impacts upon social relations, while social relations shape the use of the

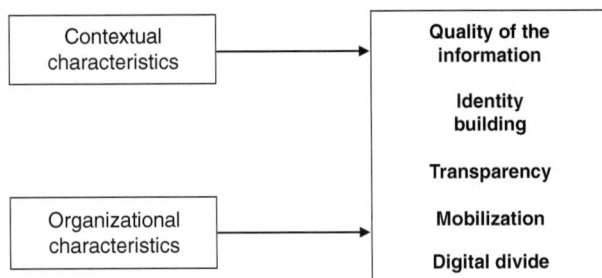

Figure 8.1   Explanatory model

Internet as a technology. Assuming that offline characteristics matter in explaining the online presence of SMOs (see also Calenda and Mosca 2007), in our explanatory model we focus in particular on the role of offline characteristics in shaping the online environment (Web sites), considering contextual dimensions as well as organizational factors (see Figure 8.1).

To address the influence of context, first, we looked at the level of Internet access in the selected countries.[8] We assumed that a larger diffusion of the Internet could explain a greater investment in this medium by SMOs. Where the Internet is used less, SMOs will more likely limit their online presence to advertisements, without investing very much in other aspects of their Web sites.

Moreover, we have classified the Web sites based on the characteristics of the GJM in the respective countries.[9] We noted in other parts of our research (della Porta 2007b) that the density and format of GJM organizational networks tended to vary in the selected countries, generating two different constellations of social movements that corresponded, with some caveats, to northern and southern Europe (ibid.). These two groups are characterized by different types of networks (more integrated in the French, Italian and Spanish cases; more polarized in Germany and Switzerland and, to a lesser extent, in the UK); different organizational structures (more horizontal in the first constellation, more vertical in the second); and a different orientation towards unconventional collective action (more protest oriented in the first, more lobbying oriented in the second).

Concerning the organizational characteristics, attitudes towards the Internet could vary on the basis of the age of the group, as 'newer, resource-poor organizations that tend to reject conventional politics may be defined in important ways by their Internet presence' (Bennett

2003), while established organizations seem to have a conservative approach (Smith 1997; Tarrow 2003, p. 31). The level of resources available to an organization might facilitate a more effective use of the Internet – as some findings on political parties (Ward 2001) and NGOs (Warkentin 2001) seem to suggest. In fact, while it is quite easy and inexpensive to create a Web site and to let it float in cyberspace, a well organized, frequently updated, and interactive site demands significant investment of resources. We then expect the Web sites of large (and resourceful) organizations to perform better on the analysed dimensions than do those of smaller grass-roots groups (Pickerill 2003). We also expect other organizational features such as horizontality, formalization, and the territorial level of the group to affect Web sites' qualities in different ways.

In order to control for the effect of the relevant organizational characteristics, we have looked at some indicators on which we collected information during our research. The date of foundation of the organization is an obvious indicator of organizational age, and the budget an indicator of level of resources. Additionally, belonging to different movement areas can have path-dependent effects on the use of Web sites. We also used the absence of leadership roles or equivalent roles in charge of co-ordinating the activities of the organization (present in almost 70 per cent of the groups) as an indicator of horizontality; the presence of membership fees as an indicator of formalization; the definition of the group as local (almost one-fifth of the cases) as an indicator of the territorial scope of the action. We also looked at the main dimensions of our typology of democratic decision making: participation and deliberation.

For the dependent variables, we built five additive indexes (standardized to vary from 0 to 1) by adding up the binary indicators used for each of the mentioned qualities of Web sites, and looked at the reciprocal association among them (see Table 8.4).[10] First, the fact that not all the indexes are correlated with each other seems to confirm that different organizations tend to focus on some of the relevant functions, choosing among various techniques rather then being driven by technology (Vedres et al. 2005). Additionally, we found that provision of information is particularly related to mobilization and identity building. The Web sites that score high on these three dimensions have less hierarchical organizational models, and are more dynamic and interactive. For reasons we shall see below, transparency is not correlated with other dimensions of Internet presence: Web sites that score high on transparency, but not on other dimensions, are likely to belong to

Table 8.4 Indexes of Web sites' qualities (non parametrical correlations, Kendall's Tau-B) N = 261

Indexes of online democracy	Information provision	Identity building	Transparency	Mobilization	Digital divide
Information provision	–				
Identity building	0.295**	–			
Transparency	0.187**	0.147*	–		
Mobilization	0.317**	0.382**	n.s.	–	
Intervention on digital divide	0.182**	0.123*	n.s.	0.281**	–

Note: ** = significant at 0.01 level (2-tailed); * = significant at 0.05 level (2-tailed); n.s. = not significant.

more hierarchical organizations, being more static and less interactive. Third, online and offline mobilization is highly correlated with intervention on the digital divide. Organizations with high scores on both dimensions emerge as more concerned with empowering citizens by encouraging an active role (mobilizing in the streets and in the Net) and socializing them to the use of new technologies.

Correlation coefficients between the mentioned additive indexes and contextual characteristics show that in the group of countries more oriented towards protest and where Internet access is still limited, the Internet is more likely to be used as an instrument for offline mobilization (see Table 8.5). In the same countries, it is also more often used for identity building and information provision. The countries more oriented towards conventional forms of action and where Internet access is higher are more likely to use the Internet especially as an instrument for increasing transparency or accountability.

The first organizational characteristics we considered are particularly helpful in explaining transparency, information provision, and online mobilization. The degree of formalization and the territorial level of organizations are both correlated with the index of transparency, as informal and local groups pay less attention to formal structures. More centralized organizations seem to invest more in information provision: the presence of a division of roles is in fact associated with more attention paid to the production and diffusion of information on the Internet. The availability of material resources and age of the

Table 8.5 External and internal characteristics' influence on Web sites' qualities (Kendall's Tau-B)

Indexes of online democracy	Environmental characteristics		Organizational characteristics						
	Internet access	Constellation of the GJM	Horizontality (lack of roles)	Formalization (fee membership)	Local level group	Budget	Age of the group	Delegation of power (0=executive)	Decision-making method (0=majority)
Information provision	0.154**	0.187**	−0.242**	−0.160**	n.s.	n.s.	n.s.	n.s.	n.s.
Identity building	n.s.	0.181**	−0.125*	−0.105*	−0.126*	n.s.	n.s.	n.s.	n.s.
Transparency	−0.188**	−0.235**	0.409**	−0.257**	−0.206**	0.444**	−0.287**	−0.288**	−0.207**
Offline mobilization	0.105*	0.173**	n.s.	n.s.	n.s.	n.s.	0.141*	n.s.	n.s.
Online mobilization	n.s.	n.s.	−0.160**	−0.287**	−0.118*	n.s.	n.s.	n.s.	n.s.
Intervention on digital divide	n.s.	n.s.	n.s.	n.s.	n.s.	n.s.	n.s.	0.264**	n.s.
Total (N)	231	231	261	261	261	139	150	158	160

Note: ** = significant at 0.01 level (2-tailed); * = significant at 0.05 level (2-tailed); n.s. = not significant.

organization help in explaining the degree of transparency: unsurprisingly, older and wealthier groups are likely to be more transparent online. Mobilizing online is, in contrast, a characteristic typical of less formal organizations that seem to make use of the more innovative aspects of this medium, exploiting it as a tool to strengthen their mobilization capacities. Organizational characteristics, however, do not help in explaining the use of the Internet to intervene on the digital divide or to disseminate information concerning offline mobilizations.

We also controlled if dimensions related to democratic models employed by the analysed groups such as delegation of power (assembly vs. executive) and decision-making method (majority vs. consensus) are associated with indexes of online democracy.[11] Transparency emerged as negatively correlated with low delegation and consensual decision-making methods. This result was not unexpected: the more innovative groups in terms of democratic models are also those that are younger, less formalized, and less rich in resources. As a result, their Web sites offer less information on budget, organizational structure, and so on. In contrast, we note that the less an organization delegates power to the executive, the more likely it is to intervene on the digital divide. Newer organizations born within the cycle of protest against neoliberal globalization seem to be more aware of the risk of exclusion derived from new technologies and more willing to invest their (limited) resources on what could be conceived as the democratic deficit of the Internet.

As the GJM is a 'movement of movements', often comprising groups and individuals that belong to other social movements, we have controlled for the extent to which movement traditions (Old Left, New Left, new global, new social movements, solidarity/peace/human rights) influence our indexes of online democracy (see Table 8.6). First, while values of correlations coefficients tend to be significant, we must note that most of them are not very high. What is evident is that 'new global' organizations that emerged after the rise of the GJM – which tend to be less formalized and less rich in resources than the average – are negatively associated with the index of transparency. The opposite reason explains why SMOs belonging to 'older' movement areas such as the 'Old Left' (mainly political parties and trade unions), 'solidarity/peace/human rights' and 'new social movements' perform better on transparency. New global organizations are also weak in information provision, but they perform better in terms of using the Internet as an instrument for mobilizing people in the street and in the Net. This

Table 8.6 Social movement areas' influence on Web sites' qualities (Kendall's Tau-B)

Indexes of online democracy	Social movement areas				
	Old Left	*New Left*	*New Global*	*New Social Movements*	*Solidarity/ Peace/HR*
Information provision	n.s.	n.s.	−0.142*	n.s.	n.s.
Identity building	n.s.	n.s.	n.s.	0.138*	n.s.
Transparency	0.140**	n.s.	−0.331**	0.112*	0.160**
Mobilization	n.s.	−0.122*	0.107*	0.108*	n.s.
Intervention on digital divide	n.s.	n.s.	n.s.	n.s.	−0.146*
Total (N)	257	257	257	257	257

Note: ** = significant at 0.01 level (2-tailed); * = significant at 0.05 level (2-tailed); n.s. = not significant.

could be explained by their recent emergence and more positive attitude towards an innovative and creative use of new technologies. In the case of SMOs belonging to the new social movements area, the Internet is more actively used for strengthening and developing online identities. Solidarity/peace/human rights organizations invest even less on reducing the digital divide via their online presence. This data confirms again the problematic nature of this dimension, since the attention of different social movement areas is mainly focused on improving mobilization and transparency.

Between virtual and real: Some conclusions

The Internet has been praised not only as a new, but also as a democratic medium. To be sure, our data confirm that social movement organizations and their activists make considerable use of it, especially in their internal organizational life as well as in mobilizing the public, both through the spreading of information and through (on- and offline) protest. By reducing the costs of communication, the Internet allows for the building of transnational and cross-issue networks. In facilitating internal and external communication, it improves some fundamental qualities of democracy, in particular the options for participation and deliberation.

The analysis of the Web sites of organizations belonging to the GJM confirms that the Internet plays an important role. However, we observed that SMOs pay varying degrees of attention to the various potentialities of the Web. Overall, Web sites are used mostly for spreading information, mobilizing offline, and increasing transparency. In contrast, the use of the Internet for mobilizing online and socializing users to new technologies is particularly limited and interactivity emerges as lower than expected, although not in absolute terms in comparison with similar groups (such as NGOs).

Contextual and organizational characteristics help to explain the strategic choices made by SMOs. In an adaptation to national cultures, SMOs tend to privilege transparency and provision of information in the Northern countries, identity building and mobilization in the Southern ones. Our research confirms the role played by actors in defining the specific objectives to be reached through the use of new technologies. As Pickerill noted in research on online environmental activism: 'deterministic assumptions are challenged by an awareness that technology is not a discrete artifact which operates externally to impact upon social relations' (2003, p. 23). In fact, different SMOs tend to exploit different technological opportunities, producing Web sites endowed with different qualities. Different contexts encourage an emphasis on different characteristics, and Web sites' qualities apparently reflect organizational models. In particular, SMOs oriented towards more formal and hierarchical organizations seem to show a more traditional (and instrumental) use of the Internet, while less formalized groups tend to use more interactive tools (and identity building) available online, as well as various forms of computer-mediated protest. Movement traditions as well as democratic conceptions also play some role in influencing the different qualities of the Web sites.

Overall, our data seem to show a trend of path dependency in Web sites' characteristics: less resourceful, informal, and newer SMOs tend to develop a more innovative use of the Internet, while more resourceful, formal, and older groups tend to use it as a more conventional medium of communication. However, this observation needs to be supported by further research and empirical evidence. In fact, while we found that small, radical organizations tend to be those that more likely innovate with new communication technologies, they tend to perform less well on other Internet potentials. In parallel, some formal organizations (often better resourced) are not limiting themselves to using the Internet as a traditional information provider. The important question of how Web site potentials are implemented in their actual use still remains open.

Notes

1. A previous version of this chapter was presented as a paper at the symposium 'Changing Politics through Digital Networks: The Role of ICTs in the Formation of New Social and Political Actors and Actions', University of Florence, Italy, 5–6 October 2007. We are grateful to the conference's participants for useful comments. Although the authors share responsibility for the whole article, Donatella della Porta wrote the sections 'The Internet and social movements: An introduction', 'Web sites' qualities', and 'Between virtual and real: Some conclusions'; while Lorenzo Mosca wrote the sections 'Unconventional politics online', and 'Contextual characteristics, organizational features, and Web sites' qualities'.
2. For instance, on NGOs' Web sites in Eastern Europe, see Vedres et al. 2005; on the European Social Forum organizing process, see Kavada 2007a and 2007b.
3. Age tends to be related, but with a curvilinear trend (higher connections in average cohorts).
4. This result is consistent with other research focusing on the Europeanization of the public sphere on the Internet (Koopmans and Zimmermann 2003).
5. It must be noted, however, that these interactive tools are sometimes incorporated directly within Web sites and sometimes not. First, in our research we could only assess the presence of such tools within SMOs' Web sites; we cannot exclude the possibility that the same organizations may place interactive platforms elsewhere in cyberspace without publicizing them on their Web sites. Second, the mere existence of certain utilities such as forums and mailing lists does not tell us anything about their actual use.
6. When an email address was available, we emailed the information service and the Webmasters with questions. We asked the information service how many people managed the Web site, the average number of information requests they received in a month, the average number of messages they responded to, and the time frame of the answers. We asked the Webmaster for the number of volunteers and/or paid staff employed to maintain the Web site, the average traffic demand, the number of subscribers to newsletters and/or mailing lists/forums, the frequency of updating, and the type of software used to produce the Web site.
7. This rate was calculated considering only the Web sites that published the email address of the Webmaster and of the person responsible for the information.
8. We created a variable that assigned values varying between 0 (=0 per cent) and 1 (=100 per cent), depending on the percentage of people accessing the Internet (source: http://www.Internetworldstats.com/stats4.htm) in the country to which the organization belonged. We excluded from the analysis the 30 cases sampled at the transnational level.
9. We used a dummy variable giving value 0 to Germany, United Kingdom, and Switzerland and value 1 to France, Italy, and Spain. Also in this case, we

excluded the 30 cases sampled for the transnational level. These explorative analyses are taken from della Porta and Mosca (2006b).

10. We report significance of correlation coefficients as it is still a prevalent praxis in statistical analysis, although we are aware that its usefulness for non-random samples is debated.

11. The values of variables 'Delegation of power' and 'Decision-making method' were gathered through the organizational survey (WorkPackage no. 4).

9
The Generational Issue: The Impact of Organizations' Age on Visions of Democracy

Hélène Combes, Nicolas Haeringer and Isabelle Sommier

Introduction[1]

Organizations involved in the global justice mobilizations have been presented as developers of *emerging* forms of transnational collective engagement, proposing *innovative* ways of organizing, struggling, discussing, and 'being together' (della Porta et al. 2006). In this view, the Global Justice Movement is seen as innovative in its organizational dimension.

Various works propose a critical analysis of this perspective. Emphasizing the national roots of global justice mobilization (Sommier et al. 2008b; Agrikoliansky et al. 2005a), they insist on the complexity of the connection between the local and the transnational levels. Indeed, understanding the rise of the GJM in France requires consideration of the impact of François Mitterrand's 1981 presidential victory on the French mobilizations in the 1980s (Sommier and Combes 2007) as much as a focus on trade unionists and activists' personal trajectories in the late 1980s and early 1990s (Sommier 2003). Similarly, while analysing the emergence of global justice mobilizations in Germany, Rucht et al. (2008) do not insist only on transnational factors (such as the Zapatista uprising in 1994) but also stress the consequences of the reunification process on the German protest field.

Moreover, local and global should not be opposed to one another. Indeed, 'global can produce local' mobilizations (Sommier et al. 2008a, p. 10). Transnationalization is in fact a polysemic concept that describes at least three different processes: the internationalization of global stakes, the spreading of new challenges, and the externalization of claims that were originally nationally organized.

Such specifications enable us to take some distance vis-à-vis two visions. For some analysts (Boltanski and Chiapello 1997) or activists (Aguiton 2005), the globalization of capitalism leads mechanically to transnational forms of protest. The network structure of capitalism also explains why protest tends to be reticularly organized and to be attracted by values such as horizontality, consensus and openness. Such analysis needs qualification: organizations involved in mobilizations labelled as 'altermondialiste' are very rarely centred around transnational claims (ATTAC and People's Global Action being notable exceptions[2]), whereas Francesca Polletta's (2002) work on US social movements throughout the twentieth century shows the long history of consensus-driven and horizontal forms of organization.

Nevertheless, one should not use these reflections to completely reject the possibility for the GJM and its organizations to develop 'new' features and a real 'transnational' engagement. Indeed, many actors of contemporary movements describe themselves as being 'part of the GJM' (della Porta 2009), representing, more than a simple label, a common (micro)culture or identity principle.

This chapter will focus on these issues using the DEMOS interviews. In order to test how time influences the organizational dimension of the global justice mobilizations (including their democratic features and conceptions), we shall address generational differences among our organizations. Here, we shall reflect on whether these organizations translate their claimed 'novelty' and 'transnationality' into concrete principles and devices that would 'make a movement' out of the nebula involved in Social Forums, counter-summits, campaigns, and other forms of global justice sociability.

Focusing on the organizational dimension and the role of age is particularly important, as the GJM is based not so much on the direct enrolment of individuals (Agrikoliansky et al. 2005b, p. 13) as on the bloc recruitment of existing organizations, movements, and networks. The discussion on 'innovative principles' or 'new' forms of democracy on the one hand, and, on the other, the presence of a wide range of organizations created at different times (from trade unions born in the late nineteenth century to affinity groups lasting only as long as a protest against the 2007 G8 summit), make the issue of organizational generations far from a secondary one.

The meaning of age

In our perspective, age is connected either to change and innovation, or, conversely, to stability. Thus, it is difficult to clearly define what 'age'

means for an organization. Analysing the impact of the age of organizations on their practices and principles does not solve the issue of
the meaning of age, which can be considered from various perspectives. On the one hand, the analysis can be bound into a vision of
social movements and actors evolving in time – as they learn from past
experiences and try not to reproduce 'the same mistakes': newly born
organizations bear in mind the successes and failures of former ones.
Differences between the newest components of the mobilizations on
global justice and the oldest actors participating in it can be linked to
the innovations introduced with reference and in opposition to past
experience.

On the other hand, one could stress the fact that there are different steps in the development of any collective entity: young age
could stand, for example, for a defence against institutionalization,
routinization, and loss of radicality, or, in reverse, a factor in political
naïveté. Differences could be explained by the fact that not all organizations experience the same stage of development at the same time. One
has therefore to keep in mind the polysemic meaning of 'age' when
analysing its impact on organizations' features, claims and practices.

In order to operationalize our definition of 'age', we used the year
of foundation of the organizations included in our sample to build a
meaningful periodization. We thus distinguished four periods. In the
first, the 'old' organizations were born. This period ends with the "68'
world-wide mobilizations, as 1968 can be considered as a turning point
in the social and political fields. Organizations born before those mobilizations were part of the workers' movement as the main, if not the
only, social movement. Trade unions were often directly connected to
left political parties, while their structure was rather hierarchic and based
on delegation: the mass of members had to choose representatives at the
various levels of the organization. However, these 'old' organizations are
not all trade unions or political parties: many charity-based organizations, confessional or not, were created at the turn of the nineteenth
century.

In contrast, organizations founded after 1968 were analysed in
terms of 'new social movements' (see Touraine 1978) – that is, cultural
movements – which questioned the bases of societies rather than contesting the organization of production (see also Boltanski and Chiapello
1997). This second period, beginning in 1969 and lasting until the fall
of the Berlin Wall, is a diverse one: the economic crisis from the 1970s
contributed to a decrease in strikes and worker mobilizations, whereas
the 'new social movements' stabilized organizationally and managed to
spread their demands. In some European countries political violence

has been used by some leftist activists. There again, differences are important from one European country to the other – for instance, in the 1980s, François Mitterrand's accession to power in France, on the basis of a 'programme commun' shared by socialists and communists, did not impact social movements in the same way as Thatcher's neoliberal policies did in the UK.

The year 1989 can be considered as a relevant transnational turning point: the fall of the Berlin Wall opened a period of distrust towards 'ideologies', not to mention analysis in terms of 'end of history'. Social movements took some distance from political parties, as they were forced to reconsider the role and political importance of the communist parties.

The period opened by the fall of the Berlin Wall ends with the 'Battle of Seattle'. The protests organized by several loose networks of activists against the WTO Millennium Round in 1999 can be considered as the (mediatic) opening performance of the mobilizations on global justice. Moreover, these events play a very important role in the activist imaginary: they were horizontally organized, often by a small group of activists, using the Internet as their main resource (Barlow and Clarke 2002). Some authors have even analysed the Internet as an indispensable tool for the building of an international civil society whose shape would match that of the World Wide Web (Castells 2002; Negri and Hardt 2005). Nevertheless, it is important to remember that transnational mobilizations on global issues did not begin during (or after) the Seattle protests. Indeed, although 1999 marks their spreading and generalization, the birth of such mobilizations dates back to the early 1970s (Agrikoliansky et al. 2005b, pp. 15ff).

The organizations we studied are distributed in the following way over the four periods. Looking at the combined database, 14 per cent of the organizations were created before 1968, 19.9 per cent between 1969 and 1989, 35.6 per cent in the phase 1990–99, and 30.5 in or after the year 2000. A look at the territorial levels organizations cover pushes us to some specifications about the transnationalization of the newest groups. Indeed, the organizations born during the spread of the GJM (2000 and after) are less likely to include international levels than are the older organizations: 51.5 per cent of groups born before 1968 include an international level, whereas only 38 per cent of the most recent do (although the latter are usually connected at the transnational level through networks). The national level has undergone the same descending curve, passing from 97 per cent of organizations existing before 1968 to 64.5 per cent of those from 2000 and after. However, this last period is not the only phase of denationalization: 21.4 per cent of the groups born between 1968 and 1989 have no national level – this last phase starting right after the period that Tilly (1986) has singled out as the most important period for national protests. The youngest organizations emerge as more attracted by the smaller scales (or more bound into local activities), whereas older organizations have the most multilevel structures, existing largely at all levels.

In what follows, we will look at the different characteristics of our organizations according to generation. For heuristic purposes, we will separate the internal dimension of democracy (that is, democracy as applied to internal decision making) from the external, which refers to relations with institutions.

Organizations' age and practices of democracy

The internal dimensions can be analysed in terms of 'prefiguration'. As explained by Polletta (2002, pp. 6–7), 'the label *prefigurative* has remained popular as a way to describe movement groups whose internal structure is characterized by a minimal division of labor, decentralized authority, and an egalitarian ethos and whose decision-making is direct and consensus oriented': while experiencing concrete forms of direct democracy, organizations can shape their claims and test alternative practices.

Indeed, the GJM has put forward claims addressing democratic issues. Its actors strive for democracy to be more 'effective', 'direct', 'participatory' or 'transparent'. However, they have concentrated on more than these claims and demands: the issue of democracy in the 'movement' has been and continues to be discussed during workshops organized in Social Forums, local assemblies held in squats, and informal meetings organized at counter-summits.

Delegation

The Global Justice Movement has been identified with horizontality. Its actors have tried to avoid representative mechanisms, being eager to engage in 'direct' forms of democracy – delegation being opposed to participation. For instance, Social Forums have strictly prohibited delegation (Aguiton and Cardon 2005, p. 8). Their activists have stressed openness and reticularity, through open assemblies and affinity groups. Their organization is very often 'project-driven' (a project being, for instance, a mobilization or a campaign): in reticular universes, projects can be defined as the element around which co-operation will crystallize

(Boltanski and Chiapello 1997, pp. 157–60) before being horizontally engaged.

The degree of reticularity and, conversely, hierarchy can be analysed by looking at various indicators, related to specific features of our organizations. Reticular spaces have developed some specific characteristics (Aguiton and Cardon 2005, pp. 2–8): delegation is prohibited, decisions should be made by consensus, and the network has to expand. Each of these dimensions contributes to defining the degree of reticularity and, conversely, hierarchy of GJM organizations. Delegations can be checked through different variables such as the openness of the decision-making process and the institutionalization of the division of work (through the existence of an executive committee). A group can delegate decisions to a representative body (as, for instance, many trade unions or federations do). Conversely, it can open the decision-making process to all of its members or even choose not to distinguish members from outsiders, opening its assemblies completely. In this sense, two indicators from our questionnaire with representatives of GJM organizations allow us to test the potential effects of generation on democratic practices within groups. The first (Table 9.1) deals with persons authorized to take part in the decision-making processes within groups' assemblies (delegates only, any member of the group, or any person present at the meeting); the second focuses on the presence of an executive committee.

Recently created organizations favour openness (50 per cent of the organizations from the sample). Indeed, it appears clear that the younger the organization, the more open it is: while none of the organizations created before 1968 allows 'whoever wants to join' to participate in the decision-making process, this is the case in 4.9 per cent and 19.0 per cent

Table 9.1 Openness of the decision making process: Who participates in the decision-making of an assembly? (%)

Period	Only delegates	Members of the group	Whoever wants to participate	Other	Total
Before 1968	57.7	38.5	0.0	3.8	100.0 (n = 26)
1969–89	31.7	46.3	4.9	17.1	100.0 (n = 41)
1990–99	30.2	42.9	19.0	7.9	100.0 (n = 63)
2000 and after	11.7	36.7	50.0	1.7	100.0 (n = 60)
Total	28.4	41.1	23.2	7.4	100.0 (n = 190)

of those created from 1969–89 and 1990–99, respectively. When looking at the concrete life of organizations, this openness can become merely a formal statement. Indeed, non-constitutional mechanisms can tend to close the entry, even if it is supposed to be open to anyone: friendship and affinity as much as the lack of public information on meetings can reduce participation to the most active members, excluding potential participants as efficiently as requiring a membership card, for instance. Nevertheless, it is undeniable that these 'young' organizations tend to refuse delegation: only 11.7 per cent of them define delegates as the decision makers. Conversely, organizations created before 1968 favour delegation (57.7 per cent define delegates as the decision makers in assemblies).

If openness increases throughout the four periods, the ratio of organizations putting members at the centre of their decision-making process remains stable. Indeed, the characteristics of the assemblies and their decision-making processes are key indicators to define the democratic practices of one organization. Groups can choose a system in which only a specific group of members is in charge of implementing the decisions made in assemblies. This can lead to a professionalization of contestation, the impact and consequences of which have been analysed in various surveys, some of them stressing its contributions to the renewal of protest (Sommier 2003). But groups from other sensibilities can decide not to recur to a specialized body, considering flatness as a way to enhance democracy.

It appears here clearly that the younger the organization, the more it refuses to specialize or divide the work, at least through official recourse to an executive committee. Indeed, while 90.3 per cent of the older organizations have such a committee, only 42.2 per cent of the most recent ones do (with a continuous decrease from 82.2 per cent in the second and 73.5 per cent in the third period). Moreover, the presence of an executive committee is evenly spread at high levels in all the organizations from the first three periods: only for the last are there more organizations having no executive committee than organizations having such a committee.

Such differences can be explained by the nature of the organizations born after 1999: groups tend to be structured around an open assembly as the only space for deliberation and decision making. However, horizontality can also be linked to the youth of the organizations: being at the first stage of their life, they can be small enough to avoid the necessity for an executive committee. Similarly, they lack the resources that could enable the institution of an executive committee. Indeed, as

Polletta explained, a goal in the development of the method of consensus is to open spaces for discourses (2002, p. 7), thus justifying members' 'continued participation' (p. 13). Beyond the decision-making system, multiplying meetings is a way to reinforce the group's cohesion, through this 'continued participation'. Indeed, refusing to formalize a group in charge of the daily run-up can be a way to invite members to be frequently active in the group. This requires a large time commitment, but here, time can become a resource as young organizations mobilize in order to strengthen the ties among their members. In the same perspective, young organizations are still at a stage in which the object, project, and principles need to be discussed, as they are not always well stabilized. Thus, it is important to include all members in these discussions. Indeed, participation can be considered as 'all the more important for collective actors that have little material incentives to distribute and must therefore gain and keep the commitment of their members on the bases of shared beliefs' (della Porta and Andretta 2007, p. 2).

Decision-making method

Consensus has been defined as one of the GJM's specificities; it is linked to the choice for reticular forms of organization. However, it is not only a positive choice: the heterogeneity of the actors involved makes it difficult to agree on voting procedures, with some suggesting the principle of 'one organization–one vote', others 'one member–one vote' (Agrikolianky and Cardon 2005). But, above all, it matches activists' desires to prefigure the world for which they struggle. In this perspective, consensus would be opposed to older forms of organizations centred around hierarchy and majority vote.

As can be seen in Table 9.2, the older the organization, the less it is attracted by consensus: while only 14.8 per cent of the organizations created before 1968 make their decisions by consensus, 24.4 per cent of those created from 1969 to 1989 do so (see also Chapters 3 and 5). Consensual decision making is adopted by the majority of organizations created after 1990: 55.4 per cent of those born in the period 1990–99, and 66.1 per cent of those created from 2000 on. However, reciprocity is not obvious: organizations created in 1969–89 resort to voting more than others do, with the turning point in 1990. The use of majority vote remains quite stable until 1990, whereas consensus constantly increases.

Attraction to consensus can be analysed as a direct consequence of openness: prohibiting delegation means that individuals do not

Table 9.2 The role of consensus: How do organizations make their decisions? (%)

Period	By majority vote	By consensus	Other[a]	Total
Before 1968	59.3	14.8	25.9	100.0 (n = 27)
1969–89	61.0	24.4	14.6	100.0 (n = 41)
1990–99	29.2	55.4	15.4	100.0 (n = 65)
2000 and after	23.7	66.1	10.2	100.0 (n = 59)
Total	38.5	46.4	15.1	100.0 (n = 192)

Note: [a] This refers to hybrid decision-making processes: for the oldest organizations, it is related to their complex architecture, which mixes members and delegates as much as vote and mandate. For the youngest, it is a will to reach a consensus whenever possible, but to leave open the possibility of voting.

represent anyone else. Thus, decisions can be made only by all those present in the assembly.

Openness of the group and the meaning of membership

One of the main features of the 'new' forms of democracy would be their attraction to openness. Networks are meant to expand, that is, to connect more and more knots. This goal is clearly mentioned, for instance, in the Charter of Principles of the World Social Forum. Several social science works have opposed old forms of engagement (whose main traits would be the importance of activists' personal involvement, stability of membership over time, and formalization of engagement) to newer ones, defined by their plasticity and fluidity (Ion 1997). Collective identities are considered as less stable, and ever changing. This would translate organizationally into different relations to membership. In this section, we will focus on the way in which organizations define membership, using three different indicators: first, groups can declare themselves as being open to recruiting members, that is, as discriminating who belongs to the group from who does not; second, groups can formalize membership through cards or choose informality; third, membership can be free of charge, or, on the contrary, linked to fees, which can become an important financial resource for the group. Finally, we shall focus on another relevant characteristic of our groups: do they gather only individual members, or, on the contrary, only groups? Or do they choose a hybrid nature, welcoming both individuals and groups?

Reticular universes make a value of diversity: they aspire to connect more and more different knots. We already had a first overview of openness when we looked at the ability of non-members to participate in assemblies. We shall go more in depth here by analysing how the principle of openness is translated in the relationship with the group's members. Declaring that it is not possible to become a member of a group means, in fact, that the group refuses to discriminate members from outsiders.

Organizations created before 1989 declare being open to members more often than the most recent ones do. Moreover, closing membership appears as an option only in the third generation of organizations (after 1990): 13 per cent of the groups born between 1990 and 1999 declare not having members. The proportion grows among the youngest organizations, with this rate rising to 23.4 per cent in the last generation. Organizations born after 2000 are very often keen to open their assemblies to all, frequently refusing the very principle of membership. This is also connected to the specific culture of some horizontal networks, which are reluctant to think in terms of membership. The French Intergalactique Network, created to co-ordinate the organizations of the 2003 G8 counter-summit, is a good example. Its activists do not think in terms of 'members' but 'participants' in the group's activities: as suggested by Jacques Ion in his analysis of contemporary activism (2005), one does not become an activist because of membership, but rather because one participates in a group's activities: membership is not based on declaration and recognition but on participation.

Formalizing membership is not common: only 28.7 per cent of the organizations declare giving a card to their members. This statement contradicts a common view of membership, probably inherited from the organizational model of working class parties (communist, socialist, or social democratic) or trade unions. When becoming members, newcomers received a card, often numbered, as a way to distinguish old-timers from recent members. This symbolic attribute still plays a role in some organizations, even those recently born. For instance, during ATTAC France's crisis, open letters and emails were sometimes signed with the name of the contributor and his or her card number – the lower the number, the more legitimacy it was supposed to give. However, the fact that less than one-third of the organizations declare formalizing membership should lead scholars to rethink a whole section of the history of activism, which developed around the archetype of working class activism. In fact, informality is the rule even among 'older' organizations, supposedly the most 'classical': only 40 per cent declare giving cards to their members. This ratio decreases for the most recent periods, with 37.8 per cent of organizations in the second and 30.9 per cent in the third period formalizing membership, ending with a very low 10.4 per cent for organizations born in 2000 and after.

Actually, formalizing closure does not necessarily lead to closedness. On the contrary, it can contribute to openness by stating clearly what the boundaries of organizations are. Stating who is in and who is out also requires stating explicitly how to join – that is, how one can become a member (or leave, lose membership, be rejected). A low level of formalization does not only mean that engagement can remain fluid and plastic. Jo Freeman's analysis of feminist movements has shown the perverse effect of structurelessness on groups' efficiency and democracy. She states that lack of formalization does not mean that all members are equal, but that the structure, and consequently the power, remain implicitly distributed. This can lead to difficulties when groups decide to recruit new members, or when they not only aim at raising consciousness (of the oppression that women experience, for instance) but also engage in other political actions (Freeman 1970).

Indeed, it is possible to state that 'very often, the most formal procedures enable the achievement of an – always relative – equality in participation and handling' (Mathieu 2008). The Intergalactique network is, again, a good example of the impact of a lack of explicit structure on the openness of a group. In it, 'becoming a member' does not mean anything more than to 'be a subscriber to the group's mailing list', where activities are discussed. Subscription is based on co-optation: here, in contrast to trade unions, 'candidates' have to be rather proactive: members of the group do not recruit newcomers, but co-opt those who ask to join. In addition, joining can be quite difficult: if ties are quite weak at the beginning of a horizontal network, they strengthen through the group's activities, which can soon start to become more selective. For instance, the Intergalactique network's mailing list has not welcomed a new subscriber since 2006. Choosing not to discriminate members from outsiders can indeed make it difficult for newcomers to know how to join the group's activities.

Formalizing membership also has an impact on groups' resources: membership can be free of charge, or, on the contrary, fee-paying. The tendency towards the rise of informal activism is confirmed if we look at paid dues. There is a very clear evolution through the whole period considered: the proportion of membership without paid dues starts from 9.7 per cent for groups created before 1968, rising to 24.1 per cent for organizations founded between 1990 and 1999 and 52.1 per cent for those created after 1999.

This continuous trend can be explained in two different ways. First, declining formality would mean that forms of membership change and are regulated differently from before. Indeed, the assessment of the political influence of organizations is not (anymore) strictly related to the number of members, but to other types of resources – including the capacity to mobilize beyond active members. Indeed, new forms of protest do not necessarily require a strong commitment from their supporters, blurring the distinction between 'members', 'supporters', and 'friends'.

Second, the rise of a new activism may have led to a change in the nature of groups: membership may have become hybrid. Individuals as much as groups can join together and form a new organization. ATTAC's core group, born in France in 1999, is a good example of the potentialities, but also the limits of such a structuration. It is composed by founding organizations as well as up to 20 000 individual members (Wintrebert 2007; Haeringer 2008).

In fact, over time, the groups' nature in terms of individual versus collective members has also changed. 'Single groups', that is, direct recruitment organizations, clearly decline (see Table 9.3): only 34.4 per cent of the groups born in 2000 and after are 'single' ones, whereas this format applies to 75.6 per cent of the oldest organizations. The model of a formal membership, validated by fees and an official card, appears as applicable only to these organizations. Indeed, their decline is caused by the rising of both federations and ad hoc groups, in two different stages. Federations and networks represent only 24.4 per cent of the organizations born between 1969 and 1989, 42 per cent of those created in the following period, and 45 per cent of those in 2000 and after. The model of ad hoc groups, that is, the temporary gathering of groups on a specific collective action, emerges after 1989 (with 8.7 per cent of the organizations born between 1990 and 1999) and expands very

Table 9.3   Nature of the group (%)

Period	A single group	A federation or network	Ad hoc group or campaign	Total
Before 1968	68.8	31.2	0.0	100.0 (n=32)
1969–89	75.6	24.4	0.0	100.0 (n=45)
1990–99	49.3	42.0	8.7	100.0 (n=69)
2000 and after	34.4	45.3	20.3	100.0 (n=64)
Total	53.3	37.6	9.0	100.0 (n=210)

quickly: 20.3 per cent of the groups born after 1999 are ad hoc ones. This trend shows the evolution of activism from separate organizations to the connection of organizations active on different causes and the building of campaigns based on transnational orientations.

Generation and interactions with institutions

GJM organizations build complex relations with institutions. Indeed, these organizations strive to link global and local issues (see also Chapters 4 and 7). Taking into account that, as Craig Jenkins and Bert Klandermans stated, 'surprisingly, little attention has been paid to inter-action between social movements and the state' (1995, p. 3), we shall not end this chapter without having analysed this relation as reported by the representatives of the organizations included in our sample (see Table 9.1).

The organizations that, proportionally, collaborate most with institu-tions on the local level are those created before 1968 (67.7 per cent) and between 1968 and 1989 (59.1 per cent). The fact that organi-zations stemming from 1968 (which at that time strongly advocated their autonomy) nowadays frequently collaborate with local political institutions speaks against *path dependency*. The recent creation of the organization seems to have an impact on relations with public institu-tions at the local level, as only 34.4 per cent of those founded in the most recent period do collaborate. However, this needs to be put in perspective, since only 14.8 per cent refuse collaboration despite their recent creation (2000 and after). It is also important to emphasize that many organizations declare a critical or selective collaboration accord-ing to the type of authority, the thematic and/or the political orientation of the local institutions.

Similar results emerge when looking at relations with public institu-tions at the national level: the older the GJM organizations, the more they collaborate with national institutions; the younger they are, the less they collaborate. Among the youngest organizations, however, only 19 per cent refuse to collaborate and 23.8 per cent declare indiffer-ence towards institutions. One can actually note that the older the organizations, the less indifferent they are toward collaboration with institutions. Finally, the distribution is similar when looking at rela-tions with public institutions at the international level: here as well, the older the organizations, the more they collaborate. One can also note that with regard to the three periods of time previous to 2000 (before 1968, 1969–89, and 1990–99), the refusal to collaborate is stable: a little more than 9 per cent. In contrast, it increases to 21 per cent for the organizations created after 1999.

Organizations belonging to the same generation are therefore quite consistent in their attitudes toward institutions, regardless of the level of the institution (local, national or international) (see Table 9.4). This is clearly the case, for instance, for refusal of collaboration, which is quite stable whatever the level: the variation within the same generation is never higher than 5 per cent. More important for the organizations is the profile of the institution. Representatives of diverse French organizations pointed out that the scale is not a sufficient criterion to decide whether to collaborate with an institution: they would not have the same attitude toward UNESCO as to the World Bank, or towards the Ministry of Social Affairs as to the Ministry of the Interior. For an executive committee member we interviewed from the French Foundation Copernic, 'It depends on the closeness of the institutional actors to the association (the State is plural). It is impossible to give a general response: we have a positive relationship with some institutions (close to the ideas of the Foundation Copernic) and no relationship with neo-liberal institutions'.

We should also consider a more flexible attitude that admits lobbying and pressuring for achieving concrete results on specific issues rather than fighting uncompromisingly for global ideological positions. Furthermore, participation in advisory authorities – depending on the administrations, the governments and the topics – is often complementary to mobilization and protest action (see also Chapter 7). As Jack Goldstone notes:

> there is no reason to expect that protest and conventional political action should be substitutes, with groups abandoning the former as they become able to use the latter. While some groups may, at different times, be more 'in', in the sense of being more aligned and integrated with the institutional authorities, with other groups are more 'out' (. . .). The dynamics of protest thus have a complex and contingent relationship to a group's integration into institutionalized politics. (2003, p. 10)

In general, we can consider a growing tendency towards critical collaboration, or participation in advisory authorities, as oriented to controlling public institutions. In this active defiance, 'The goal is then to make sure that elected officials fulfil their promises, and to find the means of maintaining the initial demand of a service for the common good', through oversight, resistance and assessment (Rosanvallon 2006, p. 15).

Table 9.4 Relations with public institutions

	Institutions at the international level (n = 203)				Institutions at the national level (n = 204)				Institutions at the local level (n = 200)			
	Refusal	Indifference	Collaboration	Other	Refusal	Indifference	Collaboration	Other	Refusal	Indifference	Collaboration	Other
Before 1968	9.4	9.4	65.6	15.6	9.7	0.0	71.0	19.4	6.5	0.0	67.7	25.8
1969–89	9.1	20.5	43.2	27.3	4.5	9.1	61.4	25.0	4.5	13.6	59.1	22.7
1990–99	9.2	18.5	33.8	38.5	9.1	10.6	45.5	34.8	4.7	10.9	45.3	39.1
After 2000	21.0	30.6	14.5	33.9	19.0	23.8	19.0	38.1	14.8	13.1	34.4	37.7
Total	12.8	21.2	35.0	31.0	11.3	12.7	44.6	31.4	8.0	10.5	48.5	33.0

In contrast, the generational factor has very little effect on how the group considers the impact of experiments with participatory public decision making (participatory budget, Agenda 21) on the quality of political decisions. Whatever the date of creation, about 20 per cent of the organizations consider that those experiments do not improve the quality of political decisions, while about 40 per cent believe that they do (only the organizations created between 1969 and 1989 have a lower rate of 27.3 per cent). The rest of the organizations do not have well defined positions on this topic.

Conclusion

Various practices and features characterize the organizational components of global justice mobilizations. Older organizations use consensual decision making less often than the newest ones do. These older groups are still attracted by delegation, whereas more recent organizations tend to reject it in favour of horizontal forms of participation. Similarly, conceptions of membership vary for different generations. Age also impacts on relation to institutions, as it determines the territorial levels one organization covers.

These differences are relevant when addressing the definition of the Global Justice Movement itself. The existence of differences does not imply the impossibility of making a movement out of the heterogeneous coalition of actors involved. However, it pushes us to define this movement through its heterogeneity, plasticity and the pragmatic alliances that its actors build through a common democratic microculture.

In this perspective, co-operation develops around shared beliefs for time-limited projects such as campaigns. Indeed, these project-driven organizations accompany the decline of 'single group' and the rise of 'ad hoc' campaigns. Thus, the differences among organizations from various generations could be linked to changes in the conception of political projects and perspectives: organizations themselves tend to be defined increasingly through activities and projects rather than on the basis of a collective and conscious identity. This redefinition seems to be a main 'novelty' of the most recent organizations, whose definition of boundaries tends to diverge from those of past models: openness to and reluctance about centralization are reinforced by an attraction to consensus-driven decision-making processes.

Nevertheless, informality and the goal of openness do not mean that this openness is always concretely realized. On the contrary, rather than reducing barriers, informality can maintain them while making them more difficult to identify and hence to bypass. As our survey has shown, groups emphasizing open assemblies can, at the same time, refuse to discriminate between members and outsiders, simply because 'being a member' does not hold the same meaning for them as for older organizations. Here again, membership will crystallize around ad hoc perspectives and specific projects, based on shared affinities as much as through objective and strategic alliances. This is not only the result of a positive, conscious choice made by founders of recent organizations, unwilling to reproduce the experience of their elders. Newer organizations are, by definition, less institutionalized than older ones. They have to deal with a lack of material resources, and therefore innovate as a way to mobilize other types of resources that are more readily available.

Ad hoc alliances can indeed be highly relevant. Our analysis has shown that the organizations involved in the mobilizations on global justice do not share the same visions of democracy. Thus, they tend to gather quite fluidly around specific campaigns, rather than around big ideological visions. This container's structure is loose enough to embrace organizations with diverse practices of democracy, while still sharing democratic demands and claims. In this, it is thus a very efficient space in which to share different types of resources, for instance enabling newer organizations to participate in transnational mobilizations. In this way, the organizations that participate in mobilizations on global justice prefigure various forms of democracy in their direct experience.

Notes

1. The authors would like to thank Ilhame Hajji for her contribution to the statistical analysis and Francine Simon-Ekovich for translating several sections of this chapter.
2. It is also worth noting that the story of the national chapters of ATTAC is very much determined by political opportunities at the national level.

10
Crossing Borders: Transnational Activism in European Social Movements[1]

Mario Pianta, Raffaele Marchetti, and Duccio Zola

Introduction

Since the late 1990s, the Global Justice Movement (GJM) has emerged as a major force in the global political arena. It has successfully organized growing numbers of cross border mobilizations on a range of global issues addressing justice, peace, and democracy. How has this surge of cross-border activism been possible? In this chapter we explore the complex factors – both external and internal to social movements – that have put global issues at the centre of transnational activism in European countries (as well as around the world). While the rest of the book addresses the visions and actions of GJMOs and their conceptions and practices of democracy as a fundamental element of their cross-border mobilizations, in this chapter we aim at identifying the key sources and dynamics of transnational activism, and the characteristics of the organizations of major European countries that are most active in cross-border mobilizations.

In the next section the relevant literature is discussed, exploring the conceptual frameworks used and the analyses of the sources and mechanisms of cross-border mobilizations. In the third section, the GJM organizations surveyed in the DEMOS project are investigated in terms of the issues of contention and degree and forms of transnational activism. In order to explore the main determinants of transnational activism, a quantitative analysis is carried out in the fourth section; a number of conclusions are presented thereafter.

The dynamics of transnational contention

Social movement literature has traditionally addressed contentious politics within national contexts, focusing on the relationships with domestic political processes and state power (McAdam et al. 2001; della Porta and Diani 2006). Such an approach has recently been extended to a variety of cross border mobilizations.

A first group of studies investigated the evolution of specific nationally (or locally) based campaigns that involved some cross-border dimensions, in terms of access to (or provision of) knowledge, resources, support, legitimation or political alliances with activist organizations (and sometimes also institutions) of other countries.[2] Typical cases include instances of North–South solidarity actions (on development, child labour, popular economy projects, and so on); assistance on human rights protections (against repressive governments, supporting indigenous peoples, and so on); environmental issues (climate change, the construction of dams, the protection of forests, and so on). In these studies, the domestic contention generally concerned national governments' decisions, policies or behaviours, sometimes associated with pressures from supranational institutions, more powerful states, or multinational corporations. Such policies were opposed by national mobilizations capable of building links outside the country, usually relying on networks with expertise in confronting the same external pressures.

The advantages of transnational linkages for domestic mobilization have been pointed out by Keck and Sikkink (1998), who suggested that a 'boomerang effect' may operate when national activism benefits from alliances with international social movements or institutional actors in seeking domestic political change. The protection of human rights is perhaps the most clear cut case, where contention concerns one specific government act – the decision by repressive states to accept internationally agreed conventions on human rights, or to stop violations or lack of compliance by its agencies.[3] In this case, the opening of a transnational dimension does not substantially change the political process of national contention; using the approach of Kriesi (2004, p. 69), political opportunity structures, configuration of political actors, and context of interaction remain essentially shaped by national factors.

A second line of investigation has addressed mobilizations concerning supranational institutions – typically, opposition to the International Monetary Fund, the World Bank, or the World Trade Organization, or support for the International Criminal Court.[4] Transnational activism is of major importance in these cases, usually with a crucial co-ordinating role played by large networks of movements or organizations in many countries. Contention focuses on the multilevel system of governance of specific issues – trade, finance, development, as well as crimes against humanity. Here, social movements engage in conflict over the decisions, policies and behaviour of supranational institutions – heavily affected by the most powerful state actors, such as the US and the EU – while the role of most national governments decreases. In fact, at the national level, contention usually concerns the government's (limited) responsibility in the formation of an international consensus and the consequences that global decisions will have on the country, including the required policy actions. In these cases, political opportunity structure, configuration of political actors, and context of interaction necessarily reflect the multilevel systems of governance operating on these issues. However, these studies have generally focused on the problems of global governance, international relations and political economy, or civil society involvement, rather than on social movement dynamics; a transnational perspective on contentious politics and social movements has not yet emerged from this literature.

A third line of more specific investigations has addressed the rise of the Global Justice Movement – exemplified by the 1999 Seattle protest against the WTO, by the diffusion of World and Continental Social Forums, by the global day of protest against preparations for the US war against Iraq on 15 February 2003.[5] The specificity of such mobilizations is their focus on *global issues*, although they include a wide spectrum of actions ranging from nationally (or locally) rooted ones to the campaigns on supranational institutions.

What unifies these mobilizations – to some extent – are three basic characteristics. First, the global nature of contentious issues at stake, which are always embedded in multilevel governance. Second, novel forms of transnational mobilization have emerged, based on cross-border networks and international campaigns. Third, new identities that are aware of global responsibilities, tolerant of diversity and capable of building large alliances, appear to come forward in parallel with such movements (see Chapter 1 in this volume; della Porta 2007c).

An additional aspect is the novelty in strategies and repertoires of action. GJMOs frequently make parallel use of both radical protest and more moderate lobbying of authorities; their repertoires of action tend to evolve rapidly, with immediate diffusion of successful models and shifts of the scale of activism. However, these dynamics have often been documented also in national contexts of rapid expansion of social movements and therefore do not appear as a specificity of the GJM (della Porta and Diani 2006; Tarrow 2005). In these mobilizations, the global and national (or local) dimensions are both present from the beginning, and parallel the multilevel system of governance; the domestic contexts of contention retain their relevance, but as part of a broader, global challenge. Cross-country differences in movements' cultures, attitudes on global issues, political opportunities, and repertoires of action have therefore been found to persist (della Porta 2007c).

All three approaches address the novelty of transnational mobilizations and contribute to highlighting specific dimensions of the process. Their conclusions on the relevant dimensions of the analysis of transnational movements, however, tend to differ. Some authors emphasize the continuity between national and transnational mobilizations (Smith 2004; Giugni et al. 2006), as with the first of the approaches discussed above. But this conclusion can hardly be reconciled with the cases addressed by the second research perspective, where mobilizations develop from the start around multilevel political processes and governance systems, with key dynamics of contention taking place on a global scale. Still, the second group of studies is limited by the lack of a unified model; the diversity and specificity of these mobilizations has complicated the construction of an adequate conceptual framework for global contention.

An effort in this direction has been made by the analysis of transnational activism carried out by Tarrow (2005), which takes as its starting point the rise of cross-border mobilizations of various types. It investigates the effects of transnational activism on social actors, their claims and strategies, and the links between non state actors, states, and international politics, but does not address the factors that produced such mobilizations in the first place.[6]

Moving from its conceptualization of global issues, the approach focusing on the Global Justice Movement appears to be a promising perspective for developing an adequate multilevel framework for global contentious politics. Building on the literature discussed above, the aim of this chapter is to contribute to an understanding of the determinants of the transnational activism associated with the Global Justice Movement, focusing on GJM organizations in Europe, and shedding new light on the dynamics of global (or multilevel) contention.

In particular, we explore the relevance of the factors identified above as key characteristics of GJM mobilizations, advancing a number of hypotheses that will be tested in the empirical analysis of the next sections. The first factor concerns the diverse nature of the global issues they address, which are characterized to various extents by political opportunity structures shaped by multilevel systems of governance, by configurations of political actors that are centred on international networks and institutions, and by cross-border contexts of interaction. Therefore, we can expect that the stronger the transnational nature of the issue of contention (in particular in the cases of trade, finance, development, and perhaps in the cases of peace and environmental issues), the greater the relevance of transnational activism.

The second characteristic concerns factors internal to social movements, and in particular their organizational structures. We have already argued that in mobilizations on global issues, a major and novel role has been played by transnational networks of social organizations and movements.[7] While such coalitions have largely contributed to make cross border activism feasible also for small organizations or activist groups with little resources (of all kinds: staff, knowledge, finance, experience, and so on), there is no denying that a greater amount of resources may contribute to more sustained transnational activism. Therefore, we can expect that GJM organizations that are members of networks or campaigns and/or have more resources can be associated to a greater intensity of transnational activism.

Third, the complex question of identities should be considered. Mobilizations on global issues – which may be perceived even by activists as distant from everyday concerns and local contention – are likely to require strong motivation by both individuals and organizations. We may expect that a stronger involvement of organizations in transnational activism can be associated (both as a result and as a contributing factor) to a group identity that is largely built on involvement in such global issues.

A fourth factor to be explored concerns the strategies and repertoires of action used by the organizations; as suggested above, it is difficult to identify here a specificity of the GJM as opposed to national social movements, and therefore no clear hypothesis can be advanced.

Finally, as argued above, we should not forget the persistence of national characteristics, rooted in differences in national political contexts, opportunity structures, and movement cultures (as shown in the country studies in della Porta 2007c).

In the next sections, these factors are investigated empirically, exploring their relevance in explaining the rise of transnational activism.

The empirical analysis

The empirical evidence provided in this chapter is based on the DEMOS project survey of 210 organizations (85 per cent nationally based, from France, Germany, Italy, Spain, Switzerland and the UK, and 15 per cent transnational in character) engaged in various global issues.[8] We focus here on the information relevant for highlighting the dynamics and determinants of transnational activism. We first provide descriptive evidence for the four aspects – issues, organizational structures, identity, and strategies – that are expected to influence the participation in cross-border mobilizations. Second, we investigate various forms of transnational activism and propose a synthetic measure of their importance in the activity of GJMOs.

The determinants of global activism

The first aspect to be addressed concerns the global issues of contention that are at the root of the evolution of specific cross-border mobilizations within the GJM. Eight broad groups of global issues have been identified as principal fields of activity for the surveyed organizations: 1) democracy and human rights; 2) global economic issues; 3) development, international solidarity, and co-operation; 4) environment; 5) peace; 6) social, citizenship, and labour rights; 7) media and think tanks associated with the GJM; 8) political parties, political organizations, and trade unions participating in the GJM. A detailed description of the activities grouped in these issues, and examples of relevant organizations, are provided in the Appendix. Table 10.1 below shows the distribution of surveyed organizations across these fields of activism.[9] The most represented field is political organizations and trade unions; other major fields include democracy and human rights; social, citizenship, and labour rights; followed by media/think tanks; development and co-operation; and global economic issues. Peace and environmental issues are the least represented among surveyed organizations.

These issues are characterized by varying degrees of global or national activism. National political organizations, parties, and unions, as well as media and think tanks, are firmly embedded within national political contention, respond to domestic opportunities and contexts, and can be expected to concentrate most of their activism at the national level, even when it is associated with GJM mobilizations. A similar orientation can be expected in the case of social and labour rights, where efforts for their protection are generally carried out within specific national contexts. Not surprisingly, we find that these activities are more frequent

Table 10.1 Distribution of GJMOs by issue of activism and country (%)

Issues of activism	Transnational	France	Germany	Italy	Spain	Switzerland	UK	Total
Democracy and human rights	1.9	1.4	2.4	2.4	2.4	1.4	2.9	14.8
Global economic issues	3.8	0.5	1.4	1.0	1.0	1.9	2.4	11.9
Development, co-operation	3.3	0.5	1.4	1.0	2.9	1.4	1.9	12.4
Environment	1.0	1.0	1.0	0.5	1.4	–	0.5	5.2
Peace	–	0.5	1.4	3.3	1.4	1.0	1.0	8.6
Social, citizenship and labour rights	1.0	3.3	1.9	2.4	2.9	1.9	1.4	14.8
Media/think tanks	1.0	2.9	1.4	2.4	1.9	1.4	1.9	12.9
Political parties, trade unions	1.0	3.3	1.4	4.8	2.9	4.3	1.9	19.5
Total	**12.9**	**13.3**	**12.4**	**17.6**	**16.7**	**13.3**	**13.8**	**100.0**

among national organizations and have little relevance among transnational groups. Conversely, as already pointed out, the global dimension of contention is more relevant in the case of global economic issues and development and co-operation (issues where transnational organizations have an above average presence). Democracy and human rights, peace, and environmental issues combine a strong global nature and strong contention with national governments, who have key decision-making power on such matters; the relevance of transnational activism will therefore depend on the orientation of the specific organizations surveyed.

The second aspect to be considered concerns organizational structure, including the nature of the group and the size of its resources. The organizations surveyed in this study are equally divided between single organizations and networks or campaigns; the former are more frequent among national groups and are commonly made up by media/think tanks and parties/trade unions. The latter tend to address global democracy and global economic issues in particular and are dominant among transnational organizations. This result is associated with the ability of networks and campaigns to allow for diversity and to adapt to different sociopolitical contexts, combining a practical constraint with a preference for local autonomy and pluralism. Organizational size is likely to be a crucial element for cross-border activism. High levels of funds and specialized personnel are often needed in order to tackle complex global issues. Organizations with larger budgets (usually the older ones) tend to have more paid staff and volunteers, while networks and campaigns have smaller budgets and fewer paid staff.[10]

On the third question – identity of GJM organizations – the DEMOS survey provides information on whether organizations consider themselves as belonging to the GJM; more than 90 per cent of the surveyed groups make this statement.[11]

The fourth aspect concerns the strategies and repertoires of action of organizations. Political education and raising awareness is the most adopted strategy by surveyed organizations – almost 90 per cent – followed by protest and promotion of alternatives (75 per cent) and lobbying (50 per cent) (see Chapter 1). A key characteristic in this regard is the adoption of multiple strategies: 70 per cent of the surveyed groups deploy a multi-focus strategy (including three or four strategies), as this is considered the most effective way to have an impact on a multilevel system of governance and transnational opportunity structures. Larger budgets are associated with a higher number of strategies used.[12]

When we relate the strategies adopted to the issues of activism, we find a greater orientation towards political education, lobbying, and constructing alternatives in organizations active on democracy, global economic issues, development, and the environment. Protest is most frequent (and often the single strategy) among organizations focusing on social and labour rights, parties and unions, as well as in peace and environmental groups. The presence of multiple strategies is notable: 73 per cent of environmental groups and 60 per cent of those active on the global economy carry out all four strategies at once.

In line with the use of multiple strategies, a majority of GJM organizations engage in collaborative relationships with institutions, especially at the local (68 per cent) and national (67 per cent) levels. Collaboration with international institutions is present in 54 per cent of cases, while a refusal to collaborate is expressed by 14 per cent of the groups and indifference by 33 per cent. Older organizations with more resources are more collaborative with institutions, while networks and campaigns remain less collaborative. Organizations that collaborate with international institutions practice lobbying and protest with equal frequency, and are even more oriented towards political education and alternatives.[13]

Measuring transnational activism

GJM organizations have developed different types and forms of cross-border mobilization. In order to fully capture the novelty of the GJM, it is necessary to identify the various elements of transnational activism and to construct a valid method to measure them. We have considered four types of cross border initiatives carried out by GJM organizations. They include:

- two forms of participation in international events (*expressed by two binary variables*):

  a. *global days of action or parallel summits;*
  b. *World and European Social Forums;*

- two types of cross border relationships with other groups (*expressed by two binary variables*):

  c. *participation in transnational campaigns;*
  d. *participation in transnational networks.*

The first variable reports whether the organization has participated in global days of action (for example, those against the war in Iraq, held since 2003) or in parallel summits (that is, those organized in coincidence with official G8, WTO, IMF or WB summits). These events are relevant, as they have represented important and widespread contentious gatherings of social movements on global issues; 75 per cent of the surveyed groups have joined one of these events.

The second variable refers to the participation of the interviewed organizations in either World or European Social Forums. Since 2001, Social Forums have offered the principal meeting point for social movements at the global and continental levels. Again, more than 75 per cent of organizations participated in such events (with French and Italian groups reporting even higher participation). Conversely, less than 66 per cent took part in national and local social forums.

The third variable shows the participation of organizations in transnational campaigns, either as members or as promoters. Since the 1990s, transnational campaigns have become a key mode for cross border mobilization. Of the surveyed organizations, 80 per cent take part in transnational campaigns, particularly the British, Italian and transnational groups. More specifically, 40 per cent of cases are campaigns on social issues, and 25 per cent on democracy.

Finally, the fourth variable focuses on the participation of surveyed organizations in transnational networks. We have already pointed out the importance of participation in networks by the surveyed organizations and the relevance they have in cross-border mobilizations.

We argue that an organization with full participation in transnational mobilizations would engage in all four types of activities, and an exclusively national organization would not participate in any of them. Thus, an organization fully involved in cross-border mobilizations would have an organizational structure that is shaped by stable links to international networks, and a mode of activism that includes participation in cross-border campaigns. As a part of such activities, it would participate both in specific (and often specialized) parallel summits, and in broader gatherings of the GJM, such as World and European Social Forums. Following from this, we propose an index of transnational activism (TN4) as the logical sum of these four variables; the proposed index has values ranging from 0 (when an organization did not participate in any event, nor to transnational campaigns and networks) to 4 (when an organization did participate in at least one global day of action/parallel summit, one Social Forum, one transnational campaign, and one transnational network). The index privileges those organizations that have multiple initiatives, rather than those exclusively focused on a single activity.[14] We claim that this index provides a viable metric to measure the degree of transnational activism of GJMOs. In order to prove this case, we need to examine the empirical patterns of cross-border activism that such an index highlights.

The values of the index of transnational activism and of the four variables that constitute it are shown in Table 10.2 for all organizations and for the seven country groups. On average, the surveyed organizations show a substantial degree of cross border activism, with a TN4 value of 2.96. Looking at the four variables, participation in transnational events is more frequent than inter-organizational linkages. Participation in global days of action and parallel summits is the most common cross-border activity (90 per cent of organizations), followed by Social Forums (80 per cent), while networking (73 per cent) is more widespread than participation in campaigns (53 per cent).

National specificities are interesting to observe. Not surprisingly, transnational organizations reveal the highest degree of cross-border activism, with an average value of 3.59; we could point out that all the transnational organizations in our survey are involved in transnational networks. Italian and French organizations also are ranked high in terms of transnational activism, showing very high percentages of participation in GJM events; British and German organizations are positioned in the middle, while Spanish and Swiss cases are at the bottom of the rankings (with 22 per cent and 21 per cent for campaigning, and 54 per cent and 67 per cent for participation to Social Forums, respectively).[15]

The issue of activism is a key factor influencing cross-border activism. As Table 10.3 shows, organizations engaged in global economic issues are the most transnationalized, followed by political parties and trade unions, and groups active on development, environment and peace. Groups involved in global economic issues have high scores on all variables; almost all are part of transnational networks, as this form of organization has emerged as a viable and effective model for the contestation of global economic power. A similar pattern is followed by groups active on development and co-operation. Political parties and trade unions have the highest participation in events, where they may obtain visibility and exert influence, while they disregard involvement in networks and campaigns; the opposite pattern is shown by environmental groups. Finally, groups focused on social, labour and citizenship rights and media/think tanks are mainly active at the national/local level, with lower participation in all cross-border activities.

Table 10.2 Degree of transnational activism of GJMOs by country

Country	TN4 index	Global days of action, parallel summits (% of yes)	World and European Social Forums (% of yes)	Participation in transnational campaigns (% of yes)	Participation in transnational networks (% of yes)
Transnational	3.59	92.5	92.5	74.0	100.0
France	3.46	96.4	96.4	60.7	92.8
Germany	2.61	80.7	73.0	42.3	65.3
Italy	3.51	100.0	94.5	86.4	70.2
Spain	2.37	94.2	54.2	22.8	65.7
Switzerland	2.28	78.5	67.8	21.4	60.7
UK	2.86	79.3	79.3	65.5	62.0
Total	2.96	89.5	79.5	53.8	73.3

Table 10.3 Degree of transnational activism of GJMOs by issue of activism

Field of activity	TN4 index	Global days of action, parallel summits (% of yes)	World and European Social Forums (% of yes)	Participation in transnational campaigns (% of yes)	Participation in transnational networks (% of yes)
Democracy and human rights	2.70	80.6	80.6	45.2	64.5
Global economic issues	3.48	92.0	92.0	68.0	96.0
Development, co-operation	3.07	92.3	69.2	65.4	80.8
Environment	2.81	81.8	54.5	63.6	81.8
Peace	2.88	88.9	77.8	55.6	66.7
Social, citizenship and labour rights	2.64	87.1	67.7	45.2	64.5
Media/think tanks	2.88	85.2	81.5	51.9	70.4
Political parties, trade unions	3.12	100.0	92.7	48.8	70.7

Organizational structure plays an important role in shaping cross-border mobilizations. Looking in Table 10.4 at the values of the index of transnational activism by type of organization, we find that networks and campaigns tend to be more transnational than do single organizations. In particular, they have higher percentages of participation in parallel summits, and, despite already being networks or campaigns, they tend to participate in other campaigns and networks, thus creating an intense net of relationships. In participation in Social Forums, the values of the two types of organizations do not differ.

Economic resources appear to be a constraint for a high level of transnationalization of an organization, but the same does not apply to human resources. An organization with a higher budget tends to be more transnational (those with no budget have the lowest degree of transnationalization), but it does not need a lot of personnel to carry out cross border activism; in fact, organizations with fewer than 100 paid staff and fewer than 15 volunteers are more transnational than larger ones.[16]

Results on the identity issue are shown in Table 10.5. Organizations with a strong GJM identity tend to be (moderately) more transnational than those denying such an identity. Of the organizations with a GJM identity, 90 per cent participate in global days of action or parallel summits, 79 per cent in Social Forums (no difference with those without GJM identity), and 74 per cent in transnational networks. The clearest distinction is on participation in transnational campaigns, where the presence of groups with no GJM identity is the lowest (less than 40 per cent).

The strategies adopted by organizations have a less clear effect. The groups engaged in lobbying and promoting alternatives have (marginally) higher levels of cross-border activism, and there is little variation among the four variables on transnational activities. The most relevant result concerns the presence of multiple strategies: the more an organization adopts various strategies, the more likely it is to be involved in cross-border initiatives. Organizations collaborating with various institutions show marginal differences in their intensity of cross-border activism. As could be expected, those collaborating with international bodies show a higher degree of transnationalization than those involved at the national and local levels.

Summing up the empirical evidence provided so far, we can argue that the 210 European organizations of the DEMOS survey provide a relevant picture of the characteristics, activities, and strategies of GJMOs involved in cross-border activism. The index of transnational

Table 10.4 Degree of transnational activism of GJMOs by type of organization

Type of organization	TN4 index	Global days of action, parallel summits (% of yes)	World and European Social Forums (% of yes)	Participation in transnational campaigns (% of yes)	Participation in transnational networks (% of yes)
Single organization	2.82	85.3	80.0	50.5	66.3
Network or campaign	3.16	92.4	81.5	64.1	78.3

Table 10.5 Degree of transnational activism of GJMOs by identity

GJM identity	TN4 index	Global days of action, parallel summits (% of yes)	World and European Social Forums (% of yes)	Participation in transnational campaigns (% of yes)	Participation in transnational networks (% of yes)
Sense of belonging to GJM	3.00	90.4	79.7	55.6	74.3
No sense of belonging to GJM	2.65	82.6	78.2	39.1	65.2

activism we have proposed captures the variety of cross-border activities, providing a synthetic picture of the degree of transnational activism of European organizations involved in the GJM. These organizations engage in transnational events, join networks and campaigns on international issues, and develop an identity with a strong sense of belonging to the GJM. Despite this, the heterogeneity of organizations leads to a highly differentiated pattern of mobilization across EU countries. National differences remain important. Countries such as Italy or France, for instance, offer a sociopolitical environment that is more conducive to cross-border mobilization.

Going back to the four factors that – in our hypothesis – can play a role in influencing the degree of transnational activism of European groups, issues of contention appears to differentiate strongly among organizations, with those engaged in global economic and development issues showing a higher degree of transnational activism. Organizational structures are relevant, as networks and campaigns appear to be more viable forms of cross-border organization within the GJM. An identity centred on global issues is influential in cross-border activism. In terms of strategies, while few differences emerge among organizations, the presence of multiple strategies is indeed associated with greater cross-border activism. In the next section, a quantitative investigation of the relationships between these factors and the degree of transnational activism is presented.

Exploring the determinants of transnational activism

Building on the empirical evidence discussed above, we explore in this section the determinants of cross-border activism with a quantitative analysis relating key characteristics of the surveyed organizations with the values shown by the index of transnational activism. In this way we can test the hypotheses discussed above and assess the influence of various factors that have led European social movements to mobilize across national borders on issues of global contention. The DEMOS database allows us to carry out such an investigation, as it includes a large number of cases and offers a reliable picture of European mobilizations.

In this analysis, we aim to explain the values of the index of transnational activism (TN4, dependent variable) with a set of independent variables that reflect the four factors described above – issues, organizations, identity and strategy – while taking into account the diversity of national contexts. The independent variables used include: the eight issues of activism; the network or campaign form and the size of staff as indicators of organizational structures; the sense of belonging to the GJM in order to account for identity factors; the presence of multiple strategies and the adoption of separate strategies and forms of action in order to document repertoires of action. All variables are binary (yes/no) except in the case of size of staff and multiple strategies, where values range between 0 and 4. Country dummies are also included in the analysis in order to account for national specificities.

Owing to the nature of the dependent variable, which can assume values from 0 to 4, the analysis is carried out using an ordered logit model. The model provides results on the significance of independent variables and produces 'odds ratios' that indicate the probabilities that TN4 values have to move to a higher rank when the independent variable shifts from 0 to 1, or moves to a higher rank, while all other variables remain unchanged. An odds ratio below 1 means that the independent variable is likely to have an inverse effect on the TN4 index. In ordered logit models, the R-square is not a straightforward indicator of the goodness of fit, and a simple assessment of the strength of the model is provided by the share of cases whose TN4 values are correctly predicted.[17]

Table 10.6 reports the main results of the ordered logit estimates, showing the odds ratio and the significance of each coefficient, for two versions of the model. The results show that the model has a good ability to explain the degree of transnational activism of the surveyed organizations.

In the first model (whose results are in the first column of the table), degree of transnational activism appears to be highly and significantly related to the involvement of organizations in issues of contention associated with the global economy and (with a lower significance) to development. Organizational structures, described by size of staff, are highly significant; a larger staff contributes to greater cross-border activism. A high value and significance is found for the GJM identity variable, while the presence of multiple strategies also significantly contributes to greater transnational activism. The meaning of the odds ratio should be pointed out. Organizations active on global economic issues have more than four times the probability of being more transnationalized than those involved in other fields, while development issues make organizations twice as likely to be transnational in their activism. Groups declaring a sense of belonging to the GJM have more than five times the probability to be more transnational than those who reject such an identity. Conversely, a larger staff and the coexistence of multiple strategies – protest, lobbying, promotion of alternatives, education – have a modest effect on increasing the chances of greater cross-border activism.

The model has controlled for countries of organizations (with reference to the case of transnational ones, which is excluded from the regression); when they are based in the UK, Germany, Spain and Switzerland, there is a small (but significant) probability of showing a lower degree of transnational activism. Comparing the scores estimated by the model for the dependent variable with actual values, we find that the prediction is accurate in 54 per cent of cases. This model appears to effectively summarize the relationships between organizations' characteristics and degree of cross-border activism, confirming much of the hypotheses advanced above on the factors shaping transnational activism.

A possible weakness of this model may concern the nature of the variable on GJM identity, because it is – as we suggested in the conceptual discussion above – both a determinant and a product of transnational activism. Therefore, a second version of the model has been estimated without such a variable; the results are shown in the second column of Table 10.6.

The findings change little with this picture. The two relevant issues of activism increase their importance; the variable on global economic issues maintains its strong impact and significance; and the variable on development increases both. A more modest impact of a larger staff is combined with a new relevance of the variable on the network or campaign nature of the organization. Similarly, a minor weakening of the impact of the presence of multiple strategies is combined with the inclusion of the variable concerning the use of demonstrations as a form of action; generally, the impact on transnational activism expected from the variables on organizations and strategies is about half of that resulting from issues of contention.

The country controls in this model confirm the negative effect when the country of origin is Germany, Spain, Switzerland or the UK (the latter loses its significance). The predicted values for TN4 are correct in 50 per cent of cases.

This second model confirms the previous results and extends the range of relevant variables, discussed in the empirical analysis of the previous section, that have an influence on transnational activism.

Summing up these results, the emergence of transnational activism by European organizations appears to be associated to the four factors identified above – issues of contention, organizational structures, identity and strategies – but with major differences in relevance. Organizations

Table 10.6 The determinants of transnational activism

Variables	Model 1 ODDS RATIO	Model 2 ODDS RATIO
Issue of activism: Global economy	4.13***	4.29***
Issue of activism: Development and cooperation	2.17*	3.49**
Organizational structure: Network or campaign	–	1.84*
Organizational structure: Size of staff	1.52***	1.50**
Identity: Belonging to GJM	5.39***	–
Strategies: Presence of multiple strategies	1.50***	1.41**
Strategies: Demonstrations as forms of action	–	1.94*
Country: France	2.06	1.31
Country: Germany	0.20**	0.23**
Country: Italy	1.89	1.69
Country: Spain	0.11***	0.05***
Country: Switzerland	0.06***	0.08***
Country: UK	0.22**	0.37
No. of Observations	205	182
LR chi2	104.14	90.30
Prob > chi2	0.00	0.00
Log likelihood	−221.76	−198.62
Pseudo R2	0.19	0.18
% of Correctly Predicted Cases	54%	50%

Notes: Ordered Logit Estimates. Dependent Variable: Index of Transnational Activism (Values: 0–4). *significant at the 90% level; **significant at 95%; ***significant at 99%. Calculations carried out with STATA8.

involved in two particular issues of transnational contention – global economy and development – are very strongly 'pulled' towards cross-border mobilizations, as the transnational dimension prevails in the opportunity structures and systems of governance of such issues. Equally important is the role of an organizational identity associated with the GJM, which however has a reciprocal influence on cross-border initiatives. A more limited influence has been found for the factors describing the nature of the organization, its strategies and national background. This suggests that the move from national to transnational activism is no simple process for GJM organizations; rather, it is shaped by the issues of contention raised by European movements, by the opportunity for groups' identities to evolve, by a choice of organizational models based on networks or campaigns (and on the presence of a larger staff), and by the ability to challenge authorities using multiple strategies.

As the surveyed organizations included a group of transnational ones with no specific country of origin, we also tested whether the results could have been 'distorted' by the inclusion of these organizations that, by definition, have a greater orientation towards cross-border activism. Therefore, the two models have been estimated also on 'national' organizations only, omitting the cases of transnational ones. The results of these estimations are in Table 10A.1 (see Appendix).

The results are broadly confirmed, in terms of both significance of the variables and size of the odds ratios. The main difference is that the field of activity 'development and co-operation' loses its significance in model 1 and weakens it in model 2. In addition, the variable on multiple strategies is not significant in model 2. In the models of Table 10.6, the country controls were set in relation to the transnational group (which was left out from the independent variables). In the estimations reported in Table 10A.1, Switzerland is left out and the odds ratios therefore calculated in reference to the average of Swiss organizations; the results show a highly positive (and significant) influence of Italian and French nationalities, and a more modest positive effect of German and UK origin.

The results of this exploration of the determinants of cross-border activism appear to be robust with respect to changes in the model and in the dataset. We can therefore argue that these models capture important determinants of the move to transnational activism of GJM organizations in Europe.

Conclusions

The large mobilizations of the GJM in Europe beginning in the late 1990s and continuing up to the present (Pianta and Zola 2007) could be sustained only with the systematic involvement of organized groups, whether single organizations, networks or campaigns. This chapter has investigated the factors that led a large number of European social movement organizations to become active in the cross-border mobilizations typical of the GJM. A number of key aspects of the emerging dynamics of transnational contention have been identified, both conceptually and empirically. They differentiate the analysis of GJM mobilizations from approaches to social movements mainly focusing on domestic political contention.

A general lesson emerging from our analysis regards the complexity of the process leading organizations to cross-border activism: several complementary developments – in issues of contention and identities, strategies, and resources – must be present in order to achieve high levels of transnational activity. Within such a multidimensional process, a number of key factors stand out.

The involvement of organizations in contentious issues with a clear multilevel governance system has emerged as a major factor in the rise in transnational activism. Issues associated with the global economy – trade, finance, economic policies – and those linked to development and cooperation – poverty, aid, fair trade – are fields that strongly 'pull' organizations towards cross-border initiatives, influencing the form and content of much of their activism. In such themes, the political opportunity structure is mainly transnational; the configuration of political actors includes supranational institutions and multinational corporations, requiring systematic mobilization at the transnational level.

The same effect did not emerge for such equally global themes as democracy, human rights, peace and the environment, because on these issues national states have retained crucial powers; contention often focuses on specific governments' decisions, such as those on democratic reforms, protection of rights, participation in war, action on climate change. Moreover, a large part of the surveyed organizations carried out work on these themes at all levels (transnational, national, and local), responding to political opportunities on varying scales. Action at the national and local levels is prevalent also for organizations involved in social and citizenship rights and in media and think-tank work, leading to a lower involvement in cross-border activism. A particular case is that of the political parties and trade unions of our survey, which showed a strong involvement in the GJM and participation in global events, but *not* in networks and campaigns; a possible interpretation is that they shared the 'ideological' drive of the GJM, and saw participation in parallel summits and Social Forums as a way of exerting influence and gaining visibility; but in terms of forms of political contestation, they maintained their traditional focus on *national* political processes.

Another factor that emerges in our findings is the importance of a robust organizational form based on networks and campaigns. As we have already pointed out, this model is typical of the GJM and particularly of the mobilizations on global economic and political issues. In fact, as we argued elsewhere (Marchetti and Pianta 2008), transnational networks have played the role of 'backbones' of the GJM, preparing and supporting the various waves of mobilization on specific themes, and providing links across different issues.

The power of identity is an additional factor: the sense of belonging to the Global Justice Movement, of sharing a new transnational political project, is closely associated with transnational activism. This role may parallel, in some ways, the power of ideologies in previous waves of *national* social movements: the common rejection of neoliberal globalization could be seen as the foundation of a shared identification with global struggles. Still, the identity of the GJM includes a variety of dimensions, such as the emergence of 'pluralistic and tolerant identities' (della Porta 2007c), which have made possible the broad alliances typical of the GJM. At the root of the widespread identification with the GJM by European social movement organizations, we may find the combination of a unifying transnational political project – a vision of resistance to globalization, or of *globalization from below* (Pianta 2001b) – and a highly plural model of cross-border activism based on major events, networks and campaigns. Greater awareness of global contention may have led to higher participation in cross-border initiatives, which in turn supported an even stronger identification with the GJM. The result has been the rise in cross-border mobilizations and the close identification with the GJM of a great variety of organizations, social groups, and cultural sensibilities.

In this process, no single strategy appears to be associated with cross-border activism; rather, the ability to combine protest with the proposal of alternatives, lobbying, and education leads to transnational initiatives. Global issues are often characterized by a complex pattern of confrontations and opportunities for dialogue with international institutions, and a flexible and multiple strategy of contention is likely to characterize the organizations with higher transnational activism.

These results confirm the view proposed in this book on the novelty of the Global Justice Movement, with its 'multilevel and multiform' actions (discussed in Chapter 1) and its ability to challenge and interact with national and transnational institutions (examined in Chapter 4). In investigating the sources of cross-border activism, this chapter has found that a key role has been played by the need to address global issues and confront multilevel governance systems, alongside developments 'internal' to movements in terms of evolving identities, emergence of flexible network structures and adoption of multiple strategies. Many of these developments are associated with the importance attached to the value of democracy, both in the contention with authorities, and in the search for effective democratic practices within the GJM – themes that are investigated in several chapters of this book. This evolution has sustained the rise of the Global Justice Movement, with its pervasive transnational activism, bringing new demands for political change onto the global scene, and continuing challenges to national political processes.

Appendix: The issues of global activism of organizations

The issues of contention with which the organizations surveyed by the DEMOS project can be associated have been identified as follows, considering selected examples of themes, campaigns, and individual organizations.

In the field of democracy and human rights, we classified Social Forums, from the local to the international level (Liverpool Social Forum, Abruzzo Social Forum, Forum Social Lemanique, Forum Social Suisse, World Social Forum); human rights organizations (Amnesty, Medico International, Ligue de Droits de l'Homme); those movements using radical forms of participation and political engagement (Espacio Alternativo, Globalise Resistance, Rete No Global); and those networks that are active on global democracy issues (Reclaim Our UN, CIVICUS).

The field of global economic issues includes campaigns, networks, and organizations active on international economic issues such as financial transactions, poverty, trade, and debt (ATTAC, Seattle to Brussels, Jubilee Debt Campaign, Make Poverty History, Trade Justice Movement).

The field of development and co-operation is made up of organizations that carry out activities of co-operation with third world countries (Oxfam International, Christian Aid, Evangelischer Entwicklungsdienst); work on development issues such as agriculture and food sovereignty (Campagna EuropAfrica-Terre Contadine, Comité catholique contre la faim et pour le developpement); fair trade organizations (CTM Altromercato, Associazione Botteghe del Mondo, International Fair Trade Association); and solidarity networks (Solidarität mit Chiapas, Comitati di appoggio europei al MST brasiliano, Colectivo de Solidaridad con la Rebelion Zapatista de Barcelona).

The field on environmental issues includes Greenpeace, Friends of the Earth and Legambiente.

The field of peace includes pacifist and anti-war organizations (Tavola della Pace, Espacio Horizontal contra la Guerra, Stop the War Coalition).

The field of social, citizenship, and labour rights contains organizations, mostly grass-roots and local, involved in issues such as migration, anti-racism, and citizenship (Derechos para todos, Kanak Attak, Pajol); unemployment and precarity (Euromarches, Euromayday, Coordination des intermittents de l'Ile de France); women's, gay and lesbian rights (Asemblea Feminista de Madrid, National Association of Women, Marche Mondiale de Femmes, Arcigay).

Table 10A.1 The determinants of transnational activism in national organizations

Variables	Model 1 ODDS RATIO	Model 2 ODDS RATIO
Issue of activism: Global economy	4.86***	4.55***
Issue of activism: Development and cooperation	1.79	2.93*
Organizational structure: Network or campaign	–	1.75*
Organizational structure: Size of staff	1.63***	1.57**
Identity: Belonging to GJM	5.49***	–
Strategies: Presence of multiple strategies	1.38*	1.30
Strategies: Demonstrations as forms of action	–	1.83
Country: France	32.33***	13.87***
Country: Germany	3.26***	2.52**
Country: Italy	29.86***	18.06***
Country: Spain	1.84	0.62
Country: UK	1.92**	4.00***
No. of Observations	180	158
LR chi2	87.42	73.93
Prob > chi2	0.00	0.00
Log likelihood	−202.29	−181.04
Pseudo R2	0.17	0.16

Notes: Ordered Logit Estimates. Dependent Variable: Index of Transnational Activism (Values: 0–4). Transnational organizations are excluded from the estimate. Calculations carried out with STATA8. *significant at the 90% level; **significant at 95%; ***significant at 99%.

The seventh field comprises media and think tanks, both institutional and alternative, such as radio programmes (Radio LoRa, Radio Rampart); newspapers and magazines (Il Manifesto, Red Pepper); Web sites (Indymedia, Unimondo); and research centres (Espace Marx, Fondation Copernic).

Finally, the field of political parties and trade unions includes political parties (Rifondazione Comunista, Green Party); political organizations (Les Communistes, Giovani Comunisti, Jovenes de Izquierda Unida); and trade unions, ranging from the local to the international level (Cobas, IG Metall, Unison, International Metalworkers' Federation).

Notes

1. This chapter was prepared during Mario Pianta's sabbatical leave as a Fernand Braudel fellow at the European University Institute, Department of Political and Social Sciences. For their comments, we thank Donatella della Porta, her colleagues at the EUI, Marco Giugni, and the participants in the May 2007 ECPR workshop in Helsinki, where this paper was first presented. We thank Tommaso Rondinella and Elisabetta Segre for their suggestions on the statistical analysis.
2. Studies on cases of transnational mobilizations on different issues, countries and contexts are found in the edited books by Smith et al. (1997), Smith and Johnston (2002), Bandy and Smith (2004), Cohen and Rai (2000), della Porta et al. (1999), della Porta and Tarrow (2005), and Khagram et al, (2002).
3. On transnational mobilizations on human rights, see also Smith et al. (1998), where the results of a survey of organizations are presented; also Risse et al. (1999).
4. Cases of conflict with supranational institutions are investigated in O'Brien et al. (2000), Cohen and Rai (2000), Keck and Sikkink (1998), Khagram et al. (2002), and Glasius (2005).
5. See the Introduction and Chapters 1 and 4 in this book; della Porta (2007c); Pianta and Marchetti (2007). These global mobilizations were also investigated using the concept of *globalization from below* (Brecher et al. 2000; Pianta 2001a; Pianta and Silva 2003; della Porta et al. 2006) and studies of global civil society events (Pianta 2001b; Pianta and Zola 2007). On labour as an issue of global mobilizations, see Waterman (2001), Waterman and Timms (2004), and Silver (2003). An interesting related perspective is the analysis of global conflicts in a world-systems perspective; see Arrighi et al. (1989) and Arrighi and Silver (1999).
6. Tarrow's argument is that such a rise is shaped by the long history of cross-border activism (by 'rooted cosmopolitans' in particular) and by the opportunity structure of international politics, but no specific analysis is developed on these determinants of cross-border mobilizations; rather, the book focuses on the forms they take and on their consequences (2005, pp. 3, 11).
7. On cross-border networks, see Keck and Sikkink (1998), Khagram et al. (2002), Henry et al. (2004), Juris (2004), Katz and Anheier (2006) and Yanacopulos (2005). For an attempt at conceptualizing the role of networks, see Marchetti and Pianta (2008). On the organizational problems of a shift to global activism, see Anheier and Themudo (2002).
8. As described in the introduction to this volume, DEMOS (Democracy in Movement and the Mobilisation of Society) is a research project funded by the European Commission, Contract n. CIT2-CT2004-506026, and (for the Swiss case) by the Swiss Federal Office for Education and Science, Contract no. 03.0482. See www.demos.iue.it. Representatives of the examined organizations were interviewed using a semi-structured questionnaire. Organizations were selected to account for relevant strands of the GJM, reflecting the heterogeneity of the movement in terms of issues and ideological leanings. Given our choice to avoid the criterion of randomness, we cannot assume that our survey is representative of the universe of GJM organizations

in each country and at the transnational level. Despite this, we maintain that the statistical results are not biased by the selection process insofar as the organizations were not selected on the basis of their prior fitness to our theoretical model.

9. This is the result of the selection of survey respondents and should not be considered as an indication of the relevance of the issues addressed within the GJM. Different chapters of this book provide a detailed analysis of several aspects of the activities of the surveyed organizations; in this section we refer to such evidence for a preliminary description of the GJM.

10. See the analysis in Chapter 1 in this volume. The age of organizations has also been considered. GJM organizations were mostly founded in the last two decades, with 16 per cent founded before 1968, another 16 per cent between 1968 and 1989, 33 per cent in the 1990s, and another 33 per cent after 2000. Networks and campaigns tend to be more recently established. While older organizations often include parties, unions, and development NGOs, more recently established ones tend to focus on global economic issues and global democracy.

11. See Chapter 1 in this volume. An overall proactive attitude towards global issues characterizes these organizations, with 85 per cent perceiving the GJM's claims as positive rather than negative political demands (that is, a mobilization in favour of global justice rather than against injustice).

12. For a comprehensive analysis, see Chapter 1 in this volume.

13. For an analysis of relationships with institutions, see Chapter 4 in this volume.

14. As a consequence, we could have an organization with a low intensity but a high differentiation of transnational activities that is ranked higher than another organization engaged very intensely in a single activity. An alternative approach would consist of 'weighting' the intensity of transnational initiatives on each of these variables. However, the information from the questionnaire was not detailed enough for such a measure, and decisions on weights could introduce a distortion in the data.

15. A cross-country comparison of the results, while important in pointing out the continuing relevance of national context, is beyond the scope of this chapter.

16. The organizations most active in cross-border mobilizations are those created between 1990 and 1999. Those were the years in which transnational campaigns emerged and transnational networks became established, often in the process of involvement and contestation of the large UN world summits. Outside of that decade, degree of transnationalization does not vary much with year of foundation.

17. Significance levels here are similar to those of other regression models, but in order to further test the reliability of their significance levels, we have followed an additional procedure: the full model has been compared with a model excluding one variable at a time, and the likelihood-ratio test has been calculated on the assumption that the second model was 'nested' in the full model. For all variables this procedure has led to the same significance levels as obtained from the model estimates.

Democracy in Movement: Some Conclusions

Donatella della Porta

Social movements have been carriers of alternative visions of democracy. Experimenting in their organizational praxis, they have elaborated demands for radical changes not only in policies but also in politics. If the social movements of the 1980s and the 1990s were described as more pragmatic and single-issue oriented, our research on the Global Justice Movement testifies to its continuous interest in addressing the meta-issue of democracy, with some continuity and innovations vis-à-vis past experiences. Our organizations emerged as political actors, mobilizing in various forms in order to produce institutional changes, but also trying to practise those novelties in their internal lives. The prefigurative role of internal democratic practices acquires, as we saw, a particularly important role for the GJMOs, which stress a necessary coherence between what is advocated in the external environment and what is practised inside (see Chapter 2).

In this conclusion, I shall summarize some main results presented in the various chapters, reflecting around the main two questions presented in the introduction: which conceptions of democracy did we find in the Global Justice Movement (part 1), and how do we explain the different organizational choices (part 2)?

Which conceptions of democracy?

Similarly to the organizations we studied, our volume aims to contribute to the general debate on democracy. In this direction, I would stress, first of all, that the Global Justice Movement builds upon some visions of democracy that have long been present in the social sciences' normative and empirical analysis of democracy, but that have been (or risk being) removed or marginalized in the 'minimalistic' conceptions of democracy that became dominant in the political as well as the scientific discourse. Second, I shall argue, however, that this attention to some democratic qualities acquires new characteristics if compared with previous visions and practices of democracy in movements.

Counter-democracy and the GJM

Several studies have indicated that the crisis of representative democracy is accompanied by the (re)emergence of other conceptions and practices of democracy. Empirical research on political participation has stressed that, while some more conventional forms of participation (such as voting or party-linked activities) are declining, protest forms are increasingly used. Citizens vote less, but they are not less interested in or knowledgeable about politics (Norris 2002). While some traditional types of associations are decreasing in popularity, others (social movement organizations and/or civil society organizations) are growing in resources, legitimacy, and members.

What is more, historical and normative research has pointed at the presence of different conceptions of democracy, which pose different emphases on different democratic qualities. As Pierre Rosanvallon recently observed, 'the history of real democracies cannot be dissociated from a permanent tension and contestation' (2006, p. 11). In his vision, democracy needs not only legal legitimation, but also what he calls 'counter-democracy'. In the historical evolution of democratic regimes, a circuit of surveillance, anchored outside of state institutions, has developed side by side with the institutions of electoral accountability. Necessary to democratic legitimacy, confidence requires defiance, in the sense of instruments of external control and actors ready to perform this control; in fact, democracy develops with the permanent contestation of power. Citizens' attentive vigilance upon power-holders is thus defined as a specific, political modality of action, a 'particular form of political intervention', different from decision making, but still a fundamental aspect of the democratic process (ibid., p. 40). Actors such as independent authorities and judges, but also mass media, experts, and social movements, have traditionally exercised this function of surveillance. The latter, in particular, are considered as most relevant for the development of an 'expressive democracy' that corresponds to 'the *prise de parole* of the society, the manifestation of a collective sentiment, the formulation of a judgment about the governors and their action, or again the production of claims' (ibid., p. 26). Surveillance from below is all the more important given the crisis of representative, electoral democracy.

As our research indicated, social movement organizations take the democratic function of control seriously, mobilizing to put pressure on decision makers, as well as developing counter-knowledge and open public spaces. As we saw in Chapter 4, GJMOs interact with public institutions, at various territorial levels. In many cases, especially but not only at the local level, they collaborate with public institutions, both on specific problems and in broader campaigns. They are contracted out specific services but are also often supported in recognition of their function in building 'counter', democratic spaces. In particular, our organizations perceive themselves as controllers of public institutions, promoting alternative policies but also, more broadly, calling for more (and different) democracy. While stressing the need for more public and less private, more state and less market, they also define themselves especially as autonomous from institutions and (to use Rosanvallon's terminology) as performing democratic control of the governors. By creating public spaces, they contribute to the development of ideas and practices (della Porta 2008c). If electoral accountability has long been privileged over the power of surveillance in the historical evolution of procedural democracy, our SMOs contribute to bringing attention back to the 'counter-democracy' of surveillance.

As our research stressed, democratic surveillance acquires a special meaning given the perceived challenge of adapting democratic conceptions and practices to the increasing shift of competence towards the transnational level. In this transition, our organizations contribute to the debate on global democracy, not only by criticizing the lack of democratic accountability and even transparency of many existing IGOs, but also by asking for a globalization of democracy and actually constructing a global public sphere. Over the last decades, transnational protest campaigns have multiplied, particularly on issues such as environmental protection, gender discrimination, and human rights (della Porta and Kriesi 1999), targeting the international financial organizations as well as other IGOs. During these campaigns, common frames developed around global justice and global democracy, and transnational networks consolidated (Andretta et al. 2002, 2003; della Porta et al. 2006; della Porta 2007c). The GJMOs we have studied do indeed have global and cross-issues framing, transnationally networked organizational structures, and intense participation in protest beyond borders (see Chapter 1). They criticize globalization-as-free-market, and they accuse national and international elites of strengthening market freedom at the expense of the social rights that, at least in the North, had become part and parcel of the very definition of citizenship. However, they also call for the development of democracy at the transnational level as all the more urgent, as the international system based on sovereign nation-states seems to have evolved into a political system composed of overlapping multilevel authorities.

Participation and deliberation as democratic qualities

Rosanvallon's concept of 'counter-democracy' resonates with two parallel, although not overlapping, concepts: participatory democracy and deliberative democracy. Although representative procedural democracy is mainly based on principles of delegation and majority votes, conceptions of democracy have always balanced such principles with deliberation oriented towards the public good. In parallel, if institutional decision making is mainly controlled by a restricted class of professional politicians, the healthy functioning of democracy is linked to the presence of multiple arenas that allow for the participation of citizens. Democracy is made of rules for voting but, even more, of spaces for talking.

While theories of representative democracy have focused on electoral rules, theories of participatory democracy have stressed the importance of involving citizens beyond elections (Arnstein 1969; Pateman 1970; Barber 1984). In this vision, citizens should be provided with as many opportunities to participate as there are spheres of decision making (Pateman 1970). Distinguishing pseudo, partial and full levels of participation according to participants' potential degrees of influence on the outcome of a given event, Carole Pateman defined *full* participation as a 'process where each individual member of a decision-making body has equal power to determine the outcome of decisions' (ibid., pp. 70–1). In a similar vein, 'strong democracy' has been defined as a government in which citizens participate at least some of the time in the decisions that affect their lives (Barber 1984). Citizen power is defined as requiring citizen participation, as 'there is a critical difference between going through the empty ritual of participation and having the real power needed to affect the outcome of the process' (Arnstein 1969, p. 216).

In these conceptions, the actors of participatory democracy are mainly outside the public institutions. While in 'party democracy', participation happened mainly within and throughout political parties (Manin 1995), in a 'democracy of the public', social movements acquire increasing relevance. As highly reflexive actors, far from limiting themselves to presenting demands to decision makers, they in fact address a meta-political critique to conventional democracy (Offe 1985). The alternative they propose has usually been conceptualized in terms of participatory democracy or, to use the words of Herbert Kitschelt (1993, p. 15), of that 'ancient element of democratic theory that calls for an organisation of collective decision making referred to in varying ways as classical, populist, communitarian, strong, grass-roots, or direct democracy against a democratic practice in contemporary democracies labelled as realist, liberal, elite, republican, or representative democracy'. At least since the 1960s, social movements have in fact criticized delegation as well as oligarchic and centralized power, instead legitimating forms of direct participation and grass-roots, horizontal, egalitarian organizational models.

As observed in our research, participation has in fact maintained a relevant, though plural, meaning for the organizations belonging to the GJM (Chapter 2). As the chapter by Herbert Reiter documented, its nature as a 'movements of movements' is reflected in the presence of a plurality of conceptions and practices of democracy. In particular, participation acquires different meanings in different movement areas. In terms of organizational areas, in the Old Left, participation and delegation are seen as highly compatible, and the stress on participation appears as a recovery of the original values of democratic centralism. For the New Left, the emphasis is on direct democracy and self-organization, while the solidarity groups and new social movement organizations stress the prefigurative role of participation as 'school of democracy'. Similarly, searching for coherence between their criticism of existing democratic institutions and their internal practices, the organizations emerging with the GJM elaborate counter-models that combine concrete proposals of reform with a utopian aspect.

The concept of counter-democracy is also linked to that of deliberative democracy. With some different emphasis, in normative theory, deliberative democracy refers to decisional processes in which, under conditions of equality, inclusiveness, and transparency, a communicative process based on reason (the strength of a good argument) is able to transform individual preferences, leading to decisions oriented to the public good (della Porta 2005b). Particular attention is given, in the conception of deliberative democracy as well as by our organizations, to the discursive quality of democracy with an emphasis on four elements: the transformation of preferences, the orientation to the public good, the use of arguments, and the development of consensus.

While representative democracy is based upon the aggregation (through vote or negotiation) of exogenously generated preferences, deliberative democracy is defined as oriented to *preference (trans)formation*. In deliberative processes, initial preferences are transformed during the confrontation with the points of view of others (Miller 1993, p. 75). In particular, the interaction of diverse positions produces a change in the perception of one's own preferences (Dryzek 2000, p. 79). Deliberation (or even communication) is based upon the belief that, while not giving up my perspective, I might learn if I listen to the other (Young 1996). This requires the deliberative process to take place under conditions of plurality of values, where people have different perspectives but face common problems. In this process, a *definition of the public good* should develop as the debates draw 'identities and citizens' interests in ways that contribute to public building of public good' (Cohen 1989, pp. 18–19). This should be achieved through *rational argumentation*. Deliberative democracy is based on reason: people are convinced by the force of the better argument (Elster 1998a). In particular, deliberation should be facilitated by horizontal flows of communication, multiple contributors to discussion, wide opportunities for interactivity, confrontation on the basis of rational argumentation, attitude to reciprocal listening (Habermas 1981, 1996a).[1] Recognition of others' reasons allows for the building of *consensus*, so that decisions can be reached by convincing others of one's own argument. They must therefore be approvable by all participants – in contrast with majority-rule democracy, where decisions are legitimated by votes.

Also in this perspective, democracy develops (also or mainly) outside of public institutions. While Habermas (1996a) postulates a double-track process, with 'informal' deliberation taking place outside institutions and then, as public opinion, influencing institutional deliberation, Joshua Cohen (1989) holds that deliberative (associational) democracy develops in voluntary groups, in particular in political parties; John Dryzek (2000) singles out social movements as better positioned to build deliberative spaces, since they keep a critical view upon institutions. In similar visions, deliberation should take place in a number of enclaves, free from institutional power – social movements being among these free spaces (Mansbridge 1996). Discourse does not exclude protest: 'processes of engaged and responsible democratic participation include street demonstrations and sit-ins, musical works and cartoons, as much as parliamentary speeches and letters to the editor' (Young 2003, p. 119). If social movements nurture committed, critical attitudes towards public institutions, as Claus Offe (1997, pp. 102–3) has emphasized, deliberative democracy requires citizens 'embedded' in associative networks, able to build democratic skills among their adherents. Empirical research on the actual decision-making processes in social movements can help to qualify these statements.

As our research indicates, sometimes explicitly (we found some references to the concept of deliberative democracy in the documents of our groups) but more often not, the GJMOs adopt deliberative norms. First of all, they stress that, given a complex reality, no easy solution is at hand or can be derived from big ideologies. Many conflicts must be approached by reliance on the potential for mutual understanding that might develop in an open, high-quality debate. The notion of a common good is often recalled (for example, water as a common good, but also democracy as a common good), which should be constructed through communication, exchanges of ideas, knowledge sharing. The value of discussion among 'free and equal' citizens is mirrored in the positive emphasis on diversity and inclusion, but also in the attention paid to the development of structured arenas for the exchange of ideas, with the experimentation with some rules that should allow for horizontal flows of communication and reciprocal listening.

In particular, consensus is mentioned by half of the organizations we interviewed as a general value as well as an organizational principle in internal decision making. In fact, even though SMOs have stressed conflict as a dynamic element in society, they tend increasingly to balance it with a commitment to different values such as dialogue and mutual understanding (see Chapter 3). Consensus is presented as an alternative to majoritarian decision making, which is accused of repressing and/or alienating the minorities. Through consensual decision making, instead, not only would legitimacy increase with the awareness of a collective contribution to decisions, but the awareness of different points of view would also help in 'working on what unites', constructing a shared vision while respecting diversity.

In the GJM, consensus spread transnationally, in particular thanks to the symbolic impact and concrete networks built around the Zapatistas experience, and the successive adoption of consensual principles and practices in the Social Forum process. Dedicated publications, workshops, and training courses helped in the diffusion of consensual practices and the principle of consensus in the movement. Here as well, however, we might stress the multiple meanings attached to consensus. In particular, when coupled with an assembleary, horizontal tradition, consensual decision making is perceived as a way to reach a collective agreement that reflects a strong communitarian identity. This vision, particularly widespread among small and often local groups within the autonomous tradition, resonates with an anti-authoritarian emphasis and an egalitarian view. Group life assumes here mainly a prefigurative value. An alternative, more pragmatic view is spread in the new (even transnational) networks. Here, consensual decision making is accompanied especially by an emphasis on diversity and the need to respect it, but also to improve mutual understanding through good communication.

Which explanations for organizational diversities?

Within a general focus on participatory and deliberative qualities, visions and practices of democracy in the GJM vary. As we saw in previous chapters, debates tend to develop on two main dimensions. First, participatory conceptions that stress inclusiveness of equals (high participation) are contrasted with those based upon the delegation of power to representatives (low participation). In this sense, we studied the continued presence of direct forms of democracy that put a strong emphasis on the assembly, but also the extent to which the processes of institutionalization of social movement organizations (often stressed in social movement research in the last two decades) have spread a principle of delegation of power (see, e.g. Chapter 9). A second dimension refers to the prevalence of a majoritarian decision making based upon vote, as opposed to one that assigns a special role to public discussion, the common good, rational arguments, and transformation of preferences, as we have just mentioned. On this, we stressed how the traditional use of vote as a decision-making mechanism even within the assembleary organizational model is challenged by an emerging emphasis on values and practices that instead stress good communication.

We have used a typology of democratic forms of internal decision making that, crossing the two dimensions of participation and deliberation, identifies four democratic models: associational, which gave more weight to delegation and majoritarian voting; deliberative representative, which combined delegation with consensus; assembleary, with an emphasis on participation but also on majoritarian decision making; and deliberative participatory, with a combined stress on participation and deliberation. Our research indicated that all of these models are highly present in our movement, which emerges as diverse in terms not only of repertoires of action or organizational resources, but also internal organizations. Organizational differences reflected the presence of groups coming from various movement traditions (Old Left and New Left, new social movements and solidarity or peace movements) as well as the newly emerged groups on global issues. They also reflected their different ages and organizational types, as the 'movement of movements' is made up not only of grass-roots groups but also of parties, unions, co-operatives and NGOs (see Chapter 1). If all these diversities have created tensions within the GJM, they have also facilitated a cross-fertilization among different models: the development of new forms, such as modern networks, but also a transformation of already existing groups.

Beyond description, we also tried to explain the variance among the various models, and to understand the meanings given to them by the social movement organizations and their activists. We did the same with other aspects of democratic conceptions and practices we analysed, such as the degree of delegation (Chapter 2), the mentioning of deliberative values (Chapter 3), the strategies of interactions with public institutions (Chapter 4), the degree of oligarchy (Chapter 6), the conceptions of e-democracy (Chapter 8), and so on.

While in previous parts of our research we focused on cross-national comparison (della Porta 2007c), national political opportunities emerged here as largely insufficient explanations for organizational choices. Although cross-country differences helped in explaining the varying forms of action (less conventional when the Right is in government and the class cleavage less pacified, see Chapter 7), or the democratic qualities of Internet Web sites (more innovative in Southern countries, see Chapter 8), more relevant was the internal diversity present in each country and at the transnational level. However, given also that our sampling strategy did not allow for strong statements about the representativity of our groups (see introductory chapter), we preferred to focus on the organizational level. Following the general debates in organizational sociology, and especially of their implementation in social movement studies, we have looked for inspiration in the resource mobilization approach, but also tried to combine it with the neo-institutional recognition of the role of ideas (DiMaggio and Powell 1991a). Even though we did not pit one approach against the other as rivals, we found neo-institutionalism useful to address some of the limits that have been identified in the resource mobilization approach (Clemens and Minkoff 2004; Clemens 2005).

In our chapters, we have contrasted and specified structural and cultural explanations, instrumental and prefigurative choices. In the introductory chapter, drawing on organizational sociology, I argued that, within a broad agreement on the importance of collective actors for social mobilization, the explanations of organizational strategies have varied. First, attention has shifted to the (selective) role of the environment versus the entrepreneurial capacity of social movement organizations as agents of change. Second, and linked, there has been a shift from instrumental to normative interpretation of organizational paths: while the resource mobilization approach stressed the instrumental logic in decision making, privileging efficiency, more recently greater attention has been paid to their prefigurative logic, privileging normative concerns. In line with a neo-institutional turn in organizational sociology, the role of cognitive processes and normative motivations has been stressed, although without denying the relevance of some incentives and structures. In most of the following chapters, the relative importance of instrumental and normative, structural and cultural factors have been assessed and discussed. More than assigning final victory to one set of explanations over the others, our research helped in specifying which types of organizational characteristics (as independent variables) influence which specific democratic conceptions and practices (as dependent variables).

Indeed, different strategies to deal with institutions have emerged as influenced by the structural characteristics of our groups (see Chapter 4). The more formal, professionalized, larger (in terms of members, budget and paid staff), and territorially multilevel an organization, the more it tends to collaborate with institutions, and vice versa. When looking at democratic models, the less participative (associational and deliberative representative) organizations are more collaborative, while the others have a higher propensity to refusal but especially critical collaboration. Structures alone, however, do not explain interactions with institutions that indeed seem to belong to broader organizational conceptions and to be influenced by more general values. More critical attitudes towards public institutions emerge when values such as democracy, inclusiveness and autonomy are mentioned. Values are also embedded in movement areas: collaboration tends to decrease not only for the anarchist and New Leftist groups, but also for the new global organizations, and to be higher for not only the Old Left, but also for the new social movement areas.

References to participation and consensus are also influenced by some organizational characteristics. Even though participation as an internal principle is more likely to be mentioned where delegation in decision making is low, participation is considered as a positive general value by organizations at all levels in the scale of delegation (Chapter 2). While mentioned by large and small groups, participation in actual decision making of GJMOs decreases with their size. Similarly, critiques of delegation and the appeal to consensual values resonate more with smaller, poorer and more participatory groups (Chapter 3).

Significantly, mention of democratic values is associated with references to alter-globalist issues; in particular, consensual values are more often mentioned by groups that were founded in the most recent wave of protest on global issues, that experiment with new organizational forms (such as the modern networks) or stress horizontal structures, and that maintain a more multi-issue focus.

Triangulating multivariate regression with Qualitative Comparative Analysis, Marco Giugni and Alessandro Nai showed that delibera-tive participation is favoured by some structural characteristics (such as degree of professionalization, structuration and, even more, size). However, cultural characteristics such as identification with the move-ment and belonging to the new social movements and new global areas have an even higher explanatory capacity (see Chapter 5). In particular, certain types of values seem particularly widespread in orga-nizations that were founded after 1989, reflecting some recent cultural turns.

The importance of normative motivation is confirmed in the analysis of the impact of the size of organization. Measuring an oligarchy score (based on the number of organizational members divided by the num-ber of individuals in the main decision making body), Clare Saunders pointed at the relevance of size (as indicated by budget, members and staff), but also of organizational normatively based choices (Chapter 6). True, big organizations usually emerge as 'uglier' (at least in terms of their activists' cherished conception of democracy), privileging order-liness over creative freedom and efficacy over participation. However, cultural orientations, reflected in specific organizational choices, play an important role in either easing or opposing the trend. On the other hand, even small organizations need to invest in specific strategies (for example, the use of rotation, facilitation, seating arrangement, trans-parency) if they want to keep oligarchic tendencies in check. At the same time, even large organizations might purposively work against the (not-so-)iron law of oligarchy, combining a creative use of new tech-nology with new forms of networked decision making based on spokes councils.

A mix of structural and cultural factors also influences outwardly ori-ented strategies, which are not just instrumentally chosen but carry with them dense meanings in terms of the definition of the conflict and of one's own identity (Chapter 7). Here as well, unconventional forms resonate with more participatory conceptions of democracy, with a larger role given to the assembly and appeal to horizontal values as well as for the less professionalized ones (although not only for the informal groups) and those that do not receive public funds and are less collaborative towards institutions. Organizations active on solidarity, human rights, peace issues and NGOs are, as expected, less confrontational; this is also true for New Global groups and the modern networks, allowing for collective membership. In this case, the explanation seems linked to the characteristics of intervention at the transnational level, where action in the street is more difficult.

Structural and cultural factors also influence the extent to which and the ways in which Internet is used by the GJMOs in order to improve the democratic qualities of organizational decision making as well as of the broader society (Chapter 8). Internet is in fact used a great deal by our activists and their organizations, allowing them in particular to increase internal debates, develop networked structures, and organize protests. Organizations' Web sites contain documents informing users on global problems and promoting solutions, as well as documents on their own story and being. However, the potentials of Computer Mediated Communication are variously appreciated and implemented by our organizations. In particular, while more participatory and smaller groups use their sites for the mobilization of protest and identity building, more formal, larger, and multilevel groups seem instead to invest in increasing transparency and the general provision of information.

The relevance of structural resources, but also (and even more) of a cultural commitment is finally stressed in the analysis on the degree of transnationalization of our organizations. Based on their study of determinants of an index of transnationalization (constructed on participation in Global Days of Action, World and European Social Forums, transnational networks, and transnational campaigns), Pianti, Marchetti and Zola (Chapter 10) indicate that degree of transnationalization increases especially with reference to the nature of the issues (global development and global economy), as well as the degree of identification with the GJM. Even if resources are important, a network structure allows even smaller and resource-less groups to mobilize transnationally.

In sum, the Global Justice Movement emerges from our research as a promoter of democracy in at least two ways. On the one hand, it experiments with democracy in its internal practices; on the other, it develops proposals for democratic reform of institutions at various levels. In these ways, it emphasizes some democratic qualities that are less and less present in, and cherished by, contemporary institutions.

In the social sciences, the recent focus on democratic qualities testifies to the recognition of intrinsic tensions between different democratic values and goals. Various definitions of democracy can in fact be counterpoised, each linked to specific values. Representative democracy resonates with terms such as efficiency, delegation, individual, majoritarian, vote, institutions, procedures, instrumentality, singular, professionalism. Participatory 'counter-democracy' privileges inclusion, direct exercise of power, associative practices, discursive deliberation, the society, the process, the normative, plurality, the lay citizens. If the historical evolution of representative democracy has privileged some of these values, the renewal of democracy should bring about a re-evaluation and adaptation of elements (such as control, participation, deliberation) that were well present in the 'ancient' conceptions of democracy. Old or new (or even newest), the different elements of what Rosanvallon (2006, p. 16) defined as counter-democracy 'do not represent the opposite of democracy, but instead the form of democracy that contrasts the other, the democracy of indirect powers that are disseminated in the social body, the democracy of organized defiance as opposed to electoral legitimacy'.

The reflection on the various democratic qualities is all the more relevant within the debate on post-national, cosmopolitan democracy, its normative basis and empirical perspectives. If the national political context still cushions the impact of international shifts on national politics, growing economic interdependence goes hand in hand with 'a significant internationalization of public authority associated with a corresponding globalization of political activity' (Held and McGrew 2000, p. 27). Globalization has indeed increased the awareness of 'global commons' that cannot be defended only at the national level and challenges a hierarchical model based on territorial control (Badie 1999, p. 301). The GJMOs we have studied have contributed to a critique of existing IGOs, but also to voicing a demand for the development of global democracy (Marchetti 2008).

Note

1. Deliberation must exclude power deriving from coercion, but also avoid an unequal weighting of the participants as representatives of organizations of different sizes or influence. In fact, 'all citizens must be empowered to develop those capacities that give them effective access to the public sphere'; and 'once in public, they must be given sufficient respect and recognition so as to be able to influence decisions that affect them in a favourable direction' (Bohman 1997, pp. 523–4). Public deliberation is supposed to 'replace the language of interest with the language of reason' (Elster 1998a, p. 111).

References

AC! (2002) 'Charte', http://www.ac.eu.org (home page), accessed 12 November 2008.

ARCI (2006) Associazione Ricreativa Culturale Italiana, 'Statuto dell'Associazione ARCI', http://www.arci.it/testo.php?codice=STATUTO.

ARCI (2008) Associazione Ricreativa Culturale Italiana, '1984–1995. La fine dell'esperienza confederale, il ritorno alla centralità dei circoli e il progetto della nuova ARCI', http://www.arci.it/testo.php?codice=s9.

ATTAC Europe (2005) 'Convention of European Attac for a "Democratic Refoundation of Europe"', 16 June, http://www.italia.attac.org (home page), accessed 12 November 2008.

ATTAC France (2005) 'Debate on the constitutional treaty', 20 May, http://www.france.attac.org (home page), accessed 12 November 2008.

ATTAC Germany (2001) 'Zwischen Netzwerk, NGO und Bewegung, Das Selbstverständnis von ATTAC, 8 Thesen', October, http://www.attac.de (home page), accessed 12 November 2008.

ATTAC Italia (2002) 'La Convenzione Europea e i movimenti sociali', 20 November, http://www.italia.attac.org (home page), accessed 12 November 2008.

ATTAC Italia (2003a) 'Il movimento e la politica', 17 October, http://www.italia.attac.org (home page), accessed 12 November 2008.

ATTAC Italia (2003b) 'Report riunione regionale dei comitati Attac dell'Emilia Romagna', 22 Giugno 2003, http://www.italia.attac.org/spip/spip.php?article126.

ATTAC Italia (2003c) Statuto, 30 October, http://www.italia.attac.org (home page), accessed 12 November 2008.

ATTAC Italia (2007) 'Assemblea nazionale', February 27, http://www.attac.it (home page), accessed 12 November 2008.

ATTAC Spain (2001) 'Constitucion', http://www.attac.es (home page), accessed 12 November 2008.

ATTAC Vaud (2004) 'Bullettin d'information d'Attac Vaud', No. 10, 3 June, http://www.local.attac.org/vaud/angles/10.rtf, accessed 12 November 2008.

Agir (2002) Agir ensemble contre le chomage, *La charte des collectifs d'AC!*, www.agirensemblecontrelechomage.org/spip.php?article4.

Agrikoliansky, Eric and Dominique Cardon (2005) 'Un programme en débat: forum, formes et formats', in Eric Agrikoliansky and Isabelle Sommier, *Radiographie du mouvement altermondialiste. Le second forum social européen*, Paris: La Dispute, pp. 45–74.

Agrikoliansky, Eric, Olivier Fillieule and Nonna Mayer (2005a) *L'altermondialisme en France. La longue histoire d'une nouvelle cause*, Paris: Flammarion.

Agrikoliansky, Eric, Olivier Fillieule and Nonna Mayer (2005b) 'Aux origines de l'altermondialisme français', in Agrikoliansky, Fillieule and Mayer, *L'altermondialisme en France*, pp. 13–42.

Aguiton, Christophe (2005) *Le Monde nous appartient: Porto Alegre, Florence, Évian: les acteurs d'une autre mondialisation*, Paris: 10*18.

Aguiton, Christophe and Dominique Cardon (2005) *Le Forum et le Réseau: Une analyse des modes de gouvernement des forums sociaux*, paper prepared for the Colloque 'Cultures et pratiques participatives: une perspective comparative', Paris, 20–21 January, http://mokk.bme.hu/centre/conferences/reactivism/FP/fpDC, accessed 12 September 2008.

Alexander, Jeffrey C. (1998) 'Introduction. Civil Society I, II, III: Constructing an Empirical Concept from Normative Controversies and Historical Transformations', in Alexander, *Real Civil Society. Dilemmas of Institutionalization*, London: Sage, 1–20.

Alt.media.res Collective (2007) 'Indymedia', in Gary L. Anderson and Kathryn Herr, *Encyclopedia of Activism and Social Justice*, London: Sage.

Alternativa Antimilitarista–MOC (2004) 'Declaración Ideológica', 18 July, http://www.antimilitaristas.org/spip.php?article476, accessed 12 November 2008.

Amnesty France (2008) Amnesty International France, http://www.amnesty.fr/index.php?/amnesty/qui_sommes_nous/organisation/democratie, accessed 3 November 2008.

Andretta, Massimiliano (2005a) 'Il "framing" del movimento contro la globalizzazione neoliberista', *Rassegna Italiana di Sociologia*, 2, 249–74.

Andretta, Massimiliano (2005b) 'Movimenti e democrazia tra globale e locale: il caso di Napoli', in Francesca Gelli (ed.), *La democrazia locale tra rappresentanza e partecipazione*, Milan: Franco Angeli, pp. 281–318.

Andretta, Massimiliano and Herbert Reiter (2009) 'Parties, Unions and Movements. The European Left and the ESF', in della Porta (ed.), *Another Europe*, forthcoming.

Andretta, Massimiliano, Donatella della Porta, Lorenzo Mosca and Herbert Reiter (2002) *Global, noglobal, newglobal. Le proteste di Genova contro il G8*, Roma-Bari, Laterza.

Andretta, Massimiliano, Donatella della Porta, Lorenzo Mosca and Herbert Reiter (2003) *Noglobal – Newglobal. Identität und Strategien der Antiglobalisierungsbewegung*, Frankfurt/New York: Campus Verlag.

Anheier, Helmut and Nuno Themudo (2002) 'Organisational Forms of Global Civil Society: Implications of Going Global', in Helmut Anheier, Marlies Glasius and Mary Kaldor (eds), *Global Civil Society 2002*, Oxford: Oxford University Press, pp. 191–216.

Arcigay (2004) 'Documento proposto all'11 congresso nazionale', 20 November, http://www.arcigay.it (home page), accessed 12 November 2008.

Arcigay (2007) 'Lo statuto nazionale dell'Associazione', http://www.arcigay.it/statuto.

Arnstein, Sherry R. (1969) 'A Ladder of Citizen Participation', *Journal of the American Institute of Planners*, 35(4): 216–24.

Arrighi, Giovanni and Beverly Silver (1999) *Chaos and Governance in the Modern World System*, Minneapolis: University of Minnesota Press.

Arrighi, Giovanni, Terence K. Hopkins and Immanuel Wallerstein (1989) *Antisystemic Movements*, London: Verso.

Artisans (2005) Artisans du monde, 'Le projet associatif', http://www.artisansdumonde.org/docs/ProjetAssociatifAdM2005.pdf.

Badie, Bertrand (1999) *Une monde sans souveraineté*, Paris: Fayard.

Baiocchi, Gianpaolo (2001) 'Participation, Activism, and Politics: The Porto Alegre Experiment and Deliberative Democratic Theory', *Politics and Society*, 29(1), 43–72.

Balme, Richard and Didier Chabanet (2008) *European Governance and Democracy. Power and Protest in the EU*, Lanham, MD: Rowman and Littlefield.

Bandy, Joe and Jackie Smith (eds) (2004) *Coalitions across Borders: Transnational Protest and the Neoliberal Order*, Lanham, MD: Rowan and Littlefield.

Barber, Benjamin R. (1984) *Strong Democracy: Participatory Politics for a New Age*, Berkeley: University of California Press.

Barlow, Maude and Tony Clarke (2002) *Global Showdown: How the New Activists are Fighting Global Corporate Rule*, Toronto: Stoddart.

Barnes, Samuel, Max Kaase et al. (1979) *Political Action: Mass Participation in Five Western Democracies*, Beverly Hills and London: Sage.

Bartolini, Stefano (2000) *The Political Mobilization of the European Left, 1860–1980. The Class Cleavage*, Cambridge, UK/New York: Cambridge University Press.

Beetham, David (2005) *Democracy: A Beginner's Guide*, Oxford: One World.

Benhabib, Seyla (1996) 'Toward a Deliberative Model of Democratic Legitimacy', in Seyla Benhabib (ed.), *Democracy and Difference: Contesting the Boundaries of the Political*, Princeton, NJ: Princeton University Press, pp. 67–94.

Bennett, W. Lance (2003) 'Communicating Global Activism: Strengths and Vulnerabilities of Networked Politics', *Information, Communication & Society*, 6(2), 143– 68.

Bohman, James (1997) 'Deliberative Democracy and Effective Social Freedom: Capabilities, Resources, and Opportunities', in James Bohman and William Rehg (eds), *Deliberative Democracy: Essays on Reason and Politics*, Cambridge: MIT Press, pp. 321–48.

Boli, John and George M. Thomas (1999) *Constructing World Culture. Nongovernmental Organizations since 1875*, Stanford, CA: Stanford University Press.

Boltanski, Luc and Ève Chiapello (1997) *Le nouvel esprit du capitalisme*, Paris: Gallimard.

Brecher, Jeremy, Tim Costello and Brendan Smith (2000) *Globalization from Below. The Power of Solidarity*, Boston: South End Press.

Breines, Wini (1980) 'Community and Organisation: The New Left and Michels' "Iron Law"', *Social Problems*, 27(4), 419–29.

Breines, Wini (1989) *Community and Organisation in the New Left. 1962–1968: The Great Refusal*, New Brunswick, NJ: Rutgers University Press.

Brot für die Welt (2000) *Den Armen Gerechtigkeit 2000. Herausforderungen und Handlungsfelder*, http://www.brot-fuer-die-welt.de/downloads/gerechtigkeit 2000.pdf.

Budge, Ian (1996) *budge://the.new.challenge.of.direct.democracy/*, Cambridge: Polity Press.

Buechler, Steven M. (1995) 'New Social Movement Theories', *Sociological Quarterly*, 36, 441–64.

Calenda, Davide and Lorenzo Mosca (2007) 'Youth Online. Researching the Political Use of the Internet in the Italian Context', in Brian Loader (ed.), *Young Citizens in the Digital Age: Political Engagement, Young People and New Media*, New York/London: Routledge, pp. 82–96.

Carmin, JoAnn and Deborah B. Balser (2002) 'Selecting Repertoires of Action in Environmental Movement Organizations: An Interpretive Approach', *Organization & Environment*, 15(4): 365–88.

Castells, Manuel (2001) *The Internet Galaxy. Reflections on the Internet, Business and Society*, Oxford: Oxford University Press.

Castells, Manuel (2002) *La galaxie Internet*, Paris, Fayard.

Catholic Agency (2004) Catholic Agency for Overseas Development, 'Financial Statements 2003/2004', http://www.cafod.org.uk/annual-reviews/panels/resources-to-download/financial-statements-2003-04.

CGIL (2004) Confederazione Generale Italiana del Lavoro, 'Alcune informazioni sulla CGIL', http://www.cgil.it/ufficiostampa/cgil/chi_siamo.htm.

CGIL (2006) Confederazione Generale Italiana del Lavoro, 'Lo statuto della CGIL', http://www.cgil.it/congXV/StatutoCGIL_congrXV.htm.

Christian Aid (2005) 'Vision and Values', http://www.christianaid.org.uk, accessed 14 March 2005.

Clemens, Elisabeth S. (1993) 'Organizational Repertoires and Institutional Change: Women's Groups and the Transformation of American Politics, 1890–1920', *American Journal of Sociology*, 98(4), 755–98.

Clemens, Elisabeth S. (1996) 'Organizational Form as Frame: Collective Identity and Political Strategy in the American Labor Movement', in Doug McAdam, John D. McCarthy and Mayer N. Zald (eds), *Comparative Perspectives on Social Movements: Political Opportunities, Mobilizing Structures, and Cultural Framings*, Cambridge/New York: Cambridge University Press, pp. 205–26.

Clemens, Elisabeth S. (2005) 'Two Kinds of Stuff: The Current Encounter of Social Movements and Organizations', in Gerald F. Davis, Doug McAdam, W. Richard Scott and Mayer N. Zald (eds), *Social Movements and Organizational Theory*, Cambridge/New York: Cambridge University Press, pp. 351–65.

Clemens, Elisabeth S. and Debra C. Minkoff (2004) 'Beyond the Iron Law: Rethinking the Place of Organizations in Social Movements Research', in David A. Snow, Sarah A. Soule and Hanspeter Kriesi (eds), *The Blackwell Companion to Social Movement Research*, Oxford: Blackwell, pp. 155–70.

COBAS (2002) Confederazione dei Comitati di Base, 'Il libro bianco', http://www.cobas.it/Sito/Documenti/Materiali/AD_00_03_2002.doc.

Cohen, Jean L. and Andrew Arato (1992) *Civil Society and Political Theory*, Cambridge: MIT Press.

Cohen, Joshua (1989) 'Deliberation and Democratic Legitimacy', in Alan Hamlin and Philip Pettit (eds), *The Good Polity*, Oxford: Blackwell, pp. 17–34.

Cohen, Joshua and Charles Sabel (1997) 'Directly-Deliberative Polyarchy', *European Law Journal*, 3(4), 313–42.

Cohen, Robin and Shirin Rai (eds) (2000) *Global Social Movements*, London: Athlone Press.

Coleman, Stephen, John Taylor and Wim Van de Donk (eds) (1999) *Parliament in the Age of the Internet*, Oxford: Oxford University Press.

Combes, Hélène and Francine Simon Ekovich (2006) 'Organisational ideology and visions of democracy: The French GJMOs', in Donatella della Porta and Herbert Reiter (eds), *Organisational Ideology and Visions of Democracy in the Global Justice Movement*, WP3 Report for the Democracy in Europe and the Mobilization of Society project, pp. 105–36.

Combes, Hélène and Isabelle Sommier (2006) 'Democratic Practices in the French Global Justice Movement', in Donatella della Porta and Lorenzo Mosca (eds), *Demos WP4 – Integrated Report*, Florence, pp. 73–106.

Comité catholique (2007) Comité catholique contre la faim et pour le développement, 'Rapport moral du Président Mai 2006 à Mai 2007', http://ccfd.asso.fr/e_upload/pdf/rapportmoral2007.pdf.

Coordination (2003) Coordination des intermittents et précaires d'Ile de France, 'Charte de la Coordination', http://www.cip-idf.org/article.php3?id_article=108.

Cronqvist, Lasse (2003) 'Using Multi-Value Logic Synthesis in Social Science', paper prepared for the Second General Conference of the European Consortium for Political Research (ECPR), Marburg, September.

Crossley, Nick (2002) 'Repertoires of Contention and Tactical Diversity in the UK Psychiatric Survivors Movement: The Question of Appropriation', *Social Movement Studies*, 1(1), 47–71.

CUB (2002) Confederazione Unitaria di Base, 'Dichiarazione finale del congresso nazionale', June, http://www.cub.it (home page), accessed 12 November 2008.

Cunha, Carlos, Irene Martín, James Newell and Luis Ramiro (2003) 'Southern European Parties and Party Systems, and the New ICTs', in Rachel Gibson, Paul Nixon and Stephen Ward (eds), *Political Parties and the Internet*, New York/London: Routledge, pp. 70–97.

Dalton, Russell J. (1988) *Citizen Politics in Western Democracies. Public Opinion and Political Parties in the United States, Great Britain, West Germany, and France*, Chatham, NJ: Chatham.

Dalton, Russell J. (1994) *The Green Rainbow: Environmental Groups in Western Europe*, New Haven, CT: Yale University Press.

della Porta, Donatella (1995) *Social Movements, Political Violence and the State*, Cambridge: Cambridge University Press.

della Porta, Donatella (1996) *Movimenti collettivi e sistema politico in Italia: 1960–1995*, Rome: Laterza.

della Porta, Donatella (2005a) 'Deliberation in Movement: Why and How to Study Deliberative Democracy and Social Movements', *Acta Politica*, 40(3), 336–50.

della Porta, Donatella (2005b) 'Making the Polis: Social Forums and Democracy in the Global Justice Movement', *Mobilization*, 10(1), 73–94.

della Porta, Donatella (2005c) 'Multiple Belongings, Tolerant Identities, and the Construction of "Another Politics": Between the European Social Forum and the Local Social Fora', in Donatella della Porta and Sidney Tarrow (eds), *Transnational Protest and Global Activism*, Lanham, MD: Rowman and Littlefield, pp. 175–202.

della Porta, Donatella (2006a) *Organizational Networks in the Global Justice Movement*, WP4 Report, Democracy in Movement and the Mobilization of the Society – DEMOS, European Commission.

della Porta, Donatella (2006b) 'Ricercando nella rete: stili democratici dei siti web del movimento per una giustizia globale', *Rassegna Italiana di Sociologia*, XLVII(4), 529–56.

della Porta, Donatella (2007a) 'The Europeanization of Protest: A Typology and Empirical Evidence', in Beate Kohler-Koch and Berthold Rittberger (eds),

Debating the Democratic Legitimacy of the European Union, Lanham, MD: Rowman and Littlefield, pp. 189–208.

della Porta, Donatella (2007b) 'The Global Justice Movement: An Introduction', in della Porta (ed.), *The Global Justice Movement*, pp. 1–28.

della Porta, Donatella (ed.) (2007c) *The Global Justice Movement. Cross-National and Transnational Perspectives*, Boulder/London: Paradigm Publishers.

della Porta, Donatella (2008a) 'Eventful Protests, Global Conflicts', *Distinktion. Scandinavian Journal of Social Theory*, no. 17, 27–46.

della Porta, Donatella (2008b) 'La partecipazione nelle istituzioni: concettualiz-zare gli esperimenti di democrazia deliberative e partecipativa', *Partecipazione e conflitto*, No 0, 15–42.

della Porta, Donatella (2008c) 'Social Movements as Open Space', paper presented at the Conference on 'The Decline and Rise of Public Spaces', Berlin, Hertie School of Governance, 9–11 October.

della Porta, Donatella (ed.) (2009) *Another Europe*, London: Routledge, forth-coming.

della Porta, Donatella and Dieter Rucht (1995) 'Left-Libertarian Movements in Context: A Comparison of Italy and West Germany, 1965–1990', in Bert Klandermans and Craig Jenkins (eds), *The Politics of Social Protest: Comparative Perspectives on States and Social Movements*, Minneapolis and St Paul: University of Minnesota Press, pp. 229–72.

della Porta, Donatella and Hanspeter Kriesi (1999) 'Social Movements in A Glob-alizing World: An Introduction', in della Porta, Kriesi, and Rucht (eds), *Social Movements in a Globalizing World*.

della Porta, Donatella and Herbert Reiter (eds) (2006) *Organisational Ideology and Vision of Democracy in the Global Justice Movement*, WP3 Report, Democ-racy in Movement and the Mobilization of the Society – DEMOS, European Commission.

della Porta, Donatella and Lorenzo Mosca (2005) 'Global-net for Global Move-ments? A Network of Networks for a Movement of Movements', *Journal of Public Policy*, 25(1), 165–90.

della Porta, Donatella and Manuela Caiani (2009) *Social Movements and Europeanization*, Oxford: Oxford University Press, forthcoming.

della Porta, Donatella and Mario Diani (2006) *Social Movements. An Introduction*, 2nd edn, Malden, MA and Oxford: Blackwell Publishing.

della Porta, Donatella and Massimiliano Andretta (eds) (2007) *Global Activists. Conceptions and Practices of Democracy in the European Social Forums*, Florence: European University Institute.

della Porta, Donatella and Sidney Tarrow (eds) (2005) *Transnational Protest and Global Activism*, Lanham, MD: Rowman and Littlefield.

della Porta, Donatella, Hanspeter Kriesi and Dieter Rucht (eds) (1999) *Social Movements in a Globalizing World*, London: Macmillan.

della Porta, Donatella, Massimiliano Andretta, Lorenzo Mosca and Herbert Reiter (2006) *Globalization from Below: Transnational Activists and Protest Networks*, Minneapolis: University of Minnesota Press.

Diani, Mario (2001) 'Social Movement Networks: Virtual and Real', in Frank Webster (ed.), *Culture and Politics in the Information Age*, New York/London: Routledge, pp. 117–28.

DiMaggio, Paul J. and Walter W. Powell (1991a) 'Introduction', in Powell and DiMaggio (eds), *The New Institutionalism in Organizational Analysis*, Chicago/London: University of Chicago Press, pp. 1–38.

DiMaggio, Paul J. and Walter W. Powell (1991b) 'The Iron Cage Revisted: Institutional Isomorphism and Collective Rationality', in Powell and DiMaggio (eds), *The New Institutionalism in Organizational Analysis*, Chicago/London: University of Chicago Press, pp. 63–82.

Dissent! (2004a) Dissent! A Network of Resistance against the G8, Minutes, Newcastle Dissent Gathering, 4–5 December, http://www.dissent.org.uk (home page), accessed 12 November 2008.

Dissent! (2004b) Dissent! A Network of Resistance against the G8, Minutes, DISSENT! Gathering, Edinburgh, 18–19 September, http://www.dissent.org.uk (home page), accessed 12 November 2008.

Dissent! (2008) Dissent! A Network of Resistance against the G8, 'Introduction to the Dissent! Network', http://www.dissent.org.uk (home page), accessed 12 November 2008.

Doerr, Nicole (2006) 'Thinking Democracy and the Public Sphere beyond Borders. Language(s) and Decision-Making in the European Social Forum Process', paper presented at the XVI ISA World Congress of Sociology, Durban, 23–28 July.

Dryzek, John S. (2000) *Deliberative Democracy and Beyond*, New York: Oxford University Press.

Dryzek, John S. (2001) 'Legitimacy and Economy in Deliberative Democracy', *Political Theory*, 29, 651–69.

ESF (2006) 'Declaration of the Assembly of the Movements of the 4th European Social Forum', Athens, 7 May, http://athens.fse-esf.org/workgroups/press-office/declaration-of-the-assembly-of-the-movements-of-the-4th-european-social-forum/.

Eber, Christine E. (1999) 'Seeking Our Own Food: Indigenous Women's Power and Autonomy in San Pedro Chenalho, Chiapas (1980–1998)', *Latin American Perspectives*, 26, 6–36.

Edwards, Bob and John D. McCarthy (2004) 'Resources and Social Movement Mobilization', in David A. Snow, Sarah Soule, and Hanspeter Kriesi (eds), *The Blackwell Companion to Social Movements*, Oxford: Blackwell, pp. 116–52.

Edwards, Bob and Michael Foley (2003) 'Social Movement Organizations beyond the Beltway: Understanding the Diversity of One Social Movement Industry', *Mobilization*, 8(1), 85–105.

Eliasoph, Nina (1998) *Avoiding Politics: How Americans Produce Apathy in Everyday Life*, New York: Cambridge University Press.

Elster, Jon (1998a) 'Deliberation and Constitution Making', in Elster (ed.), *Deliberative Democracy*, pp. 97–122.

Elster, Jon (ed.) (1998b) *Deliberative Democracy*, Cambridge: Cambridge University Press.

Ennis, James G. (1987) 'Fields of Action: Structure in Movements' Tactical Repertoires', *Sociological Forum*, 2(3), 520–33.

Epstein, Barbara (1991) *Political Protest and Cultural Revolution: Nonviolent Direct Action in the 1970s and 1980s*, Berkeley: University of California Press.

Espacio Alternativo (2008) IV Encuentros Confederales Espacio Alternativo, Documento de Organización, http://www.espacioalternativo.org (home page), accessed 12 November 2008.

EuroMayDay (2004) 'Middlesex Declaration of Europe's Precariat 2004', http://
www.euromayday.org (home page), accessed 12 November 2008.
European Commission (2001) *European Governance: A White Paper*, COM(2001)
428.
Evans, Sara M. and Harry Chatten Boyte (1992) *Free Spaces: The Sources of
Democratic Change in America: With a New Introduction*, Chicago: University of
Chicago Press.
Faber, Daniela and Deborah McCarthy (2001) *Green of Another Colour: Building
Effective Partnership between Foundations and the Environmental Justice Movement.
Report by the Philanthropy and the Environmental Justice Research Project*, Boston:
Northeastern University.
Finelli, Pietro (2003) 'Un'idea partecipativa della politica. Strutture organizzative
e modelli di democrazia in Attac-Italia', in Paolo Ceri (ed.), *La democrazia dei
movimenti. Come decidono i noglobal*, Soveria Mannelli: Rubbettino.
Foro Social de Palencia (2008) 'Documento de constitución del Foro Social de
Palencia' (Ámbito provincial), http://www.communica-accion.org/fspalencia
(home page), accessed 12 November 2008.
Freeman, Jo (1970) 'The Tyranny of the Structurelessness', http://flag.
blackened.net/revolt/hist_texts/structurelessness.html, accessed 28 October
2008.
Freeman, Jo (2000 [1970]) 'The Tyranny of the Structurelessness', reproduced as
a PDF booklet from the Struggle site www.struggle.ws, accessed 13 September
2006.
Freschi, Anna Carola (2002) *La società dei saperi. Reti virtuali e partecipazione sociale*,
Rome: Carocci.
Fruci, Gian Luca (2003) 'La nuova agorà. I social forum tra spazio pubblico
e dinamiche organizzative', in Paolo Ceri (ed.), *La democrazia dei movimenti*,
Soveria Mannelli: Rubettino, pp. 169–200.
Gamson, William A. (1990) *The Strategy of Social Protest* (2nd edn), Belmont,
CA: Wodsworth (Original edn 1975).
Gamson, William A. (2004) 'Bystanders, Public Opinion, and the Media',
in David A. Snow, Sarah A. Soule and Hanspeter Kriesi (eds), *The Black-
well Companion to Social Movements*, Malden/Oxford/Carlton: Blackwell, pp.
242–61.
Gibson, Rachel, Paul Nixon and Stephen Ward (eds) (2003) *Political Parties and
the Internet. Net Gain?*, New York/London: Routledge.
Giugni, Marco and Florence Passy (1998) 'Contentious Politics in Complex
Societies. New Social Movements between Conflict and Cooperation', in
Marco Giugni, Doug McAdam, and Charles Tilly (eds), *From Contention to
Democracy*, Lanham, MD: Rowman and Littlefield, pp. 81–107.
Giugni, Mario, Marco Bandler, and Nina Eggert (2006) 'The Global Justice Move-
ment: How Far Does the Classic Social Movement Agenda Go in Explaining
Transnational Contention?' Programme Paper 24, Geneva: UNRISD.
Glasius, Marlies (2005) *The International Criminal Court: A Global Civil Society
Achievement*, London: Routledge.
Goldstone, Jack (2003) 'Bridging Institutionalized and Noninstitutionalized Pol-
itics', in Jack Goldstone (ed.), *States, Parties and Social Movements*, Cambridge:
Cambridge University Press.

Gundelach, Peter (1989) 'Effectiveness and the Structure of New Social Movements', *International Social Movements Research*, 22, 427–42.

Gurak, Laura J. and John Logie (2003) 'Internet Protests, from Text to Web', in Martha McCaughey and Michael D. Ayers (eds), *Cyberactivism. Online Activism in Theory and Practice*, New York/London: Routledge, pp. 25–46.

Habermas, Jürgen (1981) *Theorie des kommunikativen*, Frankfurt am Main: Suhrkamp.

Habermas, Jürgen (1996a) *Between Facts and Norms: Contribution to a Discursive Theory of Law and Democracy*, Cambridge: MIT Press.

Habermas, Jürgen (1996b) 'Three Normative Models of Democracy', in Seyla Benhabib (ed.), *Democracy and Difference: Contesting the Boundaries of the Political*, Princeton, NJ: Princeton University Press, pp. 21–30.

Haeringer, Nicolas (2008) 'Attac France and No Vox', in Donatella della Porta (ed.), *Microanalysis of Practices of Deliberative Democracy, WP6 integrated report*, Florence: EUI, pp. 45–70.

Hall, Peter A. (2003) 'Aligning Ontology and Methodology in Comparative Research', in James Mahoney and Dietrich Rueschemeyer (eds), *Comparative Historical Research in the Social Sciences*, Cambridge: Cambridge University Press, pp. 373–404.

Hands, Gordon (1971) 'Roberto Michels and the Study of Political Parties', *British Journal of Political Science*, 1(2): 155–72.

Harkreader, Steve and Allen Imershein (1999) 'The Conditions for State Action in Florida's Health-Care Market', *Journal of Health and Social Behavior*, 40(2), 159–74.

Held, David and Andrew McGrew (2000) *Globalismo e antiglobalismo*, Bologna: Il Mulino.

Henry, Leroi, Giles Mohan and Helen Yanacopulos (2004) 'Networks as Transnational Agents of Development', *Third World Quarterly*, 25(5), 839–55.

Hicks, Alexander (1994) 'Qualitative Comparative Analysis and Analytical Induction: The Case of the Emergence of the Social Security State', *Sociological Methods and Research*, 23(1): 86–113.

ICS (2004) Italian Consortium of Solidarity, 'Solidarietà in movimento. Le sfide della cittadinanza planetaria', VIII assemblea generale.

ICS (2008) Italian Consortium of Solidarity, 'Aiuto umanitario', http://www.icsitalia.org/index.php?module=htmlpages&func=display&pid=11, accessed 3 November 2008.

Indymedia (2001) 'Principles of Unity', http://docs.indymedia.org/view/Global/PrinciplesOfUnity.

Indymedia (2002) 'Principles of Unity', http://italy.indymedia.org (home page), accessed 12 November 2008.

Indymedia Italia (2004) 'Assemblea IX 8-8-10 ottobre 2004', http://docs.indymedia.org/view/local/PrimaParte.

International Consortium for Solidarity Italia (2004) 'Rapporto alla assemblea generale', http://www.ics.italia.org (home page), accessed 12 November 2008.

Ion, Jacques (1997) *La fin des militants*, Paris: L'Atelier.

Ion, Jacques (2005) 'Individualisation et engagements publics', in Philippe Corcuff, Jacques Ion, and François de Singly, *Politiques de l'individualisme*, Paris: Textuel.

Isole (1996) Isole nella rete, 'Statuto dell'Associazione', http://isole.ecn.org/inr/associazione/statuto.htm.

Izquierda (2004) Izquierda Unida, 'Estatutos de Izquierda Unida', http://www1.izquierda-unida.es/doc/1169750311065.pdf.

Jenkins, J. Craig (1983) 'Resource Mobilization Theory and the Study of Social Movements', *Annual Review of Sociology*, 9, 527–53.

Jenkins, J. Craig and Bert Klandermans (eds) (1995) *The Politics of Social Protest*, Minneapolis: University of Minnesota Press.

Jennings, Kent M., Jan W. van Deth et al. (eds) (1990) *Continuities in Political Action: A Longitudinal Study of Political Orientations in Three Western Democracies*, Berlin and New York: de Gruyter.

Jiménez, Manuel and Angel Calle (2006) 'Organizational Ideology and Visions of Democracy in Spanish GJMOs', in Donatella della Porta and Herbert Reiter, *Organizational Ideology and Vision of Democracy in the Global Justice Movement*, WP3 Report, Democracy in Movement and the Mobilization of the Society – DEMOS, European Commission, pp. 265–89.

Jordan, Grant and William Maloney (1997) *The Protest Business*, Manchester: Manchester University Press.

Jordan, Tim (2002) *Activism!: Direct Action. Hacktivism and the Future of Society*, London: Reaktion Books.

Jovenes (2004) Jovenes de Izquierda Unida Comunidad de Madrid, 'Programa de juventud', http://www.jovenesdeiu-madrid.org, accessed 17 March 2005.

Juris, Jeffrey S. (2004) 'Networked Social Movements: Global Movements for Global Justice', in Manuel Castells (ed.), *The Network Society: A Cross-Cultural Perspective*, London: Edward Elgar, pp. 341–62.

Juris, Jeffrey S. (2005) 'The New Digital Media and Activist Networking within Anti-Corporate Globalization Movements', *The Annals of the American Academy of Political and Social Sciences*, 597, 189–208.

Kaldor, Mary (2003) *Global Civil Society. An Answer to War*, Cambridge: Polity Press.

Katsiaficas, George (1997) *The Subversion of Politics: European Autonomous Social Movements and the Decolonisation of Everyday Life*, New Jersey: Humanity Press.

Katz, Hagai and Helmut Anheier (2006) 'Global Connectedness: The Structure of Transnational NGO Networks', in Marlies Glasius, Mary Kaldor, and Helmut Anheier (eds), *Global Civil Society 2005/6*, London: Sage, pp. 240–65.

Kavada, Anastasia (2007a) 'The "Horizontals" and the "Verticals": Competing Communicative Logics in the 2004 European Social Forum', paper presented at the General Conference of the European Consortium for Political Research (ECPR), 6–8 September, Pisa, Italy.

Kavada, Anastasia (2007b) 'Email lists as Multiple Sites of Identity Construction: The Case of the 2004 European Social Forum', paper presented at the Symposium 'Changing Politics through Digital Networks', 5–6 October, Florence.

Keane, John (2003) *Global Civil Society?*, Cambridge: Cambridge University Press.

Keck, Margaret E. and Kathryn Sikkink (1998) *Activists beyond Borders: Advocacy Networks in International Politics*, Ithaca, NY: Cornell University Press.

Khagram, Sanjeev, James V. Riker and Kathryn Sikkink (eds) (2002) *Restructuring World Politics. Transnational Social Movements, Networks, and Norms*, Minneapolis: University of Minnesota Press.

King, Gary, Robert Keohane and Sidney Verba (1994) *Designing Social Inquiry*, Princeton, NJ: Princeton University Press.

Kitschelt, Herbert (1986) 'Political Opportunity Structures and Political Protest: Anti-Nuclear Movements in Four Democracies', *British Journal of Political Science*, 16(1), 57–85.

Kitschelt, Herbert (1993) 'Social Movements, Political Parties, and Democratic Theory', *Annals of The AAPSS*, 528, 13–29.

Klandermans, Bert (1989a) 'Introduction: Social Movement Organizations and the Study of Social Movements', in Klandermans (ed.), *Organizing for Change: Social Movement Organizations in Europe and the United States, vol. 2, International Social Movement Research*, Greenwich, CT/London: JAI Press, pp. 1–17.

Klandermans, Bert (1989b) 'Introduction', in Bert Klandermans (ed.), *Organizing for Change*, pp. 215–24.

Klein, Naomi (2002) *Fences and Windows. Dispatches from the Front Lines of the Globalization Debate*, London: Flamingo.

Klinenberg, Eric (2005) 'Channelling into the Journalistic Field: Youth Activism and the Media Justice Movement', in Rodney Benson and Erik Neveu (eds), *Bourdieu and the Journalistic Field*, Cambridge: Polity Press, pp. 174–94.

Klingeman, Hans D., Richard Hoffenbert and Ian Budge (1994) *Parties, Policies and Democracies*, Boulder, CO: Westview Press.

Knoke, David (1989) 'Resource Acquisition and Allocation in U.S. National Associations', in Bert Klandermans (ed.), *Organizing for Change: Social Movement Organizations in Europe and the United States, vol. 2, International Social Movement Research*, Greenwich, CT/London: JAI Press, pp. 129–54.

Koopmans, Ruud and Ann Zimmermann (2003) *Political Communication on the Internet*, EUROPUB project research report, http://europub.wz-berlin.de/Data/reports/WP4/D4-5%20WP4%20Integrated%20Report.pdf, accessed 6 November 2007.

Koopmans, Ruud and Dieter Rucht (1995) 'Social Movement Mobilization under Right and Left Governments: A Look at Four West European Countries', Berlin: Wissenschaftszentrum Berlin für Sozialforschung. Discussion Paper FS III 95–106.

Kriesi, Hanspeter (1989) 'New Social Movements and the New Class in the Netherlands', *American Journal of Sociology*, 94, 1078–16.

Kriesi, Hanspeter (1995) 'The Political Opportunity Structure of New Social Movements: Its Impact on their Mobilization', in J. Craig Jenkins and Bert Klandermans (eds), *The Politics of Social Protest*, Minneapolis: University of Minnesota Press.

Kriesi, Hanspeter (1996) 'The Organizational Structure of New Social Movements in a Political Context', in Doug McAdam, John D. McCarthy, and Mayer N. Zald (eds), *Comparative Perspective on Social Movements*, Cambridge/New York: Cambridge University Press.

Kriesi, Hanspeter (2004) 'Political Context and Opportunity', in David A. Snow, Sarah A. Soule, and Hanspeter Kriesi (eds), *The Blackwell Companion to Social Movements*, Oxford: Blackwell, pp. 67–90.

Kriesi, Hanspeter, Ruud Koopmans, Jan Willem Duyvendak and Marco G. Giugni (1995) *New Social Movements in Western Europe. A Comparative Analysis*, Minneapolis: University of Minnesota Press.

Leach, Darcy K. (2005) 'The Iron Law of *What* Again? Conceptualizing Oligarchy', *Sociological Theory*, 23(3), 312–37.

Legambiente (2007) 'Statuto Nazionale', http://www.legambiente.eu/documenti/2007/1004_VIII_congresso/statuto08.pdf.

Lijphart, Arend (1999) *Patterns of Democracy: Government Forms and Performance in Thirty-Six Countries*, New Haven, CT: Yale University Press.

Lipsky, Michael (1965) *Protest and City Politics*, Chicago: Rand McNally & Co.

Lofland, John (1996) *Social Movement Organizations. Guide to Research on Insurgent Realities*, Hawthorne, NY: Aldine Transaction.

London Social Forum (2003) *Why a London Social Forum now*, http://www.londonsocialforum.org (home page), accessed 12 November 2008.

London Social Forum (2005) *About us*, http://londonsocialforum.org.uk/about.htm, accessed 22 March 2005.

Mahoney, James and Gary Goertz (2006) 'A Tale of Two Cultures: Contrasting Quantitative and Qualitative Research', COMPASSS Working Paper.

Manin, Bernard (1995) *Principes du gouvernement représentatif*, Paris: Flammarion.

Mansbridge, Jane (1996) 'Using Power/Fighting Power: The Polity', in Seyla Benhabib (ed.), *Democracy and Difference: Contesting the Boundaries of the Political*, Princeton, NJ: Princeton University Press, pp. 46–66.

Mansbridge, Jane (2003) 'Rethinking Representation', *American Political Science Review*, 97(4).

March, James G. (ed.) (1988) *Decisions and Organizations*, Oxford/Cambridge, MA: Blackwell.

March, James G. and Johan P. Olsen (1989) *Rediscovering Institutions. The Organizational Basis of Politics*, New York: Free Press.

Marchetti, Raffaele (2008) *Global Democracy: For and Against. Ethical Theory, Institutional Design and Social Struggles*, London: Routledge.

Marchetti, Raffaele (2009) 'Mapping Alternative Models of Global Politics', *International Studies Review*, 11(1), 133–56.

Marchetti, Raffaele and Mario Pianta (2008) 'Understanding Networks in Global Social Movements', University of Urbino working paper.

Margolis, Michael and David Resnick (2000) *Politics as Usual. The Cyberspace 'Revolution'*, Thousand Oaks, CA: Sage Publications.

Marsh, Alan (1977) *Protest and Political Consciousness*, Beverly Hills and London: Sage.

Mathieu, Lilian (2008) 'Un "nouveau militantisme"? À propos de quelques idées reçues', *ContreTemps*, http://contretemps.eu/node/127, accessed 28 October 2008.

McAdam, Doug, Sidney Tarrow and Charles Tilly (2001) *Dynamics of Contention*, Cambridge: Cambridge University Press.

McCarthy, John D. and Mayer N. Zald (1973) *The Trend of Social Movements*, Morrilltown, NJ: General Learning Press.

McCarthy, John D. and Mayer N. Zald (1977) 'Resource Mobilization and Social Movements, a Partial Theory', *American Journal of Sociology*, 82(6), 2323–41.

McCarthy, John D. and Mayer N. Zald (1987a) 'Appendix: The Trend of Social Movements in America: Professionalization and Resource Mobilization', in Zald and McCarthy (eds), *Social Movements in an Organizational Society. Collected Essays*, New Brunswick, NJ/Oxford: Transaction Books, pp. 337–91.

McCarthy, John D. and Mayer N. Zald (1987b) 'Resource Mobilization and Social Movements: A Partial Theory', in Zald and McCarthy (eds), *Social Movements in an Organizational Society*, pp. 15–42.

McCarthy, John D., David W. Britt and Mark Wolfson (1991) 'The Institutional Channeling of Social Movements in the Modern State', *Research in Social Movements, Conflict and Change*, 13, 45–76.

Melucci, Alberto (1985) 'The Symbolic Challenge of Contemporary Movements', *Social Research*, 52, 789–816.

Melucci, Alberto (1999) *Challenging Codes, Collective Action in the Information Age*, Cambridge: Cambridge University Press.

Menard, Scott (2002) *Applied Logistic Regression Analysis. Quantitative Applications in the Social Sciences (106)*, Thousand Oaks: Sage.

Meyer, John W. and Brian Rowan (1977) 'Institutionalized Organizations: Formal Structure as Myth and Ceremony', *American Journal of Sociology*, 83, 340–63.

Meyer, Megan (2004) 'Organizational Identity, Political Contexts, and SMO Action: Explaining the Tactical Choices Made by Peace Organizations in Israel, Northern Ireland, and South Africa', *Social Movement Studies*, 3(2), 167–96.

Michels, Robert (1962 [1911]) *Political Parties: A Sociological Study of the Oligarchical Tendencies of Modern Democracy*, New York: Free Press.

Michels, Robert (1959 [1915]) *Political Parties: A Sociological Study of the Emergence of Leadership, the Psychology of Power and the Oligarchic Tendencies of Organisation*, New York: Dover Publications Inc.

Miller, David (1993) 'Deliberative Democracy and Social Choice', in D. Held (ed.), *Prospects for Democracy*, Cambridge: Polity Press, pp. 74–92.

Minkoff, Debra C. (1999). 'Bending with the Wind: Strategic Change and Adaptation by Women's and Racial Minority Organizations', *American Journal of Sociology*, 104(6), 1666–1703.

Minkoff, Debra C. (2001) 'Social Movement Politics and Organization', in Judith R. Blau (ed.), *The Blackwell Companion to Sociology*, Oxford: Blackwell Publishers.

Minkoff, Debra C. and John D. McCarthy (2005) 'Reinvigorating the Study of Organisational Processes in Social Movements', *Mobilization*, 10(2), 289–308.

Mitzal, Barbara (2001) 'Civil Society: A Signifier of Plurality and Sense of Wholeness', in Judith R. Blau (ed.), *The Blackwell Companion of Sociology*, Oxford: Blackwell, pp. 73–85.

Monbiot, George (2003) *The Age of Consent: A Manifesto for a New World Order*, London: Harper Perennial.

Mosca, Lorenzo (2005) 'The Environmental Issue in the Global Justice Movement. Some Findings from the Italian Case', paper presented at the 3rd ECPR Conference, Budapest, 8–10 September.

Mosca, Lorenzo (2007) 'A Double-Faced Medium? The Challenges and Opportunities of the Internet for Social Movements', *EUI Working Papers*, MWP 2007/23.

Mosca, Lorenzo and Daria Santucci (2008) 'Petitioning Online. The Role of E-Petitions in Web-Campaigning', in Sigrid Baringhorst, Johanna Niesyto, and Veronika Kneip (eds), *Political Campaigning on the Web*, Bielefeld: Transcript, forthcoming.

Myers, Daniel J. (2001) 'Social Activism through Computer Networks', in Orville Vernon Burton (ed.), *Computing in the Social Science and Humanities*, Urbana: University of Illinois Press, pp. 124–39.

Negri, Toni and Michael Hardt (2005) *Multitude*, Paris: La Découverte.

Neidhardt, Friedhelm and Dieter Rucht (2001) 'Protestgeschichte der Bundesrepublik Deutschland 1950–1994: Ereignisse, Themen, Akteure', in Dieter Rucht (ed.), *Protest in der Bundesrepublik. Strukturen und Entwicklungen*, Frankfurt am Main: Campus, pp. 27–70.

Norris, Pippa (2001) *Digital Divide. Civic Engagement, Information Poverty and the Internet Worldwide*, Cambridge: Cambridge University Press.

Norris, Pippa (2002) *Democratic Phoenix. Reinventing Political Activism*, New York: Cambridge University Press.

O'Brien, Robert, Anne Marie Goetz, Jan Aart Scholte, and Marc Williams (2000) *Contesting Global Governance: Multilateral Economic Institutions and Global Social Movements*, Cambridge: Cambridge University Press.

O'Brien, Rory (1999) 'Social Change Activism and the Internet: Strategic Online Activities', http://www.web.net/~robrien/papers/netaction.html, accessed 6 November 2007.

Oates, Sarah and Rachel Gibson (2006) 'The Internet, Civil Society and Democracy: A Comparative Perspective', in Sarah Oates, Diana Owen, and Rachel Gibson (eds), *The Internet and Politics: Citizens, Voters and Activists*, New York/London: Routledge, pp. 1–19.

Oberschall, Anthony (1973) *Social Conflict and Social Movements*, Englewood Cliffs, NJ: Prentice Hall.

Offe, Claus (1985) 'New Social Movements: Changing Boundaries of the Political', *Social Research*, 52, 817–68.

Offe, Claus (1997) 'Microaspects of Democratic Theory: What Makes for the Deliberative Competence of Citizens?', in Alex Hadenius (ed.), *Democracy's Victory and Crisis*, New York: Cambridge University Press, pp. 81–104.

Olesen, Thomas (2005) *International Zapatismo: The Construction of Solidarity in the Age of Globalization*, London: Zed Books.

Otra Democracia (2008) Otra democracia es posible, 'Contenidos ideològicos', http://otrademocraciaesposible.net/wiki/bin/view/Main/IdeariO, accessed 3 November 2008.

OWINFS (2008) Our World is Not for Sale, http://www.ourworldisnotforsale. org/about.asp, accessed 12 November 2008.

Panebianco, Angelo (1982) *Modelli di partito*, Bologna: Il Mulino.

Parker, Tessa, Marilyn Taylor and Mick Wilkinson (2004) 'From Protest to Partnership? Voluntary and Community Organizations in the Democratic Process', in M.J. Todd and G. Taylor (eds), *Democracy and Participation. Popular Protest and New Social Movements*, London: Merlin Press, pp. 307–25.

Pateman, Carole (1970) *Participation and Democratic Theory*, Cambridge: Cambridge University Press.

Pax Christi (2001) 'Mozione conclusiva Assemblea nazionale', 29 April, http://www.paxchristi.it (home page), accessed 12 November 2008.

Pax Christi Germany (1948) 'Statuten der deutschen Sektion von Pax Christi', http://www.paxchristi.de/fix/files/doc/Statuten.pdf.

Pax Christi UK (2008) Pax Christi (UK Section), 'About Pax Christi', http://www.paxchristi.org.uk/about.HTML, accessed 3 November 2008.

Peacelink (1991) Statuto, http://www.peacelink.it (home page), accessed 12 November 2008.

Pénélopes (2001) Marina Galimberti, 'La démocratie participative au service de la cause des femmes', http://www.penelopes.org/archives/pages/docu/mondiali/demo2.htm.

Peoples' Global Action (2002) 'Peoples' Global Action Manifesto', http://www.nadir.org/nadir/initiativ/agp/en/pgainfos/manifest.htm.

Pianta, Mario (2001a) *Globalizzazione dal basso. Economia mondiale e movimenti sociali*, Rome: ManifestoLibri.

Pianta, Mario (2001b) 'Parallel Summits of Global Civil Society', in Helmut Anheier, Marlies Glasius and Mary Kaldor (eds), *Global Civil Society 2001*, Oxford: Oxford University Press, pp. 169–94.

Pianta, Mario and Duccio Zola (2007) 'La montée en puissance des mouvements altermondialistes', in Isabelle Sommier, Olivier Fillieule, and Eric Agrikoliansky (eds), *La généalogie des mouvements altermondialistes*, Paris: Karthala.

Pianta, Mario and Federico Silva (2003) *Globalisers from Below. A Survey on Global Civil Society Organisations*, Rome: Globi Research Report.

Pianta, Mario and Raffaele Marchetti (2007) 'The Global Justice Movements. The Transnational Dimension', in della Porta (ed.), *The Global Justice Movement*, pp. 29–51.

Piazza, Gianni and Marco Barbagallo (2003) 'Tra globale e locale. L'articolazione territoriale del movimento per una globalizzazione dal basso: i social forum in Sicilia', paper presented at the annual congress of the Società Italiana di Scienza Politica, Trento, September.

Pichardo, Nelson A. (1997) 'New Social Movements: A Critical Review', *Annual Review of Sociology*, 23, 411–30.

Pickard, Victor (2006a) 'United yet Autonomous: Indymedia and the Struggle to Sustain a Radical Democratic Network', *Media Culture and Society*, 28(3), 315–36.

Pickard, Victor (2006b) 'Assessing the Radical Democracy of Indymedia: Discursive, Technical and Institutional Constructions', *Critical Studies in Media Communication*, 23(1), 19–38.

Pickerill, Jenny (2003) *Cyberprotest. Environmental Activism Online*, Manchester: Manchester University Press.

Piven, Frances Fox and Richard Cloward (1979) *Poor People's Movements: Why They Succeed, How They Fail*, New York: Vintage.

Podilchak, Walter (1998) *Fun in Social Movements*, International Sociological Association, Association Paper.

Polletta, Francesca (2002) *Freedom is an Endless Meeting. Democracy in American Social Movements*, Chicago: University of Chicago Press.

Ragin, Charles (1987) *The Comparative Method*, Berkeley: University of California Press.

Ragin, Charles (2000) *Fuzzy-set Social Science*, Chicago: University of Chicago Press.

Ragin, Charles (2006) 'Set Relations in Social Research: Evaluating Their Consistency and Coverage', *Political Analysis*, 14, 291–310.

RCADE (2001) 'Final draft about the organization, 5th general meeting', http://www.rcade.org (home page), accessed 12 November 2008.

Reclaim Our UN (2005a) 'Call to Action: September 10th and 11th 2005. Introduction', http://www.reclaimourun.org/calltoaction/introduction.htm.

Reclaim Our UN (2005b) Draft Resolution on UN Reform. 6th Assembly of the United Nations of the Peoples. 'Save the United Nations!'

Perugia, 8–10 September, http://www.reclaimourun.org (home page), accessed 12 November 2008.

Reitan, Ruth (2007) *Global Activism*, London: Routledge.

Reiter, Herbert (2006) 'Organizational Ideology and Visions of Democracy of Italian GJMOs', in Donatella della Porta and Herbert Reiter, *Organizational Ideology and Visions of democracy in the Global Justice Movement*, WP3 Report, Democracy in Movement and the Mobilization of the Society – DEMOS, European Commission, pp. 224–64.

Rete Lilliput (2001) 'Criteri di fondo condivisi', http://www.retelilliput.org/index.php?module=ContentExpress&func=display&ceid=34&meid=.

Rete Lilliput (2003) 'Piano di Lavoro', http://www.retelilliput.org (home page), accessed 12 November 2008.

Rete Lilliput (2004), 'Documento di sintesi delle assemblee plenarie', http://www.retelilliput.org (home page), accessed 12 November 2008.

Rete Lilliput (2005) 'Assemblee macroregionali nord e centro unificate, Fidenza 3 settembre 2005', http://www.retelilliput.org/modules/DownloadsPlus/uploads/Vita_da_Rete/Macroregionali/Macroregionali_autunno_2005/VerbaleMacroCentroNord05.pdf.

Rete Lilliput (2006a) 'Capaci di futuro. Documento finale IV assemblea nazionale, Roma, 12 marzo 2006', http://www.retelilliput.org/modules/DownloadsPlus/uploads/Vita_da_Rete/Incontri_Nazionali/IV_Assemblea_nazionale_-_marzo_2006/DocumentoFinaleRoma2006.pdf.

Rete Lilliput (2006b) 'Capaci di futuro. IV assemblea nazionale della Rete Lilliput, Roma, 10-11-12 marzo 2006. Parte II: Sessioni tematiche', http://www.retelilliput.org/modules/DownloadsPlus/uploads/Vita_da_Rete/Incontri_Nazionali/IV_Assemblea_nazionale_-_marzo_2006/sessioni_tematiche.pdf.

Rete Lilliput (2007a) 'Essere rete … oltre la rete. Per un orizzonte politico condiviso', http://www.retelilliput.org/modules.php?op=modload&name=News&file=article&sid=438.

Rete Lilliput (2007b) 'Essere rete … oltre la rete. Per un orizzonte politico condiviso'. Atti della V assemblea nazionale della Rete Lilliput, Portici (Napoli), 25-26-27 maggio 2007, http://www.retelilliput.org/modules/DownloadsPlus/uploads/Vita_da_Rete/Incontri_Nazionali/V_assemblea_nazionale/atti.pdf.

Rete Lilliput (2008a) 'Agire un'altra politica. Costruire e praticare la democrazia. Atti del seminario sulle forme di partecipazione politica organizzato da Rete Lilliput, Roma, Città dell'Altra Economia, 5–6 aprile 2008', http://www.retelilliput.org/modules/DownloadsPlus/uploads/Vita_da_Rete/Incontri_Nazionali/Seminario_su_Partecipazione_Politica_2008/atti_def.pdf.

Rete Lilliput (2008b) 'Criteri di fondo condivisi', http://www.retelilliput.it (home page), accessed 12 November 2008.

Rete Lilliput (2008c) 'L'Europa che vogliamo', http://www.retelilliput.org (home page), accessed 12 November 2008.

Rifondazione (2002) Partito della Rifondazione Comunista, 'Documento preliminare alle tesi congressuali. V congresso nazionale', http://www.rifondazione.it/archivio/congressi/v/doc/documento.html.

Rifondazione (2005) Partito della Rifondazione Comunista, 'L'alternativa di società. Mozione 1, V congresso nazionale', http://www.rifondazione.it/archivio/congressi/vi/documenti/doc1.html.

Rifondazione (2008) Partito della Rifondazione Comunista, 'Statuto del Partito della Rifondazione Comunista – Sinistra Europea', http://home.rifondazione. it/xisttest/images/bibi/statuto_vii_rev.pdf.

Risse, Thomas, Steve Ropp and Kathryn Sikkink (1999) *The Power of Human Rights: International Norms and Domestic Change*, Cambridge: Cambridge University Press.

Rochon, Thomas R. (1998) *Culture Moves. Ideas, Activism, and Changing Values*, Princeton, NJ: Princeton University Press.

Rommele, A. (2003) 'Political Parties, Party Communication and New Information and Communication Technologies', *Party Politics*, 9(1), 7–20.

Rootes, C. (ed.) (2000) 'Environmental Movement Organisations in Seven European Union States', interim report to EC DG XII on contract ENV4-CT97-0514.

Rosanvallon, Pierre (2006) *La contre-démocratie. La politique a l'age de la defiance*, Paris: Seuil.

Rose, Richard (2005) 'A Global Diffusion Model of e-Governance', *Journal of Public Policy*, 25(1), 5–27.

Rosenthal, Naomi and Michael Schwartz (1989) 'Spontaneity and Democracy in Social Movements', in Bert Klandermans (ed.), *Organizing for Change, vol. 2, International Social Movement Research*, Greenwich, CT/London: JAI Press, pp. 33–59.

Rucht, Dieter (1989) 'Environmental Movement Organizations in West Germany and France: Structure and Interorganizational Relations', in Bert Klandermans (ed.), *Organizing for Change*, pp. 61–94.

Rucht, Dieter (1990) 'The Strategies and Action Repertoire of New Movements', in Russell J. Dalton and Manfred Küchler (eds), *Challenging the Political Order: New Social and Political Movements in Western Democracies*, Cambridge: Polity Press, pp. 156–75.

Rucht, Dieter (1994) *Modernisierung und Soziale Bewegungen*, Frankfurt am Main: Campus.

Rucht, Dieter (1996) 'The Impact of National Contexts on Social Movements Structure', in Doug McAdam, John D. McCarthy and Mayer N. Zald (eds), *Comparative Perspective on Social Movements*, Cambridge/New York: Cambridge University Press, pp. 185–204.

Rucht, Dieter (1999) 'Linking Organisation and Mobilization: Michel's Iron Law of Oligarchy Revisited', *Mobilization*, 4(2), 151–69.

Rucht, Dieter (2004a) 'The Internet as a New Opportunity for Transnational Protest Groups', in Maria Kousis and Charles Tilly (eds), *Threats and Opportunities in Contentious Politics*, Boulder, CO: Paradigm Publishers, pp. 70–85.

Rucht, Dieter (2004b) 'Movement Allies, Adversaries, and Third Parties', in David A. Snow, Sarah A. Soule, and Hanspeter Kriesi (eds), *The Blackwell Companion to Social Movements*, Malden/Oxford/Carlton: Blackwell, pp. 197–216.

Rucht, Dieter (2005) 'Un movimento di movimenti? Unità e diversità fra le organizzazioni per una giustizia globale', *Rassegna italiana di sociologia*, 46, 275–306.

Rucht, Dieter (2006) 'Critique of Capitalism in the Era of Globalization – Old Wine in New Bottles?', in Ingo K. Richter, Sabine Berking, and Ralf Müller-Schmid (eds), *Building a Trans-national Civil Society. Global Issues and Global Actors*, Basingstoke: Palgrave Macmillan, pp. 109–34.

Rucht, Dieter, Barbara Blattert and Dieter Rink (1997) *Soziale Bewegungen auf dem Weg zur Institutionalisierung. Zum Strukturwandel 'alternativer' Gruppen ind beiden Teilen Deutschlands*, Frankfurt am Main: Campus.

Rucht, Dieter, Simon Teune and Mundo Yang (2007) 'The Global Justice Movements in Germany', in della Porta (ed.), *The Global Justice Movement*, pp. 157–83.

Rucht, Dieter, Simon Teune and Mundo Yang (2008) 'La genèse des mouvements altermondialistes en Allemagne', in Sommier, Fillieule, and Agrikoliansky (eds), *Généalogie des mouvements altermondialistes en Europe*, pp. 115–42.

Ruzza, Carlo (2004) *Europe and Civil Society, Movement Coalitions and European Governance*, Manchester/New York: Manchester University Press.

Salazar, Debra J. and Don K. Alper (2002) 'Reconciling Environmentalism and the Left: Perspectives on Democracy and Social Justice in British Columbia's Environmental Movement', *Canadian Journal of Political Science*, 35(3), 527–66.

Saunders, Clare (2007) 'The Local and the National: Relationships among Environmental Groups in London', *Environmental Politics*, 16(5), 742–6.

Saunders, Clare and Massimiliano Andretta (2009) 'The Organizational Dimension: How Organizational Form, Voice and Influence Affect Mobilization and Participation', in della Porta (ed.), *Another Europe*, forthcoming.

Scharpf, Fritz W. (1997) *Games Real Actors Play: Actor-Centered Institutionalism in Policy Research*, Colorado/Oxford: Westview Press.

Schlosberg, David, Stephen Zavestoski and Stuart Shulman (2005) 'To Submit a Form or Not to Submit a Form, That Is the (Real) Question. Deliberation and Mass Participation in U.S. Regulatory Rule-Making', paper presented at the WPSA.

Schmidt, Alvin J. (1973) *Oligarchy in Fraternal Organizations: A Study in Organized Leardership*, Detroit: Gale Research.

Schmidt, Vivien (2006) *Democracy in Europe: The EU and National Politics*, Oxford: Oxford University Press.

Schumacher, Edward (1973) *Small is Beautiful, A Study of Economics as if People Mattered*, London: Blond and Briggs Ltd.

Scott, W. Richard (1983) 'The Organization of Environments: Networks, Cultural, and Historical Elements', in J.W. Meyer and W.R. Scott (eds), *Organizational Environments. Ritual and Rationality*, Beverly Hills, CA: Sage, pp. 155–75.

Scott, W. Richard (1991) 'Unpacking Institutional Arguments', in Walter W. Powell and Paul J. DiMaggio (eds), *The New Institutionalism in Organizational Analysis*, Chicago/London: University of Chicago Press, pp. 164–82.

Shefter, Martin (1977) 'Party and Party Patronage: Germany, England and Italy', *Policy and Society*, 7, 403–51.

Silver, Beverly (2003) *Forces of Labour. Workers' Movements and Globalization since 1870*, Cambridge: Cambridge University Press.

Sinistra giovanile (2005) 'Sognatori si diventa. Il Manifesto dell'Italia che vuole cambiare', document approved by the 2005 national congress, http://www.sglive.it/primo%20piano/sognatori%20si%20diventa.htm http://home.rifondazione.it/xisttest/images/bibi/statuto_vii_rev.pdf.

Smith, Jackie (1997) 'Characteristics of the Modern Transnational Social Movement Sector', in Smith, Chatfield, and Pagnucco (eds), *Transnational Social Movements and Global Politics. Solidarity beyond the State*, pp. 42–58.

Smith, Jackie (2004) 'Transnational Processes and Movements', in David A. Snow, Sarah A. Soule, and Hanspeter Kriesi (eds), *The Blackwell Companion to Social Movements*, Oxford: Blackwell, pp. 311–35.

Smith, Jackie and Hank Johnston (eds) (2002) *Globalization and Resistance. Transnational Dimensions of Social Movements*, Lanham, MD: Rowman and Littlefield.

Smith, Jackie, Charles Chatfield and Ron Pagnucco (eds) (1997) *Transnational Social Movements and Global Politics: Solidarity Beyond the State*, Syracuse, NY: Syracuse University Press.

Smith, Jackie, Ron Pagnucco and George A. Lopez (1998) 'Globalizing Human Rights: The Work of Transnational Human Rights NGOs in the 1990s', *Human Rights Quarterly*, 20, 379–412.

Smith, Jackie et al. (2007) *The World Social Forum*, Boulder, Co.: Paradigm.

Sommier, Isabelle (2003) *Le renouveau des mouvements contestataires à l'heure de la mondialisation*, Paris: Flammarion.

Sommier, Isabelle and Hélène Combes (2007) 'The French Global Justice Movement', in della Porta (ed.), *The Global Justice Movement*, pp. 103–28.

Sommier, Isabelle, Olivier Fillieule and Eric Agrikoliansky (2008a) 'Introduction', in Sommier, Fillieule and Agrikoliansky (eds), *Généalogie des mouvements altermondialistes en Europe*, pp. 11–39.

Sommier, Isabelle, Olivier Fillieule and Eric Agrikoliansky (eds) (2008b) *Généalogie des mouvements altermondialistes en Europe*, Paris: Editions Karthala.

Soule, Sarah A., Doug McAdam, John D. McCarthy and Yang Su (1999) 'Protest Events: Cause or Consequence of State Action? The U.S. Women's Movement and Federal Congressional Activities, 1956–1979', *Mobilization*, 4(2), 239–56.

Spicer, Andre and Markus Perkmann (2008) 'Translating and Organisational Form: The Case of Indymedia', Working Paper, Warwick Business School and University of Loughborough.

Staggenborg, Suzanne (1988) 'The Consequences of Professionalization and Formalization in the Pro-Choice Movement', *American Sociological Review*, 53(4), 585–606.

Steiner, Jürg, André Bächtiger, Markus Spörndli, and Markus Steenbergen (2004) *Deliberative Politics in Action: Analysing Parliamentary Discourse*, Cambridge: Cambridge University Press.

Stop the War Coalition (2008) 'About us', http://www.stopwar.org.uk/index. php?option=com_content&task=blogcategory&id=24&Itemid=41, accessed 3 November 2008.

Sunstein, Cass (2001) *Republic.com*, Princeton, NJ/Oxford: Princeton University Press.

SWP (2004) Socialist Workers Party, 'Post-Conference Bulletin December 2004', http://www.swp.org.uk.

Tan, Alexander, C. (1998) 'The Impacts of Party Membership: A Cross National Analysis', *Journal of Politics*, 60(1), 188–98.

Tarrow, Sidney (1989) *Democracy and Disorder. Protest and Politics in Italy, 1965–1975*, Oxford/New York: Oxford University Press.

Tarrow, Sidney (1998) *Power in Movement*, Cambridge/New York: Cambridge University Press.

Tarrow, Sidney (2003) *Global Movements, Complex Internationalism, and North– South Inequality*, paper presented at the workshop on Contentious Politics,

294   *References*

Columbia University, http://www.ksg.harvard.edu/inequality/Seminar/Papers/
Tarrow.pdf, accessed 6 November 2007.
Tarrow, Sidney (2005) *The New Transnational Activism*, Cambridge: Cambridge
University Press.
Taylor, Verta and Nella van Dyke (2004) "'Get up. Stand up": Tactical Repertoires
of Social Movements', in David A. Snow, Sarah A. Soule and Hanspeter Kriesi
(eds), *The Blackwell Companion to Social Movements*, Malden, Oxford, Carlton:
Blackwell Publishing, pp. 262–93.
Teune, Simon and Mundo Yang (2006) 'Visions of Democracy in German GJMOs',
in Donatella della Porta and Herbert Reiter (eds) *Organisational Ideology and
Visions of Democracy in the Global Justice Movement*, WP3 Report for the
Democracy in Europe and the Mobilization of Society project, pp. 137–66.
Tilly, Charles (1978) *From Mobilization to Revolution*, Reading, MA: Addison-
Wesley.
Tilly, Charles (1986a) *The Contentious French*, Cambridge: Harvard University
Press.
Tilly, Charles (1986b) *La France conteste, de 1600 à nos jours*, Paris: Fayard.
Tilly, Charles (1995) 'Contentious Repertoires in Great Britain. 1758–1834', in
Mark Traugott (ed.), *Repertoires and Cycles of Collective Action*, Durham, NC:
Duke University Press, pp. 15–42.
Torino Social Forum (2008) 'Proposta di struttura organizzativa', http://www.
lacaverna.it (home page), accessed 12 November 2008.
Touraine, Alain (1978) *La voix et le regard*, Paris: Seuil.
Trechsel, Alex, Raphael Kies, Fernando Mendez and Philippe Schmitter
(2003) *Evaluation of the Use of New Technologies in Order to Facilitate
Democracy in Europe*, report prepared for the Scientific Technology Assessment
Office, European Parliament, http://edc.unige.ch/edcadmin/images/STOA.pdf
(accessed 6 November 2007).
van Os, Renée, Nicholas W. Jankowski and Maurice Vergeer (2007) 'Political
Communication about Europe on the Internet during the 2004 European
Parliament Election Campaign in Nine EU Member States', *European Societies*,
9(5), 755–75.
Vedres, Balazs, Laszlo Bruszt and David Stark (2005) 'Shaping the Web of Civic
Participation: Civil Society Web sites in Eastern Europe', *Journal of Public Policy*,
25(1), 149–63.
Veltri, Francesca (2003) 'Non si chiama delega, si chiama fiducia. La sfida orga-
nizzativa della Rete Lilliput', in Paolo Ceri (ed.), *La democrazia dei movimenti.
Come decidono i noglobal*, Soveria Mannelli: Rubbettino.
Verts, les (2007) 'Pour changer la société, inversons la tendance', http://
lesverts.fr/IMG/pdf/pr2007_0.pdf.
Wall, Melissa A. (2007) 'Social Movements and Email: Expressions of Online
Identity in the Globalization Protests', *New Media & Society*, 9(2), 258–77.
Walsh, Sarah (2001) *Participation in Friends of the Earth. A Guide* (internal
document).
Ward, Stephen (2001) 'Political Organisations and the Internet: Towards a The-
oretical Framework for Analysis', paper presented at the ECPR conference,
Grenoble, 6–11 April.
Warkentin, Craig (2001) *Reshaping World Politics. NGOs, the Internet and Global
Civil Society*, Lanham, MD: Rowman and Littlefield.

Waterman, Peter (2001) *Globalisation, Social Movements and the New Internationalism*, London: Continuum.

Waterman, Peter and Jill Timms (2004) 'Trade Union Internationalism and Global Civil Society in the Making', in Helmut Anheier, Marlies Glasius, and Mary Kaldor (eds), *Global Civil Society 2004/5*, London: Sage.

Whitworth, Andrew (2003) 'Communicative Rationality and Decision Making in Environmental Organizations', *Research in Social Movements, Conflicts and Change*, 24, 123–53.

Wintrebert, Raphaël (2007) *Attac, la politique autrement? enquête sur l'histoire et la crise d'une organisation militante*, Paris: La Découverte.

Wombles (2004) 'Reflections and Analysis: the Wombles, the ESF & Beyond', http://www.wombles.org.uk/article20060454.php, accessed 13 November 2008.

Wombles (2008) 'Background to the Wombles', http://www.wombles.org.uk/article20060318.php, accessed 3 November 2008.

World Social Forum (2002) 'Charter of Principles', http://www.forumsocialmundial.org.br/main.php?id_menu=4&cd_language=2.

Yanacopulos, Helen (2005) 'The Strategies that Bind: NGO Coalitions and their Influence', *Global Networks*, 5(1), 93–110.

Young, Iris Marion (1996) 'Communication and The Other: Beyond Deliberative Democracy', in Seyla Benhabib (ed.), *Democracy and Difference: Contesting the Boundaries of the Political*, Princeton, NJ: Princeton University Press, pp. 120–35.

Young, Iris Marion (2003) 'Activist Challenges to Deliberative Democracy', in James S. Fishkin and Peter Laslett (eds), *Debating Deliberative Democracy*, Malden, MA: Blackwell, pp. 102–20.

Zald, Mayer N. and John D. McCarthy (1987) 'Introduction', in Mayer N. Zald and John D. McCarthy (eds), *Social Movements in an Organizational Society. Collected Essays*, New Brunswick, NJ/Oxford: Transaction Books, pp. 45–47.

Zald, Mayer N., Calvin Morrill and Hayagreeva Rao (2005) 'The Impact of Social Movements on Organizations: Environment and Responses', in Gerald F. Davis, Doug McAdam, W. Richard Scott, and Mayer N. Zald (eds), *Social Movements and Organizational Theory, Cambridge Studies in Contentious Politics*, Cambridge/New York: Cambridge University Press, pp. 253–79.

Zittel, Thomas (2003) 'Political Representation in the Networked Society: The Americanization of European Systems of Responsible Party Government?', *Journal of Legislative Studies*, 9(3), 1–22.

Zola, Duccio and Raffaele Marchetti (2006) 'Organizational Ideology and Visions of Democracy: The Transnational GJMOs', in D. della Porta and H. Reiter (eds), *Organizational Ideology and Visions of Democracy in the Global Justice Movement*, DEMOS WP3 report, Florence: EUI.

Index